D1478953

THE TRIAL THAT NEVER ENDS

Hannah Arendt's *Eichmann in Jerusalem* in Retrospect

GERMAN AND EUROPEAN STUDIES

General Editor: Jennifer J. Jenkins

The Trial That Never Ends

Hannah Arendt's *Eichmann in Jerusalem* in Retrospect

EDITED BY RICHARD J. GOLSAN
AND SARAH M. MISEMER

UNIVERSITY OF TORONTO PRESS
Toronto Buffalo London

Toronto Buffalo London
www.utppublishing.com
Printed in the U.S.A.

ISBN 978-1-4875-0146-4

Printed on acid-free, 100% post-consumer recycled paper
with vegetable-based inks.

(German and European Studies)

Library and Archives Canada Cataloguing in Publication

The trial that never ends : Hannah Arendt's *Eichmann in Jerusalem* in retrospect / edited by Richard J. Golsan and Sarah M. Misemer.

(German and European Studies)

Includes bibliographical references and index.
ISBN 978-1-4875-0146-4 (cloth)

1. Arendt, Hannah, 1906–1975. Eichmann in Jerusalem. 2. Arendt, Hannah, 1906–1975 – Criticism and interpretation. 3. Eichmann, Adolf, 1906–1962 – Trials, litigation, etc. 4. War crime trials – Jerusalem. 5. Good and evil – History – 20th century. 6. Holocaust, Jewish (1939–1945). I. Golsan, Richard Joseph, 1952–, editor II. Misemer, Sarah M., editor III. Title. IV. Series: German and European Studies

DD247.E5T75 2017 940.53'18092 C2016-906480-8

University of Toronto Press acknowledges the financial assistance to its publishing program of the Canada Council for the Arts and the Ontario Arts Council, an agency of the Government of Ontario.

Canada Council for the Arts Conseil des Arts du Canada

Funded by the Government of Canada Financé par le gouvernement du Canada

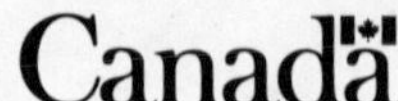

This book is dedicated to the memory of Phil Watts, Professor of French and Comparative Literature at Columbia University, whose idea this was.

Contents

Acknowledgments

Many of the chapters included here were first presented at a conference entitled "Hannah Arendt's *Eichmann in Jerusalem*: 50 Years On," held at the Melbern G. Glasscock Center for Humanities Research at Texas A&M University on 23–5 January 2014. The conference was part of the Glasscock Center's "World War II and Its Global Legacies Initiative." We would like to thank our contributors whose generous donations made that initiative and the Eichmann conference possible. These include the offices of the Provost, the Vice President for Diversity, the Dean of Faculties, and the Departments of History, Philosophy, International Studies, Hispanic Studies, and Communication at Texas A&M University. Most especially we would like to thank Melbern G. Glasscock, the France/TAMU Institute (*Centre d'Excellence*), the French Cultural Services in New York, and the Scowcroft Institute of International Affairs at the Bush School of Government and Public Service, and its Director, Andrew Natsios, and Assistant Director, Don Bailey. Thanks are also due to our wonderful Glasscock Center staff members Donna Malak, Hannah Waugh, Desirae Embree, and Kelsey Morgan. Desirae and Kelsey prepared the final version of the manuscript of this book. At the University of Toronto Press we would like to thank Rebecca Wittmann and Richard Ratzlaff for their untiring support of this project, as well as the anonymous readers of the manuscript whose comments were most helpful in improving the final product.

Acknowledgments

THE TRIAL THAT NEVER ENDS

Hannah Arendt's *Eichmann in Jerusalem* in Retrospect

Introduction

Arendt in Jerusalem: The Eichmann Trial, the Banality of Evil, and the Meaning of Justice Fifty Years On

RICHARD J. GOLSAN AND SARAH M. MISEMER

More than a half-century after its conclusion, the trial of SS Lieutenant Colonel Adolph Eichmann in Jerusalem in spring and summer 1961 remains as memorable and thought-provoking as ever. Attracting worldwide attention at the time, the Eichmann trial sparked debate and controversy from the outset. From a legal standpoint, some dismissed it as a "show trial" and a "political trial" without legitimacy in international law. For others, the importance and significance of the Eichmann trial went well beyond the legal concerns that it raised. In Israel, it marked a crucial step and a foundational moment in the creation and consolidation of Israeli national identity.[1] Having achieved statehood only slightly more than a decade earlier, the Jewish people were now, for the first time in modern history, in a position not only to confront their tormentors but also to "deliver justice" to them in their own sovereign state. For Corey Robin this was "the true miracle of the Eichmann trial."[2] The Eichmann trial also put an unforgettable face to Nazi bureaucratic and administrative horror in the person of the balding, twitching, and evasive "man in the glass box." More so than other higher-ranking Nazi leaders, including his superiors Heinrich Himmler and Reinhard Heydrich, Eichmann became, as a result of his testimony and presence at the trial, Nazism's most visible and representative figure, after Adolph Hitler of course. Finally, as intended by the prosecution, for the first time since the war the Eichmann trial gave voice on a global stage to the victims of the Nazi genocide. Their riveting testimonies launched what Annette Wieviorka has labelled the "Era of the Witness," very much still with us today.[3] For these reasons as well as others, the Eichmann trial has arguably eclipsed the Nuremberg trials as *the* most memorable trial of Nazism and the destruction and havoc that it wreaked.

A major reason – if not the major reason – that the Eichmann trial continues to fascinate and also to inspire debate among historians, philosophers, psychologists, legal scholars, and others is Hannah Arendt's classic work *Eichmann in Jerusalem: A Report on the Banality of Evil.* Appearing two years after the trial itself in 1963, *Eichmann in Jerusalem* is based on a series of five articles originally written for the *New Yorker* magazine about the trial, significant portions of which Arendt had witnessed in person. Despite its journalistic origins, however, Arendt's book was never intended to be merely a factual account, or record of the trial.[4] Indeed, *Eichmann in Jerusalem* raised vital questions concerning the nature of Nazi (and human) evil, Jewish responsibility in the Holocaust, and the law's capacity to come to terms with unprecedented crimes like those committed in the name of the Third Reich. According to Susan Neiman, "*Eichmann in Jerusalem* is not a piece of journalism; it is one of the best pieces of moral philosophy the Twentieth Century has to offer."[5]

From the outset, *Eichmann in Jerusalem*, and the ideas, interpretations, and theses it presents have proven to be highly controversial and also divisive. Moreover, in the heated and frequently ad hominem exchanges it generated especially upon publication in 1963, the actual ideas Arendt presented and the historical, moral, and legal positions she took were often misrepresented and even deliberately distorted. For Arendt's defenders, her critics sought to turn her discussion of the Eichmann trial into a "paper" trial of Arendt herself, her moral and intellectual acumen, and even her status as a Jew. As a result, if as Neiman contends *Eichmann in Jerusalem* is a landmark work of moral philosophy it remains nevertheless a work that has been repeatedly misread and misunderstood, even up to the present, as we shall see. And because, as the chapters in this collection demonstrate, it is impossible to divorce contemporary interpretations of Arendt's contribution from the history of the debates (misguided as they have often proven to be) *Eichmann in Jerusalem* has generated, a brief account of these debates, and the issues they raised, is helpful here.

In 1963 controversy centred, first, on Arendt's assertions concerning the complicity of Jewish leaders in the implementation of the Holocaust, and especially her claim in *Eichmann in Jerusalem* that had the Jewish leaders not been present and the Jews left leaderless, many more would have survived. The passage that most offended and indeed enraged Arendt's critics at the time – and which many of them quoted in their reviews – reads as follows:

> Wherever Jews lived, there were recognized Jewish leaders, and these leaders, almost without exception, cooperated in one way or the other,

> for one reason or another, with the Nazis. The whole truth was that if the Jewish people had really been unorganized and leaderless there would have been chaos and plenty of misery but the total number of victims would hardly have been between four and a half and six million people.[6]

Yehuda Bauer, among others, has argued for the inaccuracy of this claim by noting that in the Soviet territories, where there was no Jewish leadership in the form of *Judenrate*, (Jewish Councils established by the Nazis), the destruction of Jews was "still more efficient" than in places where these councils existed – in Poland, for example.[7] But at the time of the 1963 controversy, Arendt's factual error along these lines, while noted by critics like Lionel Abel[8] among others, was arguably less important than other concerns, and in particular what many saw as Arendt's disdain, even hatred, for her own people. Most famously, at the height of the controversy Gershom Sholem accused Arendt of lacking "love for the Jewish people," to which Arendt equally famously replied that she loved only her friends and that "the only kind of love I know and believe in is the love of persons," not ethnicities or nationalities. She added, however, that "wrong done by my own people naturally grieves me more than wrong done by other people."[9]

Robin has written recently that Hannah Arendt's friend Mary McCarthy exaggerated only slightly when she wrote in an essay entitled "The Hue and Cry" published in the winter 1964 issue of *Partisan Review*, that nearly all Arendt's hostile reviews came from Jews.[10] Indeed, according to McCarthy, "Gentiles" like herself who were favourable to the book were in the eyes of Arendt's Jewish critics simply incapable of understanding it. Among these Jewish critics she was made to feel like "a child with a reading defect in a class of normal readers."[11] While the two sides of the divide were not as neatly defined as McCarthy suggests, there is no doubt that Arendt's most violent critics – with the exception of figures like Michael A. Musmanno, whose incendiary and prosecutorial review in the *New York Times* on 19 May 1963 helped set off the controversy[12] – were Jewish colleagues. And although these violent reactions had the positive effect of alerting the larger "American intellectual or academic world" to the book's importance and implications, they also exposed a deeper wound.[13] Irving Howe writes in his intellectual biography *A Margin of Hope* that the vitriol, the "excesses of speech and feeling," unleashed by *Eichmann in Jerusalem* were ultimately a kind of necessary "pressure-valve" release for all the pent-up feelings of guilt over the Holocaust. This guilt was "pervasive, unmanageable, yet seldom allowed to reach daylight,"[14] and it was shared by these Jewish intellectuals. Perhaps this sense of culpability is manifest in Norman Podhoretz's lament in his own essay on *Eichmann in Jerusalem* that, here as elsewhere, Arendt makes "inordinate demands on Jews," calling on them to be "better than other people, to be braver, wiser, nobler – or be damned." But then, as Arendt's response to Gerhom Scholem cited above indicates, she made such harsh or difficult demands on Jews precisely *because* they were her own people.

If *Eichmann in Jerusalem* provoked considerable outcry by Jewish intellectuals and Jewish organizations on the subject of the Jewish leaders' complicity in the Holocaust, the ways in which the former responded to Arendt's perceived attacks and their justifications of why these leaders acted as they did varied in interesting and also problematic ways. For Abel, perhaps Arendt's most egregious offence was that she essentially reduced these leaders to stereotypes – "knaves or fools" – and roundly condemned them without ever attempting to understand their psychology or divine their motives.[15] For Podhoretz, by contrast, Arendt damned the Jewish leaders as part of an account of the trial geared to dazzle and impress a "sophisticated, modern sensibility." In the "perversity of [her] brilliance" (the subtitle of Podhoretz's essay on Arendt and *Eichmann*) Arendt strove for titillation over understanding, which explains in part her "cavalier treatment" of the evidence. Behind all Arendt's dazzling rhetorical brilliance, however, Podhoretz detected a very sinister message: "she is saying that if the Jews had not been the Jews, the Nazis would not have been able to kill so many of them."[16]

As Robin observes, many of Arendt's critics argued that she was either "too close" or "too far" from the Jewish leaders she condemned to pass judgment on these leaders for their actions as well as their motives. That is, she was "too close" because not enough time had elapsed to properly assess these men in objective, historical terms, and "too far" in that Arendt "wasn't there" at the time and therefore had no way to truly understand the situation in which these men found themselves. But if many of Arendt's critics contented themselves with following these lines of argument, some, especially Podhoretz, demonstrated the perversity of their *own* reasoning in conjuring bizarre or highly speculative arguments to justify these leaders' actions. In his September 1963 essay in *Commentary*, Podhoretz compares the Jewish leaders' accommodation of Nazi demands with the pre-war policy of appeasing Hitler and the Nazis by citing the case of Jacob Gens in Vilna. Podhoretz quotes Gens as claiming "with a hundred victims I save a thousand people, with a thousand ten thousand." He then argues that Gens, like other Jewish leaders, was "simply following a policy of appeasement, and there was nothing in the least 'extraordinary' about it." Podhoretz adds: "As many historians have pointed out, the policy of appeasement was not in itself foolish or evil."[17] The comparison is surprising, not to say counter-intuitive and paradoxical. First, regardless of the opinion of "many historians," appeasement of Hitler was, and is, perceived as shameful and tragically misguided by most. So comparing the strategy of Jewish leaders to the pre-war policy of appeasement could only serve to emphasize these leaders' own shame, their own compromises – not to mention the fact that, as Podhoretz describes this strategy, it implicitly, at least, justifies the sacrifice of some Jewish lives to save others. Second, having along with others condemned Arendt for judging and condemning Jewish leaders for their attitudes and actions, Podhoretz indulges in the same process, if for the different end of justifying the leaders, along with their deeds. Like Podhoretz, Abel also attacked Arendt for claiming to understand and judge the Jewish leaders and their motives, and then himself judges and exonerates them on the grounds that they were isolated from a largely unresponsive West and therefore had no choice but to collaborate with the Nazis.

If the anger of critics like Podhoretz and Abel over Arendt's criticism of Jewish leaders in *Eichmann in Jerusalem* led them to exaggerate or misread her positions – Arendt certainly never implied or stated, for example, that it was because Jews were Jews that Nazis were able to kill so many of them – the problem became more acute in their discussions of her interpretation of Eichmann himself. Abel's claims along these lines are particularly egregious. In his essay in the *Partisan Review* Abel states first that for Arendt Eichmann was a "mere cog in the machine," a claim that can certainly not be substantiated with reference to Arendt's text. Second, Abel claimed that Arendt was unable to distinguish between "the man she saw in the witness box" and "that man who sent millions to their death." (Abel's assertion in this instance is shared by more recent critics of *Eichmann in Jerusalem,* as will be discussed.) Third, and perhaps most problematically, Abel argues that Arendt's assessment of Eichmann is not political, moral, or personal, but aesthetic. As such, it casts the accused in a more favourable light than the Jewish leaders. Eichmann, Abel writes, is "considerably less ugly"[18] than the Jewish leaders in Arendt's "aesthetic" reading. Later in the essay, he reiterates this claim: "Eichmann is aesthetically *palatable* [my emphasis] while his victims are aesthetically repulsive," but he provides no specific examples from the text to support either judgment.

In his own essay on Arendt, Podhoretz offers a similar critique of Arendt's "aesthetic" approach but in a purely linguistic sense. Arendt, according to Podhoretz is culpable of "developing," "refining" and "virtually justifying" Eichmann's's discourse, and to such an extent that she erases his anti-Semitism: "The man around the corner who makes ugly cracks about Jews is an anti-Semite, but not Adolph Eichmann who sent several million Jews to their deaths."[19] If Eichmann were an anti-Semite, that would be "uninteresting" according to Podhoretz, and acknowledging that would undercut the brilliance and flair of Arendt's morally vacuous analysis.

If Arendt's critics in 1963 – or at least representative figures like Abel, Podhoretz, and Irving Howe – largely misconstrued her position on the responsibility of Jewish leaders and her reading of Eichmann, their interpretation of the "banality of evil" Eichmann represented and embodied was even more vexed. Or, at least, their understanding of it was highly simplistic. In his memoir Howe suggests that the banality of evil that Eichmann represented meant that he was "simply a cog impelled more by bureaucratic routine than ideological venom."[20] By way of further explanation, he adds: "the killers, it seemed, looked pretty much like you and me."[21] For his part, Podhoretz offered only the reflection that Arendt's transformation of the "brutal Nazi" into the "banal Nazi" is of a piece with her characterization of the Jew not as a "virtuous martyr" but as an "accomplice in evil."

Arendt's supporters were quick to challenge many of the most egregious claims made about *Eichmann in Jerusalem,* and also the ad hominem attacks made on its author (Abel and Podhoretz were certainly not alone in this regard).[22] In "The Hue and Cry" McCarthy denounced those who insinuated, slanderously and wrongly at least in her view, that Arendt was guilty of an 'infatuation with her own ideas, a love-hate affair with totalitarianism, a preference for butchers over their victims, for the strong over the weak, for – why not say it? – the Nazis over the Jews."[23] She also observed, caustically: "it is hardly credible to me that any reader, no matter how stupid, could really imagine that Miss Arendt divides guilt equally between Eichmann and the Jews, let alone that she views Eichmann as a lovely object in contrast to the Jewish dead."[24] And, she concluded, if Abel liked "Eichmann better than the Jews who died in the

Crematorium" after reading *Eichmann in Jerusalem*, that is his problem, not Arendt's.[25]

But if McCarthy's defence of her friend in "The Hue and Cry" involved barbed and also ad hominem comments directed at her attackers, the essay also sought to address frankly the more substantive criticisms directed at *Eichmann in Jerusalem*. And it is here that McCarthy's essay proves invaluable. First, in responding to Podhoretz's claim in particular that Arendt had failed to deal with the motives of Jewish leaders while spending hundreds of pages analysing Eichmann, McCarthy responds that Arendt simply didn't *have* to deal with the former's motives: for the average person and reader, these motives – as opposed to Eichmann's – were entirely comprehensible. McCarthy also challenged the validity as well as the logic of insisting that Eichmann was a "moral monster," by observing that in making this claim one makes him less, and not more, guilty by consigning him to the category of "beasts and devils." Moreover, in calling him a monster to his face during the trial the prosecutor Gideon Hausner actually made Eichmann feel more innocent rather than guilty by denying his humanity, and thereby sparing him the moral and ethical responsibility for his crimes. At the heart of the controversy over *Eichmann in Jerusalem*, McCarthy concluded, was the need felt by most people to "make the criminal fit the crime." For Arendt's critics, however, her analysis clearly did not accomplish this.

Like McCarthy, Daniel Bell and Dwight McDonald did not mince words in responding to Arendt's attackers. Nor for that matter did they withhold their own criticisms of *Eichmann in Jerusalem*. But for both, their main concern (like McCarthy's) was to explore dimensions of Arendt's book that her fiercest critics had distorted or ignored, or to account in broad terms precisely why *Eichmann in Jerusalem* had stirred such controversy. In "Alphabet of Justice" Bell, rather than denounce Arendt's own rhetoric as had Podhoretz, took seriously her discussion of Eichmann's language as well as Nazism's "language rules." Unlike Arendt herself, for whom Eichmann's stilted language was primarily proof of his "thoughtlessness," for Bell the "function of slogans and catch-phrases" Eichmann spouted "was to submerge the sense of individual responsibility in some cosmic enterprise."[26] Dwight McDonald, for his part, focused on the kind of evil the accused embodied, and the incommensurability between Eichmann's mediocrity and the horrendous dimensions of his crime: "That five million Jews could have been slaughtered by contemptible mediocrities like Eichmann must be hard for the survivors to accept: it trivializes the horror, robs it of meaning. It must be especially hard to take that he wasn't even a serious anti-Semite – in fact, he wasn't a serious anything."[27] Recalling the tragic national backdrop against which the 1963 debate took place, McDonald noted as well that Lee Harvey Oswald was also "mediocre," and that many if not most Americans found it difficult if not impossible to accept that Oswald and Oswald alone had been responsible for the murder of the glamorous young President John F. Kennedy.

At the conclusion of his essay, McDonald touched once again on Arendt's criticism of Jewish leaders and the ire that she inspired among her critics and even some of her defenders. At the heart of the reactions of these individuals, McDonald surmised, was the belief that Jews and Israel were "untouchable" and that in criticizing both as she had Arendt had transgressed the ground of decency and also intellectual debate. For McDonald, this position was not only wrong, it was dangerous: "I am old-fashioned enough (as of the thirties) to still find these favored, special exceptional categories of race or nation morally suspect and intellectually confusing."[28]

Looking back at the 1963 controversy over *Eichmann in Jerusalem*, it is clear that the exchanges often failed to fairly or fully comprehend and represent the complexities and implications of Arendt's discussions in her book of Jewish responsibility, the motivations and character of the accused, and the meaning of the "banality of evil." Nor was consensus among her critics on any of these issues achieved.[29] That said, even in its inconclusiveness as well as in the distortions it generated, the 1963 controversy opened the way to further discussion and debate – as well as further distortions and misunderstandings. Moreover, phrases and terminology Arendt employed in her book – words like "thoughtlessness" to describe one of Eichmann's most fundamental characteristics, and especially of course the "banality of evil" – have taken on a life of their own, and moved well beyond the confines of the Eichmann trial and Nazism itself.

The phrase "the banality of evil," and the concept or idea it supposedly captures, have subsequently inflected discussions of other political crimes and abuses, as well as other historic trials. For example, to the degree that the "banality of evil" has (wrongly) come to mean simply a "bureaucratic" crime committed for personal advancement and carried out in the name of a monstrous "efficiency," it was readily invoked during the 1997–8 trial in France of former Vichy official Maurice Papon on charges of crimes against humanity. A kind of poor man's Eichmann (if one construes the banality of evil in the ways just described), Papon was responsible for the round-up and deportation of Jews from the Bordeaux region from 1942 to 1944. He had also, like Eichmann, argued in his own defence that in carrying out these actions he was doing his job efficiently to the best of his ability and that others were responsible for the killing machine destroying Europe's Jews.[30] Claiming that Papon's crime was a "desk crime,"[31] one commentator went on to assert that it was the Vichy bureaucracy itself – in which Papon served only as a "cog" – that was murderous in this fashion. In this way, the banality of evil became falsely synonymous with a political regime, not an individual. Earlier, those who had misinterpreted Arendt's argument made a similar dubious assumption, arguing that Arendt's characterization of Eichmann's evil constituted her assessment of the essence of Nazi evil as well.

With regard to Arendt's thought itself, Richard Bernstein has observed recently that the "banality of evil" has continued to be misconstrued by critics because some assume that the expression refers to a general theory proposed by Arendt concerning the nature of evil, which it does not. Rather, according to Bernstein, Arendt was "calling attention to a factual phenomenon" she observed in Eichmann. Bernstein also notes that invoking "the banality of evil" to sum up the entirety of Arendt's reflections on evil necessarily simplifies her thought on the subject by avoiding the twists and turns it took over time. Indeed Arendt not only changed her mind about the nature of radical and Nazi evil, she also rephrased her definition of the banality of evil in different contexts once the expression had been coined and become the subject of controversy. Under any circumstances, according to Bernstein the crucial distinction for Arendt that many critics and sceptics of the banality of evil have overlooked (and continue to overlook) is the "distinction between the doer and the deeds. The 'banality of evil' describes the character and motivation of the doer (Eichmann), not his deeds – the monstrous actions that he committed, and for which he was fully responsible. She categorically rejected the 'cog' theory."[32]

If the expression "the banality of evil" remains at the centre of discussions of Arendt's philosophy as well as historical mass crimes from the Nazis on, it is not simply because it is a linguistic catchphrase or an apparent oxymoron that seems to resonate felicitously when one thinks of such crimes and criminals. Robin writes that in its very articulation it threatens something "vital," something "fundamental": "it puts at risk one of the Twentieth Century's most precarious moral ideas: the notion that despite no longer having an objective or shared foundation for our sense of what is good, or right, or just, we do know what is evil." Moreover, in challenging a shared sense of what is evil, it makes the latter even more insidious by insisting on its fundamental *superficiality.* As Arendt wrote in her 1963 response to Scholem: "It is indeed my opinion now that evil is never 'radical,' that it is only extreme, and that it possesses neither depth nor any demonic dimension. It can overgrow and lay waste to the whole world precisely because it spreads like a fungus on the surface."[33]

Like Arendt's conception of the "banality of evil," her reflections on Jewish complicity and culpability in the Holocaust have remained controversial. And because they stir such visceral reactions among many of her critics, as they did in 1963, the responses themselves, and the language used in these responses, often seem to be artefacts from that time. In the recent exchanges over Bettina Stangneth's *Eichmann before Jerusalem* (to be discussed shortly) one of Arendt's most outspoken critics was Richard Wolin, who wrote in 2014 that in her "rush to judgment, Arendt made it seem as though it was the Jews themselves, rather than the Nazi persecutors, who were responsible for their own destruction."[34] If this statement is reminiscent of the more extreme statements made earlier by the likes of Podhoretz or Abel, it also reflects a consistent position on Wolin's part over many years. In a 1996 essay appearing in *History and Memory*, Wolin had also criticized Arendt's "highhandedness" and "insensitivity" in her discussion of Jewish leaders in *Eichmann in Jerusalem*, and – also like Arendt's earlier critics, and especially Scholem – lamented Arendt's "lack of love" for her own people.[35] Whether or not one agrees with Wolin (and with Arendt's earlier critics) these criticisms do little if anything to advance the discussion of the flaws in Arendt's understanding of the responsibility of the Jewish leaders.

Published to commemorate the fiftieth anniversary of the trial in 2011, Deborah Lipstadt's *The Eichmann Trial* generally takes a more measured tone in assessing Arendt's criticism of the *Judenrate* by noting that some Jewish leaders wanted nothing to do with them, and by stressing that figures like Abba Kovner, who testified at Eichmann's trial, accused them of betrayal. Lipstadt is also judicious in her account of Arendt's factual errors, certainly more so than the most outspoken of her 1963 critics. This is not to say, however, that Lipstadt is uncritical of Arendt in other important ways. Although not a major bone of contention in 1963, Lipstadt calls attention to Arendt's absences from the courtroom during the trial, which are not acknowledged in *Eichmann in Jerusalem.*

For Lipstadt this omission borders on intellectual dishonesty and ultimately casts the validity of at least some of Arendt's conclusions in doubt.[36] More centrally – and certainly more directly reminiscent of the 1963 controversy – Lipstadt also faults Arendt for being "unable to acknowledge that the Final Solution, despite its 'universal implications,' was not a great rupture with all that had come before but was the outcome of anti-Semitism that was scripted culturally and theologically into the bedrock of European culture."[37] While many would argue with Lipstadt's claim that the Holocaust was the logical outcome and of a piece with a centuries-old European anti-Semitism, it is in keeping with both prosecutor Gideon Hausner's opening statement at that trial and the position taken by the Israeli government. This position, of course, Arendt vehemently opposed.[38]

Like Lipstadt, in his 2004 book *Becoming Eichmann: Rethinking the Life, Crimes, and the Trial of a "Desk Murderer,"* David Cesarani is generally fair-minded and thorough in his assessment of the merits and weaknesses of *Eichmann in Jerusalem.* Like Lipstadt, Cesarani also positions his discussion against the backdrop of the 1963 controversy. But, referring to Arendt's own harsh words for Jews in her book, in the *New Yorker* articles that preceded it (which Cesarani claims contained harsher anti-Jewish remarks still[39]), as well as in correspondence between Arendt and McCarthy and Arendt and Karl Jaspers, Cesarani on occasion veers toward the familiar perspectives, if not the tone, of the 1963 debate in discussing Arendt's supposed disdain for her fellow Jews and her fundamental anti-Semitism. This leads Cesaranai to the following striking – and familiar – claim: "Because his [Eichmann's] disdain for Jews found more than an echo in her attitudes towards them, she was *preprogrammed* not to register his anti-Semitism or not to take it seriously. To have confronted Eichmann's prejudices would have meant taking a hard look at her own."[40]

In emphasizing what is in his view Arendt's inability, or refusal, to recognize the extent and virulence of Eichmann's anti-Semitism, Cesarani, of course, brings us up to the present and to current debates over Arendt and *Eichmann in Jerusalem.* These centre primarily on the depth and profundity of Eichmann's race hatred, his performance during the trial, and Arendt's misreading of him. The renewal of the debate on these issues has resulted from the publication of Bettina Stangneth's *Eichmann before Jerusalem: The Unexamined Life of a Mass Murder* (2014). Stangneth's book is based upon years of painstaking research and the exploration of newly available materials, including

Eichmann's own notes as well as taped interviews before his arrest in Argentina. The portrait of Eichmann that emerges from her research offers a very different view of the man who personified for Arendt the "banality of evil." In Stangneth's book, Eichmann is a cruel and fanatical Nazi for whom the war – "his war" as Stangneth puts it – never ended. He was also, she continues, a gifted actor and con man, a chameleon of sorts who "acted out a new role for every stage of his life, for each new audience, and every new aim."[41] He had disguised himself very successfully to escape capture after the war and make his way to Argentina. When he was caught there by the Mossad and secreted back to Israel and put on trial for "crimes against the Jewish people," Eichmann knew he needed a new "act" in order to survive. Stangneth writes in fact that "Eichmann-in-Jerusalem was little more than a mask" and that Hannah Arendt "fell for his trap."[42] But unlike so many of Arendt's earlier critics, Stangneth does not attack Arendt or her motives. She argues instead that while *Eichmann in Jerusalem* remains an essential reference point, it has for too long inflected and indeed shaped our understanding of the accused. Stangneth writes: "Ever since *Eichmann in Jerusalem* was published in 1963, every essay on Adolph Eichmann has also been a dialogue with Hannah Arendt."[43]

One of the challenges Stangneth's *Eichmann before Jerusalem* itself faces is reconciling the author's claim that Eichmann was a consummate actor and was performing at every stage of his life to please those around him. If this is the case, why would he not have been "performing" his racial hatred and fanaticism, in order to please his Nazi superiors? Regardless, Stangneth is certainly correct that efforts to understand Adolph Eichmann, his actions and motives, have too long lived under the shadow of *Eichmann in Jerusalem.* By the same coin, Arendt's book and the intentions and views of its author, as this introduction has attempted to show, have themselves also too long been informed – "preprogrammed" to use Cesarani's term – by earlier readings and misreadings going back now for several decades.

One of the challenges of the present volume, then, is to rethink Arendt's interpretations and analyses in *Eichmann in Jerusalem* in new and original ways. Another is to take stock of how a work which Neiman has described as "one of the best works of moral philosophy the Twentieth Century has to offer" has influenced and informed interpretations of subsequent events and trials, developments in international law, along with courtroom dynamics and courtroom testimony in this, the age of the witness. Because Arendt's ideas and analyses presented in *Eichmann in Jerusalem* have generated the enormous critical and theoretical response they have over several decades it is also important to reconsider the most significant of these responses here. Finally, Arendt's analyses in *Eichmann in Jerusalem*, while fascinating and important in their own right, are certainly not independent of her other work, and this work, where relevant, needs to be addressed as well.

Each of these challenges is met in *The Trial That Never Ends.* Unlike other recent collective works on Hannah Arendt and her work,[44] all the essays gathered here take *Eichmann in Jerusalem* as their starting point, although by no means their end point. The result, it is hoped, is an imaginative and many-voiced dialogue on a work that tells us so much more about crucial historical, philosophical, psychological, and moral issues of the recent past and present than does the mediocre, and ultimately terrifying, man who inspired it.

In his lead-off chapter, Henry Rousso offers a concise account of the political and historical background and impact of the Eichmann trial, and stresses its seminal contribution to the memory of the Holocaust and the unprecedented nature of the Nazis' crimes. This contribution, he adds, is often overlooked, or overshadowed, by the emergence of memory on a global scale, and the memory of the Holocaust in particular, in the 1970s and 1980s. Rousso also carefully traces the construction of the legal edifice in Israel that made it possible to try and judge Eichmann, and addresses the court proceedings themselves through a discussion of the strategy of the prosecution and some of the more powerful testimonies given in the trial.

The next two chapters, by Dana Villa and Daniel Conway, take a fresh look at Hannah Arendt's discussion of the motives and mind of the accused as they are analysed in *Eichmann in Jerusalem*. Eichmann's "conscience" and his troubling "normality" serve as touchstones for Villa, who notes that for Arendt, "Eichmann is a 'representative perpetrator' not because he was a 'desk murderer' or because he lacked motives, but because he stands for all those non-fanatical 'good Germans' who became willing instruments of horror *because their conscience demanded it.*" That is, the conscience of Eichmann and other "normal" Germans had become synonymous with the murderous aims of the Reich. And, Villa observes, the prosecution's attempt (as well as that of recent commentators on the trial like Shoshana Felman) to subsume this new reality into a "monumental history" of the trial, whose main function was to give voice to and sacralize the victims of the Holocaust as a culmination of the age-old persecution of the Jews, misses the real meaning and originality of the proceedings as analysed by Arendt.

For Daniel Conway, the key to understanding both Eichmann and what Arendt made of him lies in her detecting in the accused a "new type of criminal." The emergence of this new type of criminal, Conway argues, also marks the emergence of a "new, deadly, and altogether unrecognized manifestation of evil," one whose "banality" bears the closest scrutiny. But in her effort at reportage on the man and trial itself and her fascination with other traits that the accused embodied, Arendt obscured this important discovery of a new type of criminal.

Valerie Hartouni's chapter moves in a different direction than those of Villa and Conway, and examines Eichmann's testimony before the court and the expectations placed on that testimony, especially by the judges themselves. While the judges and perhaps the court itself anticipated "some sort of emotional display," perhaps a show of contrition, Eichmann's vacuous responses, Hartouni argues, opened the door for Arendt to understand the "thoughtlessness" of the accused. So while Eichmann's testimony "may have escaped legal resonance and understanding in the court," in the logos that it articulated Arendt "found the beginnings of an answer to a set of political questions about genocide's preconditions."

More overtly critical of Arendt than the other authors in this volume, Russell Berman explores Arendt's troubling (!) opposition to the Supreme Court's decision to integrate public schools in Little Rock on the very debatable grounds that the more society becomes equal, the more those who are marked for difference by colour, for example, will be resented and persecuted. As Berman quotes Arendt, "it is therefore quite possible that the achievement of social, economic, and educational equality for the Negro may sharpen the color problem in this country instead of assuaging it." For Berman, Arendt's comments on desegregation are indicative of a profound conservatism, and suggest possibly that Arendt may have had "difficulty with ethnic communities." Turning to *Eichmann in Jerusalem*, Berman speculates that Arendt's anti-Zionism on display in the book is reflective of the German Jew's "contempt" for the *Ostjuden* and the *Sephardim*, and that her refusal to interrogate Eichmann's "ethnic stereotypes and anti-Semitism" may well be attributable to her reluctance to examine her own views on these issues.

Carolyn Dean's chapter is also critical of Arendt, but along different lines. For Dean, Arendt's impatience with the victims' testimony, her desire that it be "free of sentimentality and self-indulgence," prefigures a more current discourse that criticizes an "overwrought Jewish memory" while arguing for the efficacy of a "minimalist" testimony that assumes it is all the more persuasive for being so. Dean notes that Tzvetan Todorov's work on Primo Levi is precisely reflective of this attitude and bespeaks the idea that "the exemplary victim" is "the survivor who manifests 'extraordinary reticence.'" But in discussing Saul Friedländer's masterful two-volume history of the Nazi persecution and destruction of the Jews, Dean notes that Friedländer recognized the limits of this kind of minimalism in portraying the suffering of the victims of Nazi persecution, and gave them back their voice and *authenticity* in not subjecting their experience to an overriding and distanced historical narrative. In failing to recognize that her own reactions to victims' testimonies were dictated by a Manichaen opposition between sobriety and "kitsch," Arendt proved herself incapable of creating a solidarity with the vulnerability of these victims.

The next two chapters included here grapple directly with the legal implications of Hannah Arendt's account of the Eichmann trial. For Leora Bilsky, Arendt's critique of witness testimony that was not directly related to the question of the accused's guilt or innocence has led some to characterize her wrongly as a strict "legalist." Moreover, in dismissing this "didactic" function of the trial, Arendt has apparently fallen out of step with the practices of current international tribunals and truth commissions. Bilsky argues, however, that both of these views wrongly limit the scope of Arendt's thinking, and that she was in fact "less concerned with protecting the law from so-called extralegal purposes than with preserving and creating the necessary conditions for politics in general, and for politics in transition to democracy in particular." In illustrating her argument Bilsky examines Arendt's thought in the wider context of her other writings besides *Eichmann in Jerusalem*, and tests these ideas in the context of contemporary Argentina and the implications and practices related to the individual's "right to the truth."

In his chapter, Lawrence Douglas examines Hannah Arendt's criticism of the legal framing of the Eichmann trial, first, in order to show that for Arendt a court weighing such spectacular crimes must do more than simply do justice to the accused. It must also take into account the distinctive nature of state-sponsored atrocity." But if Israeli law and the Israeli court fell short, Douglas's discussion shows that postwar West German law dealing with the crimes of the Nazis was even more stunted and obtuse. Not only did German jurists challenge the notion of retroactivity, which made Nuremberg possible, they insisted that German "criminal law alone" provide the basis for the punishment of Nazi crimes by German courts. And conceptually, this meant that "acts of extermination and genocide" would be treated as "ordinary crimes," "ordinary murder."

In focusing her discussion around Bettina Stangneth's *Eichmann before Jerusalem*, Seyla Benhabib in the final chapter brings us up to the present, and to current debates about Eichmann. These debates focus on the nature of Eichmann's crimes and his guilt, and the validity of the core concepts and ideas that made Arendt's *Eichmann in Jerusalem* so powerful and controversial. As Benhabib notes, the discussion of the trial of Adolf Eichmann inevitably entails the "trial" and often the condemnation of Hannah Arendt herself along with her ideas and even her relations. The repetition of this scenario, according to Benhabib, not only misjudges Arendt (again) but also relies on a slanted or partial reading of Stangneth's important book.

The chapters collected in this volume will not close the discussion of either the 1961 trial of Adolph Eichmann or Hannah Arendt's extraordinary book about its meaning and import. Rather they serve as a reminder that extraordinary crimes like those of the Nazis, and the motivations and actions of individuals, "normal" or otherwise, in dark times, must be constantly kept in mind and carefully scrutinized if we are to understand and perhaps come to terms with the violence and traumas of the present, recent past – and the future.

NOTES

1 See especially Tom Segev, *The Seventh Million: The Israelis and the Holocaust* (New York: Hill and Wang, 1993).

2 Corey Robin, "The Trials of Hannah Arendt," *The Nation*, 12 May 2015.

3 Annette Wieviorka, *The Era of the Witness* (Ithaca, NY: Cornell University Press, 2006).

4 More journalistic accounts include Harry Mulisch's *Criminal Case 40/61: The Trial of Adolph Eichmann* (Philadelphia: University of Pennsylvania Press, 2005); and Sergio Minerbi's *The Eichmann Trial Diary: An Eyewitness Account of the Trial That Revealed the Holocaust* (New York: Enigma Books, 2011).

5 Susan Neiman, "Banality Reconsidered," in *Politics in Dark Times: Encounters with Hannah Arendt*, ed. Seyla Benhabib (New York: Cambridge University Press, 2010), 305.

6 Hannah Arendt, *Eichmann in Jerusalem: A Report on the Banality of Evil* (New York: Penguin Books, 1992), 125.
7 Yehuda Bauer, *Rethinking the Holocaust* (New Haven, CT: Yale University Press, 2001), 77.
8 Lionel Abel, "The Aesthetics of Evil," *Partisan Review* (Spring 1963): 211–30.
9 Hannah Arendt, letter to Gershom Scholem, in *The Jewish Writings* (New York: Schocken Books, 2007), 467.
10 And, Robin adds, many Jewish organizations as well as the State of Israel itself.
11 Mary MacCarthy, "The Hue and Cry," *Partisan Review* (Winter 1964): 82.
12 Among other transgressions, Musmanno accused Arendt of criticizing the prosecutor Gideon Hausner because the latter made "mincemeat" of Eichmann's defence, the implication being that Arendt was sympathetic to Eichmann. He also argued that, because Arendt stated that trials such as the Eichmann trial could not deter further crimes, she was therefore arguing that it was "a terrible mistake to punish Eichmann at all." Both claims are simply ludicrous.
13 Irving Howe, *A Margin of Hope: An Intellectual Biography* (San Diego, CA: Harcourt, Brace, Jovanovich, 1982), 274.
14 Ibid.
15 Abel, "Aesthetics of Evil," 222.
16 Norman Podhoretz, "Hannah Arendt on Eichmann: A Study in the Perversity of Brilliance," *Commentary*, 1 September, 1963, 6.
17 Ibid., 5.
18 Abel, "Aesthetics of Evil," 223.
19 Podhoretz, "Hannah Arendt on Eichmann," 8.
20 Howe, *Margin of Hope*, 272
21 Ibid.
22 In a review of Gideon Hausner's *Justice in Jerusalem* in her book *Practicing History* (New York: Knopf, 1981), Barbara Tuchman claimed that Arendt revealed a "conscious desire to support Eichmann's defense" (121). In an earlier essay attacking Arendt's "pseudo-profundity," Lionel Abel had already criticized Arendt's "method of thinking, her lack of a definite discipline, her unclear writing, and her unacknowledged dependence on the ideas of others" (129).
23 McCarthy, "Hue and Cry," 83.
24 Ibid., 84.
25 Ibid., 83.
26 Daniel Bell, "The Alphabet of Justice," *Partisan Review* 30, no. 3 (Fall 1963): 426.

27 Dwight McDonald, letter included in exchange entitled "More on Eichmann," *Partisan Review* 31, no. 2 (Spring 1964): 265.
28 MacDonald, letter, 269.
29 In "The Hue and Cry" Mary McCarthy makes the point that Arendt's aim was never to offer a definitive, unimpeachable portrait of the accused. But her critics, rather than taking up the challenge to develop an alternative portrait of Eichmann, contented themselves with criticizing Arendt's (87).
30 See Papon's interview with Annette Lévy-Willard in *The Papon Affair*, ed. Richard J. Golsan (New York: Routledge, 2000), 162–6.
31 See Bertrand Poirot-Delpech, *Papon: Un crime de bureau* (Paris: Stock, 1998).
32 Richard Bernstein, "Is Evil Banal? A Misleading Question," in *Thinking in Dark Times: Hannah Arendt in Ethics and Politics*, ed. Roger Berkowitz, Jeffrey Katz, and Thomas Keenan (New York: Fordham University Press, 2010), 131.
33 Arendt, "A Letter to Gershom Scholem," in *The Jewish Writings* (New York: Schocken Books, 2007), 471.
34 Richard Wolin, 'The Banality of Evil: The Demise of a Legend," *Jewish Review of Books* (Fall 2014).
35 See Richard Wolin, "The Ambivalences of German-Jewish Identity: Hannah Arendt in Jerusalem," *History and Memory* 8, no. 2 (Fall-Winter 1996): 9–34.
36 Deborah Lipstadt, *The Eichmann Trial* (New York: Schocken Books, 2011), 180. For a detailed account of Arendt's comings and goings during the trial, and the impact they arguably had on her perceptions, see David Cesarani, *Becoming Eichmann: Rethinking the Life, Crimes, and Trial of a "Desk Murderer"* (New York: Da Capo Press, 2007).
37 Lipstadt, *Eichmann Trial*, 183.
38 While Liptstadt's tone remains judicious throughout, other remarks made about Arendt border on the kinds of ad hominem attacks of her 1963 critics. In discussing Arendt's "many voices" Lipstadt claims that a strident Arendt, critical of the Jews and Israel, appealed to "Mary McCarthy and her set" because "it freed them from self-censor when they spoke of Jewish matters" (180). Lipstadt also mentions Arendt's defence of her "former lover" Martin Heidegger and her efforts to protect the former Nazi, although the point of mentioning this is unclear. Finally, channelling Norman Podhoretz, Lipstadt writes: "Hannah Arendt sometimes seemed more interested in turning a good phrase than on understanding its effect" (184).
39 Cesarani, *Becoming Eichmann*, 349.
40 Ibid., 346; emphasis added.

41 Bettina Stagneth, *Eichmann before Jerusalem: The Unexamined Life of a Mass Murder* (New York: Knopf, 2014), xviii.

42 Ibid., xxii.

43 Idid.

44 See, for example, Seyla Benhabib, ed., *Politics in Dark Times: Encounters with Hannah Arendt* (Cambridge: Cambridge University Press, 2010); Dana Villa, ed., *The Cambridge Companion to Hannah Arendt* (Cambridge, UK, and New York: Cambridge University Press, 2000); and Berkowitz, Katz, and Keenan, eds, *Thinking in Dark Times.*

Chapter One

Judging the Past: The Eichmann Trial[1]

HENRY ROUSSO

Never had Israel lived the horror of the Holocaust as it did in those months … The terrifying stories that broke forth from the depths of silence brought about a process of identification with the suffering of the victims and survivors.

—Tom Segev, 1993[2]

On the one hand, the trial undoubtedly played a major part in forming my personality as a first-grader, and as a man today. It assured me in my self-confident Israeli-ness. Eichmann was confined in a glass booth and I was roaming free, walking past the People's House – now the Gerard Bachar Center – on to school and back home. Sometimes I walked alone by the People's House, looked around and then spat toward the detainee behind the bulletproof glass, just to prove (almost) to him and to myself that I was not afraid. I liked my streets and trusted that the soldiers would guard the beast well and not let it roam the jungle and hunt me and my dear ones. I had a father from Germany, a mother from Hebron, and two sisters, all of us named after dead people whom we had not known. Today, I cannot escape the feeling that the glass cage has expanded so much that it confines us and disconnects us from the world, from the universalism and humanism that I wish to be a part of.

—Avraham Burg, 2008[3]

The Eichmann trial would be of no use to me. Reading the transcripts, it became clear to me that the trial had been conducted by ignorant people: the historians at the time had done too little research, the president and the judges were poorly informed; Hausner, the chief prosecutor, thought that pompous moralizing flights of rhetoric compensated for what he lacked in knowledge … [there was also] the shocking way in which the trial was directed unjustly and put much of the responsibility and the blame for the extermination on the *Judenräte*. This became the subject of a bitter dispute between Gershom Scholem and Hannah Arendt, who followed the trial and, in her book *Eichmann in Jerusalem*, showed a partiality, a lack of compassion, an arrogance, and a failure of comprehension for which he was right to reproach her.

—Claude Lanzmann, 2009[4]

Three quotations, three different sensibilities, and three categorically divergent judgments by three figures of contemporary Judaism, uttered long after the event that was the trial of Adolph Eichmann. Taken together, they point to the ongoing controversy that surrounds an event that should have created some sort of moral, if not political, consensus: the conviction, fifteen years after the war ended (and before any possible statute of limitations ran out), of one of the central figures in the Nazi extermination of Europe's Jews. This was a crime without precedent in history, whose singularity the immediate postwar trials such as the Nuremberg Tribunal failed to address.

The first quotation above is from the historian Tom Segev, who did groundbreaking research on the memory of the Shoah in Israel. The second is that of an Israeli politician and former Jewish Agency president and Knesset speaker Avraham Burg, who was in charge of the dossier of despoiled Jewish property during the 1990s. Both of these figures triggered fierce controversies by questioning the sometimes-excessive role the memory of the Shoah has played in Israel's domestic and foreign policy in recent years. In their statements, both recall that the issue came to the fore, not when the State of Israel was created in 1948 but, thirteen years later at the 1961 Eichmann trial. This is not a minor detail; it underscores the fact that the genocide was not decisive in the accession to statehood of Palestine's Jewish communities. If the immense physical and psychological wound that was the Shoah did not close in 1945, neither did it become a major focus of national memory until after 1961, and therefore in a completely different historical and political context.

The third judgment raises another set of questions which had not been raised at the time: Can a trial modify the representation of the past, a collective memory, and a national identity? Is a trial the best place to witness, or to write, History? In the passage quoted Claude Lanzmann takes up again doubts concerning and criticisms made of

Hannah Arendt – even if he attacks her for other reasons – and of her historical work that constitutes both an act of judgment and a vector of memory.

The fiftieth anniversary of the trial, which opened on 11 April 1961, offered an opportunity to look back at the event through different eyes. Not that the time elapsed necessarily provides greater critical distance. On the contrary, as Avraham Burg's comments attest, the controversies over the Shoah in the Israeli-Palestinian conflict are fiercer now than they were fifty years ago. Rather, the Eichmann case brought up new kinds of issues concerning the relationship between justice and memory and politics and history, issues that have become considerably more complex and significant over the past quarter-century. Contemporary conceptions of justice with multi-pronged political aims that stemmed from the need to judge Nazi crimes took shape during the Second World War and led to the first international tribunal in 1945. These ideas have spread around the planet since the fall of the Berlin Wall, the collapse of the Soviet system, the demise of apartheid in South Africa, and the end of military dictatorships in Latin America. These conceptions gave national or international penal action several simultaneous roles. These include a *repressive* role in punishing criminals; a *reparative* role by contributing to the recognition of victims; a *transitional* role in facilitating the shift from war to peace, from dictatorship to democracy, in particular through the process of judgment; a *reconciliatory* role, in helping to rebuild a shattered national or regional unity; and finally a *memorial and historic* role, in producing a record of the past event with the aim of educating present and future generations, especially through the documents and testimonials gathered. In many ways, the Eichmann trial can be considered the forerunner if not an essential step in these developments.

In any case the Eichmann trial was a seminal event whose impact was overlooked ten to twenty years later with the emergence of a European and international consciousness of Nazi crimes, in particular the Final Solution, in the 1970s and 1980s. It was not until well after the Jerusalem trial that the memory of the Shoah, and even memory *tout court* became cardinal values of our epoch. And it took half a century later for Western societies to acknowledge the Nazi genocide's unprecedented nature and scale and to face a new imperative to remember and demand recognition of the victims and their descendants – an obligation to undertake moral, political, financial, and legal forms of reparation. This was an unprecedented situation. It was not until later that memory served as a model for the recognition of other genocides and mass crimes, and inspired the trials of some of those responsible for these crimes. And it is only recently that the right to remember has become inscribed in the panoply of "human rights."

Politics

Eichmann's trial was a political affair because it was Prime Minister Ben-Gurion who made the decision to capture him. When Ben-Gurion announced the news to the Knesset on 23 May 1960, the deputies were dumbstruck. Their astonishment did not come from the capture itself. It was not uncommon at the time for former Nazis to be arrested and tried. In addition to the Allies' trials of Nazi criminals in Germany or other European countries (mainly in 1945–9) from 1949 to the early 2000s the Federal Republic opened approximately 100,000 criminal proceedings, of which 6,500 led to sentences and prison terms. Around 17,700 of these proceedings were undertaken as a result of investigations by the German Special Prosecutor's Office for Nazi crimes (Zentrale Stelle der Landesjustizverwaltungen zur Aufklärung nationalsozialistischer Verbrechen). The agency, created in December 1958, two years before Eichmann's capture, yielded to international pressure and intensified its work mainly after the Jerusalem trial, which served to spur on these efforts.[5]

Their surprise did not arise from the fact that the accused was Eichmann, whose exact role in the Final Solution was little known. Rather, it was because Ben-Gurion's stunning announcement signalled a shift in Israeli policy. When a Mossad commando caught up with Eichmann in Argentina on 11 May 1960, it was not the result of a long-term and relentless manhunt. The Israelis did not make tracking down former Nazis a top priority before or after 1948. Eichmann had been spotted in Argentina as soon as he got there in 1950, but he was not a target. Israeli officials were more preoccupied by their current enemies, the Arab countries, than by their former foes. However, a turning point came in 1959. This was perhaps due to the uncertainty that followed in the wake of the Suez Crisis three years earlier, which had turned the political advantage to Israel's adversaries, including especially Nasser, the Egyptian leader. That is when Ben-Gurion decided to authorize an operation to capture Ricardo Klement, alias Adolf Eichmann. This was the first time the Jewish state took action and decided to punish, in a legal framework, one of those who wanted to wipe out the Jewish people. The trial was to be the first physical and symbolic face-to-face confrontation between one of the extermination's masterminds and the new Jewish state. This event was obviously laden with symbolic and historical meaning. But it was not without risks.

The trial was political because the Israeli government desired, organized, and orchestrated it down to the slightest details. The Israeli government did this in order to consolidate national identity and to show the world that the young state was entitled, empowered, and willing to defend the interests and the memory of Jews, living or dead, throughout the world.

Justice

Eichmann was the only person sentenced to death and executed in Israel. Years later, another case made headlines when John Demjanjuk, a former Sobibor guard, was extradited from the United States, where he had fled after the war. He was sentenced to death in Jerusalem in 1988 but acquitted in 1993 on appeal due to lack of proof of his true identity. He was eventually brought to trial in Munich in 2009 and sentenced to five years in prison on 12 May 2011.[6] This is not insignificant. There is a huge gap between the scope of the Nazis' crimes and the number of people who could and should have been held accountable for them and the number of sentences handed down in postwar Europe. For Israel, it is not a gap but a chasm: one man paid the price for nearly six million victims. The Jewish state launched no major proceedings after Eichmann.

On moral and political grounds, Israel chose justice instead of vengeance, although some Jewish resistance groups did advocate revenge in 1945. The option of vengeance – used for example against the Palestinian terrorists who massacred Israeli athletes at the 1972 Munich Olympic Games – was discarded. What act of vengeance could be commensurate with the enormity of the Nazi crime? Nevertheless a thirst for revenge overtook Israeli opinion when Eichmann was caught in 1960. Consequently, legal and political officials wanted not only to protect the defendant, who was enclosed in a bulletproof glass cage, but even more so to hold a trial that would be as fair as possible considering the event's exceptional magnitude.

As a result, Eichmann was granted a trial before an ordinary civilian court, the Jerusalem district court, and offered all the safeguards of free expression over a considerable period of time. The trial lasted for four months, from 11 April to 14 August 1961. This does not include the sentencing hearings in December 1961 and the appeal in March 1962.

In order to make the trial feasible in the context of an "extraterritorial" judgment, it was necessary to pass several new laws (such as one allowing foreign lawyers to plead in Israel – the *lex Servatius*, named after Eichmann's lawyer) and to take special measures. The state paid the defence team and granted immunity to some of the German witnesses, former Nazis who were also subject to prosecution in Israel. Consequently, none of the latter made the trip to Jerusalem and their testimonies were collected in the form of written depositions. The defence was given the possibility of filing its conclusions in writing and limiting its oral plea to what was essential. Most of the trial's historians have pointed out a number of departures from formal legality, starting with the capture itself, which led to a half-hearted United Nations Security Council resolution on 23 June 1960 condemning the infringement of Argentina's sovereignty but acknowledging the need to try a criminal like Eichmann.

The rules were also bent in the exercise of the rights of the defence: Eichmann did not have a lawyer present during questioning; the prosecution used the testimony of some Nuremberg defendants, including Dieter Wisliceny, who had died in the meantime; and it even called a judge in that trial, Michael Musmanno, to the stand. Those technical and legal arrangements gave the prosecution an edge but alone could not cast doubt on the trial's fairness, especially since, as many observers pointed out, the three judges, starting with presiding magistrate Landau, played an essential arbitrating role.

The legal controversy actually broke out long before it was decided to try Eichmann under the 1950 law punishing Nazis and their collaborators. Until then the law had been applied only in approximately twenty-eight cases. These cases consisted of Jewish survivors accused of "collaboration" with the Nazis, members of the Jewish police or Jewish councils in the ghettos, kapos in the camps, and so forth.[7] Eichmann was the first Nazi indicted under the law. The law itself caused much ink to flow because it distorted certain legal principles considered to be immutable. The law applied only to crimes committed during the Nazi period and the Second World War, specified in Article 15 as the period between 30 January 1933 and 8 May 1945. It was, therefore, by definition, retroactive. It also applied to crimes committed outside Israeli territory. In addition, it authorized the prosecution of crimes that had already been adjudicated elsewhere. In some instances, it allowed for exceptions to the rules on evidence. These innovations responded to the unprecedented nature of Nazi crimes and the difficulty of fitting them into existing legal frameworks. The 1950 law took up old (war crimes) as well as more recent (crimes against humanity) criminal categories, both of which were applied for the first time at Nuremberg. It also established a new category (crimes against the Jewish people), which sparked many disputes but reflects the genocidal nature of the crimes against the Jewish people. For the most part, it was based on the 1948 convention on genocide being discussed at the same time but which did not apply to the crimes committed during the war because the 1948 convention was non-retroactive. "Crimes against the Jewish people" is the only one of the three charges that does not have a universal character because it is limited, by definition, to a singular crime. The Nazis committed war crimes as well as crimes against humanity against many other groups of people, and the Allies also committed crimes that could have been prosecuted under the same charges. But only the Jews fell victim to a systematic extermination plan implemented throughout Europe, "genocide" as Raphael Lemkin precisely defined it in 1943 to designate the unprecedented and unique nature of the mass murder of the Jews. This singular criminal category gave Israel the legitimacy to speak on behalf of all Jews, living and dead, which again underscores the Eichmann trial's political dimension. This was the first time the law was applied to a senior Nazi official and not an "indigenous" collaborator.

In addition, unlike later cases in France or Germany (e.g., the Barbie and Papon trials in France), there were no civil actions. The state, speaking for the victims, prosecuted, tried, and convicted Eichmann. In a speech to the Knesset on 27 March 1950, Justice Minister Pinhas Rosen, who was still in office in 1961, justified the need for such a law two years after the creation of Israel. "This bill," he said,

> is the expression of the revolutionary transformation that has occurred in the political situation of the Jewish people. Whereas other peoples enacted laws to judge Nazis and their collaborators shortly after and sometimes even before the end of the war, the Jewish people, the list of whose grievances against the Nazis is the longest and gravest of all, did not possess the political power that would have enabled it to bring the Nazi criminals and their collaborators to justice until the foundation of the State. It did not have the political power to request that those criminals be handed over for trial by its own courts, as the present bill provides. In that

> regard, things have changed. As we know, the Nuremberg International Military Tribunal judged the main Nazi criminals, who did not limit their crimes to a determined country, and their collaborators: at the time, it was thought, the other criminals would be tried in the countries where they committed their crimes and by the courts of the peoples against whom those crimes were perpetrated. We are one of those peoples, in fact the people that suffered more from those crimes than any other.[8]

Rosen stated what for him was obvious: the new law would give Israel the legal means to punish the Nazis and their collaborators just as Poland, Norway, Belgium, Bulgaria, and Hungary (the countries he mentioned in his speech) had punished the criminals who had occupied their land, as well as their accomplices. This principle derived from the decisions made by the Allies at the 30 October 1943 Moscow Conference and the 8 August 1845 London agreement setting up the International Military Tribunal (IMT). They latter recommended a division of labour among individual countries that would try defendants accused of committing crimes on their soil, and an international court that would judge more general crimes that were not perpetrated in a specific territory. Rosen recalled that in most European countries, special courts, such as courts of justice and civic chambers in France, carried out the purges, whereas the Israeli law called for ordinary courts, which in theory gives defendants the best safeguards. That was the case for Eichmann. In that sense the law, which was passed as the purges were still under way in many European countries (in France the process came to a close with the 1953 amnesty act) helped make the State of Israel an ordinary country and the Jews a people like any other. Except for the fact that they "suffered the most" from Nazi crimes, this was an assertion that Poles or Soviets could contest. The charges of "crimes against the Jewish people," used against Jewish "collaborators," can be considered similar to the concept of "crime against the nation," largely used in the purge processes at the same time, starting with France, which in 1944 invented the crime of "national indignity" to punish collaboration with the enemy on a wide scale.[9]

Once the proceedings began, controversy continued on the nature of the indictment drafted by Attorney General Gideon Hausner, who wanted to emphasize all the suffering of the European Jews and judge the genocide in all of its dimensions. The task was all the more complicated because it was challenged by the court, which wanted to keep the trial within acceptable bounds. The defence was concerned with maintaining focus on the defendant's actions. Eichmann himself did not measure up to the role he was expected to play, although he actively participated in the trial. The controversy continued after the court sentenced the former Nazi to death and executed him. Justice is not vengeance. Nevertheless, in some cases it does fulfil the desire to make criminals pay the supreme price and satisfy the need for cathartic violence. Here again, Israel merely followed the example *for a single case*, set by European countries which sentenced thousands of Nazis and collaborators to death and executed them after 1945, often in conditions that were not nearly as fair.

History

In any political trial where the charges often surpass the defendant's own responsibility and touch on large-scale criminal processes, the court must understand events that already belong to the past. It must also know that its decision might weigh on the national or international community's futures. Both sides must have the opportunity to duly state their cases in relation to the charges. Only those concerning the accused must be examined in depth, and in theory the court must only hear the testimonies or examine the documents within that framework. In short, this kind of trial must be as ordinary as possible. But since 1945, when for the first time a whole political system was put on trial before a court, cases involving Nazism and, later, other criminal political systems, have produced, deliberately or not, a legal and judicial narration of history. At Nuremberg, the events were recent, the passions and the ashes still hot, and the protagonists still in the harsh light of the events under examination. In Jerusalem, time had already elapsed; the generations born during the war had reached adulthood.

Eichmann in Israel seemed like an uncertain figure caught between a past that was often misunderstood or swept under the rug and a very different present, almost cut off from its roots. So much was the latter the case that the judges heard, for the first time in a courtroom, an American historian, Salo Baron, discuss the context of the 1930s and 1940s during the 24 April 1961 session, even though the trial's protagonists had lived through the period. All three judges were born in interwar Poland or Germany. By way of introduction, Baron expressed the odd feelings he harboured. "I appear here as a witness, not an eyewitness or a jurist, but as a historian," he said.

> It is known that a historian who studies contemporary history is always confronted with a double problem. The first problem is: does one already have a historical perspective? Generally, one does not, until the passage of several decades, at least. The second problem is: does one have documents? These are usually locked away and not available. One does not know about events that happened until fifty years later, or more. It seems to me that precisely in this regard, there is a difference. The period before the Second World War is so remote from this generation, and sometimes so forgotten even by people who lived through it, that already, it seems to me, we have a historic perspective which usually is lacking in such cases. And with regard to documents, perhaps we are fortunate that many of the German archives were captured by the Allies and many of them have already been published.[10]

Baron brought up two ideas that are crucial for understanding the Eichmann trial's relationship to history. First, although less than a generation had gone by, the immediate postwar world, and in particular the world of European Jewry, seemed to belong to another era. Hence the role attributed to the trial (and to the historian) was to recall not just the crime, but also the memories of what European Jewish life was like before the crime. That situation prompted a rift that Holocaust historiography was to reflect on in the years that followed: what is the most urgent and necessary story to tell? That of the criminals, of Nazism, and of the genocidal mechanisms employed? Or that of the victims, and their destroyed and mostly vanished world? Second, like the Nuremberg trial, the Eichmann case was a turning point in the emergence of an interpretation of Nazism in general and of the extermination of the Jews in particular because of the mass of information gathered and discussed through the testimonies or documents collected. Contrary to a widespread cliché in the 1990s, there are few historical events for which so much documentation was accessible so quickly. But the interpretations expressed during the trial were dependent, at least in the beginning, on the historical references then available, in particular the Nuremberg records and the work of Léon Poliakov and Gerald Reitlinger.[11] Raul Hillberg's seminal work, *The Destruction of the European Jews*, the first edition of which was published in 1961, was still unknown. The vision of history articulated at the trial has the Final Solution starting with the invasion of Poland in 1939 or even earlier, with the forced emigration in which Eichmann played a key role. The extermination of the Jews was seen as a rationalized centralized policy implementing a premeditated plan following a long-formulated criminal intention with no real connection to other extermination policies. That is the framework in which the prosecution sought to prove that Eichmann was "the architect of genocide," assuming that all the initiatives went from the centre out to the periphery. That thesis underestimated the role of chaos in the Nazi-occupied eastern territories and of the local initiatives in 1941–2 that were to lead to the decision to kill every European Jew. The willing collaboration of other countries was not a key issue: the Frenchman Georges Wellers mentioned Vichy's responsibility in arresting Jews during the Vél' d'Hiv' roundup, managing the Drancy camp and deporting children, themes that became places of memory in the 1990s, but at the time the information elicited no particular reactions, including in France. *Le Monde* devoted only a quarter-page to it on 10 May 1961 (the story made the cover of the German magazine *Bild* the next day), and a few Communist Jewish Resistance fighters accused Wellers of underplaying the responsibility of French collaborators.[12]

The Eichmann trial brought up thorny issues that relate the history both of the persecutions as well as of Zionism. In one of the history's ironies, Eichmann, the only Nazi official ever tried in Israel, was also the only one who had close contacts with Zionist organizations. This was the case in Berlin and Vienna in 1937–8. It was also the case in Budapest in 1944, when he oversaw the extermination of Hungary's Jews, in a spasm of Nazi violence and efficacy. Several witnesses recalled those episodes, including Franz Meyer, Pinhas Freudiger, Joel Brand and Hansi Brand.

The trial also spent a good deal of time on the Kasztner affair, which was still fresh in the minds of Israelis and everybody involved in the case. Kasztner, a Hungarian who led a rescue network, tried negotiating with Eichmann to save Jews bound for death in exchange for trucks to be delivered to Germany via the Jewish Agency in Palestine. In 1952 Kasztner, living in Israel by then, was denounced as a "collaborator." Three years later, in 1955, he lost a libel suit. Benjamin Halevi, one of the three Eichmann trial judges, wrote the decision, almost explicitly accusing him of having collaborated. He was assassinated in Tel Aviv in March 1957. In January 1958 an appeals court quashed the first judgment, ruling that Kasztner had indeed been the victim of libel and was therefore innocent.

The memory of that tragedy, which shook Israeli public opinion and rattled its politicians, hovered over the Eichmann trial and justified the comparison with postwar Europe: the prosecution of Nazi criminals stirred up less passion than the trial of real or imagined indigenous collaborators. But there was a big difference. The Jewish "collaborators," not to mention the members of the Jewish Councils that were extensively discussed at the trial and sparked fierce controversy after Arendt's book came out, were often themselves sent to their deaths. There is no way their situation could be compared to that of the European elites who sided with the Reich out of ideological sympathies. That might seem obvious to us now, but it was not in Israeli society at the time.

The Eichmann trial was the first of its kind where the initiators also sought to produce a controlled, finalized narrative of history. In that sense, its contribution to the history of Nazism is real, although biased. It offers a coherent, but not a comprehensive, account of the Final Solution by covering the forced emigration policy (1937–40), the mass executions in the East (1941), and the establishment of the first death camps and the earliest deportations (1941–2). It also covered the application of the Final Solution in various countries, including France and, especially, Hungary, where, as noted, Eichmann played a decisive role. Jewish Resistance movements were discussed as well. This was a chapter Attorney General Hausner deliberately added, in consultation with Ben-Gurion, in order to nuance the effect on young Israelis of the dark toll of millions of innocent, defenceless civilians led to their deaths like sheep to the slaughter. Not all of those episodes had a link to Eichmann, but they fulfilled the needs of a trial conceived as a history lesson – the first of its kind. The narrative relied on numerous documents, many of which were unearthed for the trial, hundreds of witnesses' individual accounts and exceptional testimony from inside the Nazi machine, including that of the accused himself. The extent to which Eichmann was an uncommon defendant has not been stressed enough. That is probably due to a faulty interpretation of Arendt and her thesis on the "banality of evil," which generations of occasionally ill-informed commentators have tirelessly taken up.[13]

In addition to his importance in the structure of the extermination apparatus and his ties to Zionist organizations, Eichmann was one of the few chatty Nazis after the war. Arendt does not take that into account when she calls him an "ordinary man," a passive defendant, even a "clown."[14] Research carried out recently has helped to establish that between 1956 and 1962, in Argentina and, later, Israel, Eichmann wrote or corrected nearly eight thousand pages of oral transcriptions, a huge task. They include reports, fragments of memoirs, interviews with the former Nazi Willem Sassen partly used during the trial, and even a novel the defendant wrote in Argentina.[15] They also include the original handwritten version, with marginal notes in Eichmann's hand and discovered in 2011 by Fabien Théofilakas, of a 1957 text: "My statement concerning 'Jewish Questions' and the German Reich's National Socialist government's efforts to solve the whole complex of issues in 1933–1945." The text was used in the trial but Eichmann's notes clearly indicate that the text was intended as an "open letter" to Chancellor Adenauer that apparently he never received. We also know today from the work of Bettina Stangneth that some of the writings were intended for a work that would have been a rough outline of a defence. They also make it clear that Eichmann wanted to return to Germany, even if he had to be tried there.[16] It is therefore easier to understand why Eichmann was a particularly active defendant in Jerusalem, participating in a trial for which he had probably been preparing for years. Another important recent find by Fabien Théofilakas, unknown to historians until now, are the notes he took in his glass booth. These round out other texts produced in Israel, in particular his annotated police examination and two versions of his memoirs.[17]

Memory

The Eichmann trial was undoubtedly a milestone in the emergence of a collective memory of the Shoah in Israel. Here the term "collective memory" is used in the traditional sense defined by Maurice Halbwachs, that is, a set of social representations at the crossroads between shared individual memories and an official narrative for the purpose of forging unity, "the historical memory." The traces of the Holocaust were obviously present as soon as the first death camp survivors began straggling back home in 1945–6, but the political investment in the trial 1960–1 helped produce the first official account intended for sharing between, on the one hand, the generations who lived through the tragedy, and, on the other, those born after the war or those from countries outside Europe, such as Sephardic Jews from the Arab countries.[18]

The collective memory in question had a face: the 110 witnesses who took the stand, all but two of them Jews (Pastor Grüber and Judge Musmanno), out of a total 118 planned. In addition there were sixteen defence witnesses, all former Nazis whose depositions were taken in Germany.[19] The witnesses' words, broadcast on the radio, echoed like voices from a past on which the young Hebrew state wished to turn its back. And yet the witnesses' testimony is the best-known and most commented-upon aspect of the trial. Many have recognized this fact afterwards in other contexts.[20]

And yet for all that, can the Eichmann trial be called a decisive turning point in collective memory of the Holocaust? That question makes sense today only if we take into account what the memory of the Holocaust has actually become in the last twenty years. First, the very notion did not emerge as such until the 1980s; the term "collective memory" and "memory of the Shoah" were seldom used before then. The increasing value placed on memory; the involvement of civil society; the emergence of national and international public commemorative efforts and practices; and the steady demand for survivors' testimonies (as opposed to their spontaneous production) are recent phenomena, emerging long after the trial. All have taken on an importance that was still unimaginable in the 1960s.

In the 1960s former Nazis and collaborators were convicted in a new wave of trials, those in Frankfurt (1963–5) and Stuttgart (1969) being the most famous. Next came the trials in Cologne of the Sipo-SD officers in France, including Theodor Dannecker, Eichmann's man in Paris (1979–80), the Klaus Barbie trial in Lyon (1987), the Versailles trial of the French *milicien* Touvier (1994), and the trial of Vichy functionary Maurice Papon in Bordeaux (1997–8). These cases, which often had in common the actions of the Ludwigsburg Special Prosecutor's Office or survivors' organizations like Beate and Serge Klarsfeld's Association of the Sons and Daughters of the Jewish Deportees of France, have gradually raised courtroom testimony to the status of vectors of memory, giving witnesses and victims a central place they did not have in the postwar proceedings or even the Eichmann trial, where no civil parties were allowed to join the prosecution's case.

The Eichmann trial, therefore, was probably an essential step after Nuremberg and, as many commentators have pointed out, very different from it. Genocide was not the focus at Nuremberg. Was that possible at a trial where Nazi policy as a whole was being judged? The series of Allied trials had a collective dimension, essential for understanding the Third Reich's key strategic decisions: the annexation policies, the invasion of Poland, the plundering of occupied Europe, forced labour, and so forth. The Eichmann trial, in contrast, focused on the Final Solution through the career of a single individual. Although witnesses played an important part at Nuremberg, they were less prominent than in Jerusalem, where their testimony was one of the trial's raisons d'être.

And yet, it is hard to argue that the Eichmann trial alone ushered in an "era of the witness": survivors took the stand more to testify on behalf of the dead than to accuse the executioner of the crime of which they were victims.[21] Mass testimonies following episodes of extreme violence first appeared during and after the First World War, in particular in the writings of officers and soldiers. This was a new phenomenon resulting from the thresholds crossed by the conflict's cruelty. A small number of Shoah testimonies emerged as soon as the Second World War ended. These brought up another set of questions, extensively debated for thirty years, about their *reception* and *assimilation*, a process that cannot be reduced to merely counting the writings published before the 1960s. Moreover, there are major variations: Primo Levi's *If This Is a Man*, which came out in Italy in 1947, met with little notice at first, whereas *The Diary of Anne Frank*, published posthumously in Holland the same year, became a worldwide bestseller. Ultimately, the judicial symbolism of courtroom testimony – the swearing-in of witnesses, examination and cross-examination (for tactical reasons or modesty or both, Eichmann's lawyer abstained from that possibility), the testimony's public nature and the implications for the case being tried – give it a singular character, especially in Jerusalem. It is not so much the "deposition" that draws attention and constitutes a "place of memory" as the substance and tone of the testimony itself and, even more so, the singularity of the discourse. In that regard, it is significant that most of the filmed images of this kind of testimony, whether at the Eichmann or the Barbie trial, were afterwards used abundantly in particular in educational settings where isolated clips are detached from their judicial context, as if that context does not really matter.

The transformation of justice into a vector of memory has changed the balance of power within the courtroom. In any case, it is concomitant with a major shift in contemporary criminal justice, that is, the importance granted to the victim. In a way, it may be said that in the long run the Eichmann trial marked the transition between the era of the witness, which began with the twentieth century's first catastrophe, and the era of the victim, a transition that took shape with the emergence of the memory of the Shoah in the 1980s and 1990s. This put an end to the heroic, patriotic wartime and postwar culture that Israel and the European countries developed immediately after the Second World War.[22]

The trial established a public account of the Shoah in Israel. It helped awaken Jewish memory worldwide, especially in the United States, although recent research has tried to show that a memory of the Shoah already existed within the American Jewish community, which had many survivors in its ranks as soon as the war was over.[23] It resonated in Germany, rife with contradictions between the official desire to move on and the younger generations' increasingly relentless pressure to reassess the past. However, it would be a mistake to confuse the global dimension of the event, which mobilized the international press, at least in the beginning, and the scope of the consciousness raising it accomplished outside Jewish communities and the countries involved. The trial did not draw notice in the Communist bloc, except in the German Democratic Republic, which sought to use it against the other Germany. In Egypt, Lebanon, Syria, and Jordan, which had a huge number of Palestinian refugees – then in the midst of a psychological and political battle against Israel – perceptions were not the same as in the Western countries. Despite some variations, and in a press largely under government control (except in Lebanon), the issues discussed in relation to the trial had to do almost exclusively with political propaganda. The Arab media took no interest in the historical facts in play. First, the Arab press challenged the legitimacy of Israel's claim to try Eichmann, his arrest having violated Argentinian sovereignty. In addition, the idea of complicity, if not equivalence, between Nazism and Zionism, was floated, and the Kasztner episode exploited. This was also the moment when the comparison between the Shoah and the Nakba, the catastrophe of the Palestinian people, began to spread, especially in the wake of an Arab League directive asking that that point be emphasized. And this despite the fact that the trial testimony itself revealed day after day the utter impossibility of making such a comparison. Many articles and cartoons contested the claims concerning the magnitude of the crime and, in a contradiction typical of postwar anti-Semitism, evinced open sympathy for Eichmann, "who had the honor of killing five million Jews" while criticizing him for "not finishing the job."[24] The trial also gave Israel an opportunity, in many official speeches, to recall the wartime presence in Germany of the grand mufti of Jerusalem, Hadj Amin al-Husayni, one of the main Palestinian leaders, and his ties to Eichmann. Attorney General Hausner emphasized the connection, using logic that had more to do with the situation in the 1960s than with those facts' relevance to the crimes of which the defendant stood accused.[25] The mufti's overt collaboration with Nazi Germany was based on the idea "the enemy of my enemy is my friend," the enemies being, on the one hand, the British, against whom he took the same nationalistic stance as other independence militants who had contacts with the Reich (such as India's Subhas Chandra Bose and some Egyptian activists); and on the other the Jews, who sought to set up a Jewish state in Palestine. The historical analysis is inextricably caught up in a process of manipulating the past. The originality here lies in the symmetry of the accusations made to denounce, on the one side, the Zionist foe (and its "ties" with Eichmann) and, on the other, the Palestinian enemy and its "collaboration" with the Reich. But the processes cannot be compared: the intention of the Shoah was to kill all the Jews, and the Palestinians of 1960 could not be held collectively responsible for what the mufti did in 1941.

The Eichmann case played only a marginal role in France. It mainly found an echo among Jewish survivors or Resistance fighters and the Contemporary Jewish Documentation Centre, which sent documents and one of its members, Georges Wellers, to Jerusalem to testify. The trial started a week before the generals' putsch in Algiers on 23 April 1961, and Eichmann was executed two months after the Evian accords were signed on 19 March 1962, just as the repatriations from Algeria to France reached their peak. The French press covered the event, and already or soon-to-be famous intellectuals (Joseph Kessel and Robert Badinter) wrote about its importance. But it had little impact on collective representations of the Shoah, which occasionally sparked debates, although not nearly as many as it did two decades later in the 1980s. In the early 1960s memories of the Occupation were less raw but still fresh in everyone's minds. Official government choices aimed at a partial desire to forget the past and, above all, reconcile with the hereditary enemy, Germany. Six months after Eichmann's execution in December 1962, on the eve of the January 1963 Franco-German Friendship Treaty, General de Gaulle quietly ordered the release of Karl Oberg, the German police chief in France, and his assistant, Helmut Knochen. A military tribunal had sentenced both to death in 1954 but they were reprieved and spent only twenty years in French prisons. Twenty-five years later, in 1987, one of their subordinates, Klaus Barbie, was sentenced to life for crimes against humanity, while thirty-two years later, in 1994, an obscure Vichy militia member, Paul Touvier, received the same sentence. True, those sentences were only made possible by a December 1964 law abolishing the statute of limitations for crimes against humanity, passed after the Federal Republic of Germany announced a possible statute of limitations on Nazi crimes in 1965 (which was eventually rejected.) But Oberg's and Knochen's direct and central involvement in the deportation of 76,000 Jews from France was never an issue in the decisions to release them and to abolish the statute of limitations for some of their crimes. The figure of 76,000 victims had not even been established at the time; that would occur in the 1970s as a result of research by Serge Klarsfeld and the Centre de Documentation Juive Contemporaine (CDJC). The debate that *was* occurring at the time had to do with what to do with individuals who had committed crimes against Resistance members, civilians, and Jews, of course. But there was no emphasis on the Shoah's singularity, even though that lay at the heart of the Eichmann trial, an event still fresh in historical terms.

The trial's impact, then, varies less in accordance with places where Nazism left indelible traces than it does with the relationship of particular countries and national opinions with the State of Israel, or with the configurations of specific Jewish communities, or the circumstances of the moment of the country or countries in question, or the history of their own national memories. There is neither a mechanical relationship between the trial's inherent importance and its role in the long-term formation of a memory of the Shoah, nor a linear evolution in the emergence of that memory. The trial was a point of focus, an undoubtedly decisive moment in raising awareness, at least in Jewish communities. But it did not become a lasting feature in the landscape of memory until much later, in another context, and through the actions of other generations.

NOTES

1 This essay is a translation of "Juger le passé: le procès Eichmann," in *Face au passé: Essais sur le mémoire contemporaine* (Paris: Belin, 2016), 197–227. An earlier version of this essay appeared as "Réflexions sur un procès historique," in Henry Rousso, *Juger Eichmann: Jérusalem, 1961* (Paris: Mémorial de la Shoah), 2011.

2 Tom Segev, *The Seventh Million: The Israelis and the Holocaust*, trans. H. Watzman (New York: Hill and Wang, 1993), 361.

3 Avraham Burg, *The Holocaust Is Over: We Must Rise from Its Ashes*, trans. I. Amrani (New York: Palgrave Macmillan, 2008), 127–8.

4 Claude Lanzmann, *The Patagonian Hare* (New York: Farrar, Straus, and Giroux, 2009), 425.

5 Michael Greve, *Der justitielle und rechtspolitische Untgang mit den NS-Gewaltverbrechen in den sechziger Jahren* (Frankfurt-am-Main: Peter Lang, 2001). Christian-Frederic Rüter and Dick W. De Mildt, eds, *Die*

westdeutschen Strafverfahren wegen nationalsozialistischer Tötungsverbrechen 1945–1997 (Amsterdam & Maarssen: APA-Holland University Press; München: K.G. Saur, 1998).

6 The specifics of the Demjanjuk case are discussed by Lawrence Douglas in chapter 8 of this volume.

7 Segev, *The Seventh Million*, 313. Hanna Yablonka speaks of approximately thirty to forty cases in *The State of Israel vs. Adolf Eichmann* (New York: Schocken Books, 2004).

8 Archives du Centre de Documentation Juive Contemporaine (CDJC), 527-2, "Procès Eichmann, police israélienne, divers." Quotation translated from the French translation from the Hebrew, provided in 1961 by the Jerusalem District Court itself.

9 On the French case, see Anne Simonin, *Le déshonneur dans la République: Une histoire de l'indignité, 1791–1958* (Paris: Grasset, 2008). See also Henry Rousso, "The Purge in France: An Incomplete History," in *Retribution and Reparation in the Transition to Democracy*, ed. Jon Elster (New York: Cambridge University Press, 2006), 89–123.

10 Testimony of Salo Baron, session 12, 24 April 1961; the quote is from the beginning of his testimony at the Eichmann trial.

11 Léon Poliakov, *Bréviaire de la haine: Le III*e *reich et les Juifs* (Paris: Calmann-Lévy, 1951). Gerald Reitlinger, *The Final Solution: The Attempt to Exterminate the Jews of Europe, 1939–1945* (New York: Beechhurst Press, 1953). On early Holocaust historiography, see David Cesarani, *Becoming Eichmann: Rethinking the Life, Crimes, and Trial of a "Desk Murderer"* (Cambridge, MA: Da Capo Press, 2007).

12 G. Kenig, "Un témoin contre Eichmann ou pour Vichy?" *Le Presse Nouvelle* (organe de l'Union des Juifs pour la Résistance et l'Entraide), 20–1 May 1961, archives du CDJC.

13 Hannah Arendt, *Eichmann in Jerusalem: A Report on the Banality of Evil* (New York: Viking Penguin, 1963).

14 Ibid. According to Raul Hilberg, Arendt left Jerusalem three days before the questioning of the defendant began on 29 June 1961. She therefore missed the trial's second phase, when Eichmann was at the centre of the debates and spoke at length, whereas he had spoken little until then for procedural reasons. See Raul Hilberg, *The Politics of Memory: The Journey of a Holocaust Historian* (Chicago: Ivan R. Dee, 1996). Hilberg did not cite his sources, but during a conversation I had with him when *The Destruction of the European Jews* came out in French in 1988, he told me he had consulted Arendt's passport in her personal archives – a sort of revenge for her negative opinion of his book when it came out in 1959, a book which she used abundantly afterwards!

15 The excerpts from Eichmann's various writings reproduced in the exhibition (*Juger Eichmann* by Henry Russo) are in the Bundesarchiv of Koblenz, Germany. Some are from a private collection donated to the collection by Nachlass Adolf Eichmann. Others are from a collection containing the papers of his lawyer, Robert Servatius (Eichmann-Prozess All Proz 6 1960–1963). They were analysed by historians, including Christian Gerlach in "The Eichmann Interrogation in Holocaust Historiography," *Holocaust and Genocide Studies* 15, no. 3 (Winter 2001): 428–52. See also Irmtrud Wojak, *Eichmanns Memoiren: Ein kririseher Essay* (Frankfurt: Campus Verlag, 2001). Eichmann's autobiographical novel, *Roman Tucumdn* (named after the Argentine province where he lived), is in the possession of his heirs. We were unable to consult it.

16 La "Mise au point" – "Betrifft: Meine Feststellungen zur Angelegenheit" Judenfragen mid Massnahmen der nat. soz. Deutschen Reichsregiermzg zur Losung theses Komplaves in den Jahren von 1933 bis 1945, a sixty-nine-page text used during the trial (Bundesarchiv, All Proz 6/Ill. The original version, whose handwritten pages were intended for Adenauer, was unknown (N 1497/90). Historian and philosopher Bettina Stangneth also found this document, which she puts into the context of Adenauer's Germany in an essential book, *Eichmann Before Jerusalem: The Unexamined Life of a Mass Murderer*, published in April 2011, at the same time our exhibition opened. She says Eichmann started writing a book, *Die anderen Sprachen, jet! will idi spree/zen!* of which the "Betriffi" made up the central part. See *Eichnzann vor Jerusalem: Das unbehelligre Leben clues Massenmarders* (Zurich-Hamburg: Arche Literatur Verlag), 277–81.

17 Bundesarchiv, All Proz 6/165–177. These were several handwritten notebooks in which Eichmann commented on the witnesses' testimony, the prosecutor's statements, and some of the historical research mentioned, and so forth.

18 On this point see Yablonka, *The State of Israel vs Adolf Eichmann*, 189ff.

19 These figures come from official trial documents available at the CDJC.

20 Claude Lanzmann filmed several of the Eichmann trial witnesses for his documentary *Shoah*, including Michael Podchlewnik, Shimon Srebrnik, and Yitzhak Zuckerman, who appear in the final cut, and Joel Brand, Hansi Brand, Abba Kovner, and Ada Lichtmann. Information provided by Rémi Besson, who is completing a thesis on the film's history.

21 Annette Wieviorka, *The Era of the Witnesses* (Ithaca, NY: Cornell University Press, 2006).

22 On the notion of patriotic memory, see Pieter Lagrou, *The Legacy of Nazi Occupation: Patriotic Memory and National Recovery in Western Europe, 1945–1965* (Cambridge: Cambridge University Press, 2000).

23 On this question, see the opposing viewpoints of Peter Novick, *The Holocaust in American Life* (New York: Houghton Mifflin, 1999), and Hasia Diner, *We Remember with Reverence and Love: American Jews and the Myth of Silence after the Holocaust, 1945–1962* (New York: New York University Press, 2009).

24 These examples come from Meir Litvak and Esther Webman, *From Empathy to Denial: Arab Responses to the Holocaust* (London: Hurst, 2009), 123.

25 Ibid., 297ff.

Chapter Two

Eichmann in Jerusalem: Conscience, Normality, and the "Rule of Narrative"

DANA VILLA

In an essay entitled "Theaters of Justice: Arendt in Jerusalem, the Eichmann Trial, and the Redefinition of Legal Meaning in the Wake of the Holocaust," the literary critic Shoshana Felman argues that, while constituting a "conceptual breakthrough" in our understanding of the Holocaust, *Eichmann in Jerusalem* actually blinds us to the primary significance of the Eichmann trial as an event.[1]

In this essay, I begin by discussing Felman's reasons for making this claim, which I see as strangely continuous with the misreadings which have plagued the book since its publication. Such misreadings began with the original controversy, in which many of Arendt's critics – citing ten pages in the middle of a three-hundred-page book – charged that she had laid a large portion of the responsibility for the disaster on the Jews themselves.[2] In more recent times, critics have abandoned the idea that Arendt's work was somehow an exercise in "blaming the victim," focusing instead on her representation of Eichmann and its implications for our understanding of the perpetrators in general. Thus, Daniel Goldhagen argues that *Eichmann in Jerusalem* was responsible for the widespread image of the perpetrators as "thoughtless bureaucrats," a characterization he sees as fundamentally at odds with the anti-Semitic reality of "Hitler's willing executioners."[3]

Felman's argument, while appreciative of *Eichmann in Jerusalem*'s originality as a "critical legal history," marks a return to the terrain of the victims, and – perhaps – represents the case for a "third wave" of criticism of *Eichmann in Jerusalem*.[4] Invoking the recent academic fascination with the idea of law as narrative, memory of (and memorials to) the Holocaust, and the virtually un-representable nature of the trauma the survivors endured, Felman indicts Arendt not for blaming the victims, but for her unwitting complicity in depriving the victims of a voice. The Eichmann trial, Felman argues, broke the silence surrounding the Holocaust – in Israel, in America, in Germany, and around the world. Had the trial been conducted in accordance with Arendt's emphatic insistence on the strict demands of justice, the voice of the survivors would not have been heard, and the silence would not have been broken.

In the opening pages of *Eichmann in Jerusalem*, Arendt charged Israel's prime minister, David Ben-Gurion, with the intent to mount a "show trial," one less concerned with truth and justice than with indicting anti-Semitism in general and presenting the world with the lesson that, with the founding of the State of Israel, "Jews are not sheep to be slaughtered, but a people who can hit back."[5] Arendt's concern was not to cast doubt on Israel's right to try and condemn Eichmann, but rather to show how Ben-Gurion's educational agenda – aimed at both Israeli and world opinion – obscured both Eichmann's specific deeds and the unprecedented nature of the crime – genocide – he had helped commit. While Ben-Gurion and his lead prosecutor, Israeli Attorney General Gideon Hausner, wanted to use Eichmann as an excuse for a propagandistic presentation of the long history of Jewish suffering (culminating in the horrors of the Final Solution and the necessity of a Jewish state), Arendt wanted the trial to remain focused on Eichmann's deeds and his limited (but nevertheless damning) role in facilitating the Final Solution and the destruction of European Jewry.

Why did Arendt want to restrict the focus of the trial? What led her to react so violently (and, in print, sarcastically) to Ben-Gurion and Hausner's "staged" presentation of Jewish suffering, as well as to the long parade of "background" witnesses whose unimaginable sufferings often occurred in places where Eichmann had little or no authority?

In part it was revulsion at what she saw as the unashamed politicization of justice in the "official narrative" presented by the prosecution, in which Eichmann was assigned the unlikely role of chief architect and executioner of the Final Solution.[6] This explains her disdainful comments concerning Hausner's inflated rhetoric, as well as her admiring remarks about the Israeli judges who were able to rein him in a little, thereby preventing the proceedings from degenerating into a "bloody show."[7] In part it was her sense that no purpose was served by having witness follow witness, piling horror upon horror, when the events in question clearly fell outside of Eichmann's authority and range of action. The audience at the trial – described by Arendt as "filled with 'survivors,' with middle-aged and elderly people, immigrants from

Europe, like myself, who knew by heart all there was to know" – had to sit and listen "in public to stories they would hardly have been able to endure in private, when they would have had to face the storyteller."[8] This "unendurable" experience lasted over sixty-two trial sessions (out of a total of 121), as a hundred witnesses for the prosecution "told their tales of horror," even though many of these were, strictly speaking, irrelevant from a legal perspective.[9]

Yet the main reason Arendt rebelled against the narrative set out at the trial was that she felt the prosecution relied far too heavily on the trope of an age-old anti-Semitism in Europe.

So framed, the Holocaust emerged as one particularly traumatic chapter in the long story of Jewish suffering.[10] This, combined with the sheer mass of "numbing" survivor testimony read into the record, effectively hid from view "the unprecedented nature of the Nazi crime," which can be summed up in the distinction between a pogrom and a *genocide*.[11] The judgment, while correcting or steering clear of many of Hausner's exaggerations, stayed within the broad narrative frame he and Ben-Gurion had established. It achieved the most important thing – namely, it rendered judgment and justice – but it failed to rise to the most important challenge set by the trial. Sticking close to precedent and the "narrative of repetition" that is the history of European anti-Semitism, the judges were unable to fashion a legal language which adequately captured both the new type of crime (state-sponsored genocide) and the new kind of criminal represented by Eichmann – a criminal for whom motives were, in large part, superfluous. In Arendt's view, the Eichmann trial – both in its process and judgment – failed to elicit the novelty of either the crime or the criminal, and thus failed to engage the legal problem posed by Eichmann's absence of criminal intent (the problem Arendt encapsulates in the phrase "the banality of evil"). It thus failed to provide a valid legal precedent for future cases involving genocide as state policy.[12]

For Felman, seeing the Eichmann trial – whether in the prosecution's presentation or the judgment itself – as even a partial "failure" makes sense only if we stay within the confines of what she calls Arendt's "conservative legal approach." This approach – rigidly focused on the perpetrator, the trial as a legal proceeding, and the paradoxical undertaking of litigating an "historically unprecedented" crime[13] – ignores the broader significance of the trial as an event, both in Israel and the world. Indeed, Felman states her task as that of "espousing the state's [i.e., the prosecution's] vision of the trial and … highlighting differently than Arendt what I take to be the deeper meaning of the trial and, beyond its meaning, its far-reaching repercussions as an event – an event which *includes Arendt*."[14]

In order to uncover this "deeper meaning" and tease out the "far-reaching repercussions," Felman draws on the well-known typology of modes of history found in Nietzsche's *Use and Abuse of History*. Nietzsche had distinguished between a critical, a monumental, and an antiquarian approach to the past, each of which can "serve life" at various times and in various places. Felman draws on Nietzsche to suggest that Arendt's "trial report" is, in fact, a piece of "critical history" which seeks not inspiration, but liberation from the past – in this case, the historical narrative of Jewish suffering and trauma, which has the effect of "screening" or effacing the new.[15] Hence, *Eichmann in Jerusalem* is, according to Felman, essentially "deconstructive" in character. As "critical historian," Arendt (to use Nietzsche's words) aims at "shattering and dissolving the past" by "bringing this past before a tribunal, painstakingly interrogating it, and finally condemning it."[16] Only in this way can the unprecedented nature of the crime – and the criminal – emerge.

Against Arendt's "critical history," Felman argues that the "deeper meaning" of the trial becomes apparent only if we view it in "monumental" terms. By this she hardly means that we should view the Holocaust in terms of "the great moments in the struggles of individuals" which (according to Nietzsche) "form links in one single chain," challenging "dull habit, the trivial and the common" with the inspiring knowledge that great deeds were once performed.[17] No, what Felman means is that the trial itself is and ought to be seen as a *monument* to the victims. And it is a monument in a quite peculiar way. The Eichmann trial, according to Felman, was nothing less than "a groundbreaking narrative event," one which did not repeat the victim's story, but which created it historically "for the first time."[18] The Eichmann trial as an event struggles to "create a new space, a language that is not yet in existence" – a language in which the unprecedented nature of the injury takes precedence over the unprecedented nature of the crime.

How does the trial do this? According to Felman, it was precisely through the "theatrical" character that Arendt had so decried in the opening pages of her book. By creating a public, theatrical space in which the victims could, for the first time, articulate what had been private trauma into public language, the trial enacted what Felman calls a "legal process of translation," one which took "thousands of private, secret traumas" and transposed them into "one collective, public, and communally acknowledged one."[19] In her desire to focus on the crime and keep unendurable pain hidden from public view, Arendt thus missed the genuine novelty of the trial: its character as an event through which the silence of the victims was transformed into a public voice, one in which the victim's story happened – came into language – for the first time.[20] Thus, according to Felman, the Eichmann trial – far from being a "show trial" conceived by the state to teach ideological lessons – was animated, in fact, by a "legally creative vision," one which attempted and achieved nothing less than a "conceptual revolution in the victim," a revolution which contributes "not only to Jews, but to history, to law, to culture – to humanity at large."[21] Through the trial, the survivors regained their voice: they became the "authors of history" rather than its mute victims.

Felman's critique of Arendt's perspective in *Eichmann in Jerusalem* is provocative, and not merely because it uses Arendtian ideas – the emphasis on novelty, the distinction between public and private, the link between action and narrative or "storytelling" – against Arendt. It is provocative in a deeper way insofar as it argues that the significance of the Eichmann trial – its "monumental significance," as it were – is to be found precisely in the survivor testimony that Arendt considered largely irrelevant or immaterial. It is this testimony which "broke the silence" surrounding the Holocaust in Israel and – Felman implies – the world.[22] For the first time, the victims were "empowered": they gained "semantic authority" over the traumatic event.[23] In denying the import of the survivors' testimony, in viewing this aspect of the proceedings through the lens of a "conservative philosophy of law," Arendt did not merely miss the "contribution" of the Eichmann trial to the creation of a new legal language centred on the victims. Her deployment of the public/private distinction in the interest of curtailing "immaterial" testimony actively worked to "relegate the victim experience to the private realm."[24]

The Eichmann trial, then, was nothing less than an event in which Zionism (to quote Felman) "provided a tribunal (a state justice) in which the Jew's victimization [could] be for the first time *legally articulated*."[25] As such, the prosecution's focus on the long story of Jewish suffering was entirely warranted, since anti-Semitism as such really was in the dock, with Eichmann himself serving only as a symbol or "emblem."[26] Had the trial been conducted in accordance with Arendt's "conservative legal philosophy," this all-important articulation would simply never have occurred.

Felman's critique of Arendt and her proposal that we view the Eichmann trial through the new narrative frame are disconcerting, and for a number of reasons. Her suggestion that we view the trial less as a legal proceeding grappling with an unprecedented crime than as an "event" through which the victim recovers his/her voice neatly shifts attention away from "merely" legal justice to the terrain of what Felman calls "historical justice." The trial does not seek justice for Eichmann's crimes or the truth of his deeds (since he is merely, in Felman's phrase, an "emblem"), but rather "builds a monument" to Jewish suffering, a "new collective story" which not only empowers the victim but "for the first time ... create[s] what we know today as the Holocaust."[27] Just as much as Ben-Gurion, Felman sees the trial as, in a sense, completing the founding and legitimation of the State of Israel through the "discovery" of the Holocaust. Thus, the "monument" – the trial and its public testimony – is not merely a record of unimaginable suffering; rather, it generates what Felman calls a "canonical or *sacred narrative*" (emphasis in original) which grounds both collective memory *and* the state. To put the matter simply: Felman's focus on the trial as event traces the inner transformation of Zionism – and, by extension, Israeli civil religion – in light of the public appropriation of the Holocaust. The real "monument" to the victims is, of course, not the trial, but the State of Israel itself.

Let me say that there is nothing wrong with viewing the Eichmann trial in this manner, so long as we remind ourselves that this is a *retrospective interpretation* of its broad political, historical, and sociological significance and not the uncovering of an essential "deeper meaning" which Hannah Arendt had somehow simply failed to recognize. Arendt knew – or thought she knew – what Ben-Gurion and Hausner were up to, and she was repelled by it. Whether she ought to have been repelled by it is something that reasonable people can disagree about (although I think Felman and others are a little too quick in assuming that there is or can be such a thing as a good or "educational" show trial).[28] However, the oddest aspect of Felman's rereading of the Eichmann trial is not her justification of the prosecution's narrative in the name of the victim's voice and the needs of collective memory, but her assumption that Arendt viewed the proceedings in narrowly legalistic terms, failing to engage the broader moral and historical issues raised by the trial.

This assumption is quite unfounded. True, in *Eichmann in Jerusalem*, Arendt worries – as did many at the time of the trial – over questions of procedure, presentation, and jurisdiction. But she is not obsessed by them, and relegates most of what she has to say to the "Epilogue" of the original volume. Arendt might well have had a "conservative legal philosophy" – that is, one which saw the work of law as rendering justice, not telling stories or "educating" world opinion[29] – but if she did, this philosophy is not the centre of gravity of *Eichmann in Jerusalem*. Indeed, it is no exaggeration to state that Arendt was most fascinated by issues that she herself acknowledged "may not have been *legally* relevant."[30] Like so many critics before her, Felman presents us with an incredibly foreshortened version of Arendt's text, one which fails to come to terms with (or even mention) what Arendt called "the central moral, political, and even legal problems that the trial inevitably posed."[31]

What were these problems? What captured Arendt's attention in Jerusalem? What, in short, is *Eichmann in Jerusalem* about?

In answering this question, we have to note (pace Felman) that Arendt's "trial report" is only in small part a deconstruction of the "official narrative" of the trial. Arendt devotes a relatively small portion of her first chapter to questioning the motives and presentation of Ben-Gurion and the prosecution. She devotes almost seventy pages (chapters 9 to 13) to an overview of the deportation process as it occurred in various regions of Europe, the better to sort out Eichmann's responsibilities, actions, and authority from those of competing Nazi agencies, the army, and local (native) magistrates and populations – an exercise designed to correct the "general picture" painted by the prosecution of Eichmann's (supposed) comprehensive authority. But the book as a whole does not revolve around the "refutation" of the official narrative. Rather, it clearly revolves around Arendt's portrait of Eichmann himself, whom she first dismissed (in a letter to Karl Jaspers) as *"eigentlich dumm,"* but who turned out to be far more interesting than this (or the usual characterization of "thoughtless bureaucrat") allowed.[32]

What made Eichmann so interesting to Arendt? How did this somewhat ludicrous man force her to engage "the central moral and political" problems raised by the trial, and by the event of the Holocaust itself?

The answers to these questions are found in Eichmann's "normality" and (strange as it might sound) in his conscience. However "thoughtless" Eichmann might have been, he was hardly an unthinking "cog" in a bureaucratic apparatus, ready and able to provide the most efficient means to any end whatsoever. The trial revealed that he did, in fact, have a conscience, but that this conscience failed to work in the way generally assumed by Western law, moral philosophy, and religion. It failed to provide Eichmann with a clear sense of the criminality of his actions, and so failed to support the prosecution's contention that he had acted with criminal intent and in full knowledge of the transgressive quality of his actions. To be sure, Eichmann knew what he was doing in arranging the "shipments" of Jews to places like Treblinka, Chelmno, and Auschwitz, since he had seen for himself the arrangements being made for their liquidation.[33] But, for Eichmann, these actions became "criminal" only when he found himself in Jerusalem, on trial for committing them.

It is possible to explain this by saying that Eichmann was lying – that he knew full well that what he was doing was wrong, but that he did it anyway because he was a fanatical anti-Semite (and/or sadist). This, in fact, was the prosecution's stance.[34] Alternatively, one could argue that he had be so indoctrinated by Nazi ideology that he had truly come to believe that Jews really were the greatest threat to the survival of the German people. The problem was that neither of these explanations comported with the concrete reality of the man in the dock. Half a dozen psychiatrists examined him and found him entirely "normal" – a man with "not only normal but most desirable" attitudes towards his wife, children, mother, father, brothers, sisters, and friends.[35] Moreover, Eichmann vehemently denied that he had acted, as the indictment implied, out of such "base motives" as wickedness, greed, or racial hatred.[36] To quote Arendt, "as for base motives, he was perfectly sure that he was not what he called … a dirty bastard in the depths of his heart; and as for his conscience, he remembered perfectly well that he would have had a bad conscience *only if he had not done what he had been ordered to do – to ship millions of men, women, and children to their death with great zeal and the most meticulous care*."[37]

How could one do this if one were not a militant anti-Semite or a committed Nazi? How could Eichmann truthfully claim that he did what he did without ever being a fanatical Jew-hater? As Arendt emphasizes, nobody at the trial believed him in this regard:

> The prosecutor did not believe him, because that was not his job. Counsel for the defense paid no attention because he, unlike Eichmann, was, to all appearances, not interested in questions of conscience. And the judges did not believe him, because they were too good, and perhaps also too conscious of *the very foundations of their profession*, to admit that an average, "normal" person, neither feeble-minded nor indoctrinated nor cynical,

> could be perfectly incapable of telling right from wrong. They preferred to conclude from occasional lies that he was a liar – and missed the greatest moral and even legal challenge of the whole case. Their case rested on the assumption that the defendant, like all "normal persons," must have been aware of the criminal nature of his acts, and Eichmann was indeed normal insofar as he was "no exception within the Nazi regime."[38]

This passage contains in a nutshell the problem presented by the Eichmann trial, the problem the prosecution and the judges failed to engage or even really recognize. For once we acknowledge that Eichmann in fact had a conscience, and was indeed "normal" (at least by the measures of the "soul experts"), then we are confronted with the uncomfortable possibility that an "average person" – one who is neither "feeble-minded [n]or cynical" – can in fact be "perfectly incapable of telling right from wrong." The central problem presented by the Eichmann trial was not – at least not for Arendt – how the law can respond to the unprecedented crime of state-sponsored genocide, or even to the apparent absence of motive in a criminal defendant. Rather, it was what happens to our categories of moral and legal thought when we acknowledge that the "inner voice of conscience" – the "built in" moral faculty that is supposed to raise a "black flag" over criminal orders for the soldier and unjust statutes for the citizen – turns out to be a fiction? What happens when the "fail-safe" moral faculty of conscience turns out to be no more than what Nietzsche (in *Beyond Good and Evil*) describes as a "formal conscience," a function of socially defined norms and the internalization of externally given authority?[39]

The answers to these questions, Arendt quite clearly states, bore little direct relation to the proceedings of the trial, or indeed to the verdict ultimately handed down. But the question of Eichmann's "moral psychology" was clearly the most fascinating aspect of the trial for Arendt – and piqued the interest of the judges as well.[40] It lies behind Arendt's much-misunderstood thesis about the "banality of evil" – a thesis which is by no means a characterization of the extreme or radical evil perpetrated by the Nazis. Nor was it, for that matter, a thesis about the "absence of motive" found in bureaucratic "desk murderers" (as Felman assumes it is).[41] Rather, the idea of the banality of evil had to do with the peculiar mix of thoughtlessness and self-deception that Eichmann evidenced throughout the trial, a mix which testified not to any absence of conscience, but to the disconcerting ease with which the "formal conscience" (to stay with Nietzsche's term) can be "coordinated" with the social reality around it, no matter how pathological or criminal that reality may be.[42]

This concern with Eichmann's moral psychology – and the degree to which it was representative of countless other Germans and Europeans who were complicit with genocide – drives the central chapters of *Eichmann in Jerusalem,* which Arendt describes as her "report on Eichmann's conscience."[43] It is one of the more startling facts of the agitated response to *Eichmann in Jerusalem* that Arendt's announced central theme has drawn little or no critical attention.

What, then, are the main features of Arendt's "report on Eichmann's conscience"?

First, that he indeed had a conscience, and that it had not been silenced by either visceral hatred or ideological fantasy. As evidence, Arendt cites a particularly telling incident that occurred in September 1941, shortly after Eichmann had made his visits to the "killing centers" being set up in the East. In accordance with Hitler's wish – relayed by Himmler – to make the Reich "clean of Jews" as quickly as possible, Eichmann arranged a "shipment" of twenty thousand Jews from the Rhineland, along with five thousand Gypsies. And it is with regard to this first shipment that a strange thing happened. Eichmann, who was congenitally adverse to risks or acting without being totally "covered" by orders from higher up, "'for the first and last time' took an initiative contrary to orders."[44] Rather than sending the twenty-five thousand to their "final destination" in Russian territory (Riga or Minsk) – where they would have been summarily shot by the *Einsatzgruppen* – he instead directed the transport to the Lodz ghetto. Here, it is true, conditions were appalling, but immediate execution was not the order of the day. Unfortunately for Eichmann, this decision wound up causing him a fair amount of trouble, since the official in charge of the ghetto was "in no mood to receive newcomers and in no position to accommodate them," and complained vociferously to Himmler about the "horse trading tricks" Eichmann had "learned from the Gypsies."[45]

On the stand, confronted with documents relating to this incident, Eichmann stated: "Here for the first and last time I had a choice … One was Lodz … If there were difficulties in Lodz, these people must be sent onward to the East. And since I had seen the preparations, I was determined to do all I could to send these people to Lodz by any means at my disposal."[46] While his defence counsel disingenuously tried to use this incident to prove Eichmann had tried to save Jews whenever he could, and while the prosecution saw the incident as proof that

Eichmann had total authority over where every "shipment" wound up, the real significance of this incident – the only time Eichmann actually tried to save Jews – lies elsewhere. As Arendt notes, just three or four weeks later, at a meeting in Prague called by Reinhardt Heydrich (the real "engineer" of the Final Solution), Eichmann proposed employing the camps used for the detention of Russian Communists (who were to be liquidated on the spot by the *Einsatzgruppen*) for the detention and extermination of Jews as well.[47] Somehow, in the period of a few weeks, Eichmann's "innate repugnance to crime" seems to have been overcome. Judge Landau's question – the question, as Arendt puts it, which was "uppermost in the minds of nearly everyone who followed the trial" – of whether the accused had a conscience was given a disconcerting answer: "Yes, he had a conscience, and his conscience functioned in the expected way for about four weeks, whereupon it began to function the other way around."[48]

Eichmann, of course, remembered none of this. In his own mind, the decisive turning point occurred not four weeks, but four months later, at the Wannsee Conference in January 1942. Eichmann's recollection of this event – and the major role it played in eliminating any residual doubts he may have had about the policy of physically exterminating the Jews – is so central to Arendt's "report on Eichmann's conscience" that she devotes a chapter to it.[49] For it is in Eichmann's description of this event that we discover the reason why his conscience was so quickly – and easily – soothed.

Heydrich had organized the Wannsee Conference in order to see how higher career civil service men – the undersecretaries of state – would respond to the idea of the physical extermination of the Jews. These men were from various ministries (Transport, Finance, Foreign Service, etc.) whose cooperation and coordination would be absolutely vital to the implementation of the Final Solution. Going into the meeting, Heydrich, Eichmann recalled, "expected the greatest difficulties." But instead of encountering resistance to a "radical solution" of the Jewish question, Heydrich found his proposal greeted with "extraordinary enthusiasm" by all present. Not moral, but "complicated legal questions" – such as the treatment of half- and quarter-Jews (should they be killed or only sterilized?) – were raised, along with a discussion of the various methods of killing themselves.[50] For Eichmann, who served as secretary to the meeting and who was not used to mixing with so many "high personages," it was "an unforgettable day." As Arendt writes,

> Although he had been doing his best right along to help with the Final Solution, he had still harbored some doubts about "such a bloody solution through violence," and these doubts had now been dispelled. "Here now, during this conference, the most prominent people had spoken, the Popes of the Third Reich." Now he could see with his own eyes and hear with his own ears that not only Hitler, not only Heydrich ... not just the S.S. or the Party, but the elite of the good old Civil Service were vying and fighting with each other for the honor of taking the lead in these "bloody" matters. "At that moment, I sensed a kind of Pontius Pilate feeling, for I felt free of all guilt." *Who was he to judge?* Who was he "to have [his] own thoughts in this matter?"[51]

Confronted by the unanimous and enthusiastic endorsement of the new policy of physical extermination by his social betters, Eichmann's "crisis of conscience" quickly disappeared. Indeed (again quoting Arendt), "as Eichmann told it, the most potent factor in the soothing of his own conscience was the simple fact that he could see no one, no one at all, who was actually against the Final Solution."[52] The judges found all this hard to believe. Surely in the course of his duties someone had come forward and pointed out the criminality and immorality of what he was doing.

It is helpful here to recall the testimony of Pastor Heinrich Gruber. Gruber was a man of principle who represented the "other Germany," the leader of a group of Protestant clergymen who intervened during the deportation process "on behalf of people who had been wounded in the course of the First World War and of those who had been awarded high military decorations; on behalf of the old and on behalf of the widows killed in World War I" – categories the Nazis themselves had previously exempted.[53] His meetings with Eichmann on behalf of these people left him with an impression of the accused as a "block of ice" with a mercenary mentality – impressions he duly testified to at the trial. However, when asked point blank by Eichmann's defence attorney whether he, Probst, tried, as a clergyman, to influence Eichmann or appeal to his feelings, the answer was a very embarrassed "no." As Eichmann himself put it, "He [Gruber] came to me and sought the alleviation of suffering, but did not actually object to the performance of my duties as such."[54] The interventions of Gruber and others like him, who spoke on behalf of Jewish war veterans, actually had the effect of giving legitimacy to the rule under which Eichmann carried out his duties.

Thus it was that Eichmann could honestly claim that "there were no voices from the outside to arouse his conscience" once it had been set at ease by the unanimous agreement of his social betters. As Arendt put it, Eichmann "did not need to 'close his ears to the voice of conscience,' as the judgment has it, *not because he had none, but because his conscience spoke with a 'respectable voice,' with the voice of respectable society all around him*."[55] Eichmann's conscience – like many people's in Germany – was merely the internalization of this voice. He never felt the famous "sting of conscience" – not because he actively silenced the moral faculty within him (out of hatred or ideology), but because this faculty merely echoed the moral consensus of the society around him (a society which saw nothing especially wrong in making the Reich "clean of Jews").[56]

This takes us to the heart of Arendt's "report on Eichmann's conscience": to the problem posed by someone who was simply incapable of "telling right from wrong" while actively engaged in implementing a policy of genocide. Like the judges at Eichmann's trial, we assume that the conscience of any "normal" person must be something deeper, more profound, than the internalization of social opinions, norms, or positive law. But once we acknowledge – as *Eichmann in Jerusalem* forces us to do – that what we usually refer to as "conscience" is, for the most part, socially constructed, gaining depth or authenticity only when the individual reconstructs it as an ongoing dialogue of thought and judgment, we risk a kind of vertigo. No longer is it possible to claim – as Western law, moral philosophy, and theology repeatedly do – that human beings possess a kind of built-in or God-given moral compass, one which distinguishes right from wrong and which is silenced only by pathology or wickedness.

I want to be clear on this very important point. It is not that Arendt is claiming that the "voice of respectable society" all around Eichmann drowned out the voice of conscience, or that Eichmann's conscience simply shut down once it received reassurance from the "better people." No, what she is claiming is that Eichmann's conscience continued to function throughout his role in facilitating the Final Solution; that the marked zeal with which he performed his duties was less a sign of anti-Semitism than it was of a peculiar brand of conscientiousness. Once his "innate repugnance to crime" was overcome by the realization that no one around him viewed the policy of deportation and "special treatment" as, in fact, criminal, Eichmann's conscience was free to function "the other way around." It now insisted – sternly and indeed selflessly – that he carry out his duties, not merely because he had orders, but because – in the Third Reich – these particular orders had the force of law. For Eichmann, the zealous performance of his duties was not a simply a matter of bureaucratic or soldierly obedience; rather, it was a question of obeying the law in a regime where the will of the Führer was, practically and theoretically, the source of law.[57]

This is why Arendt entitles the most important chapter of *Eichmann in Jerusalem* "The Duties of a Law-Abiding Citizen," and why she pays such keen attention to Eichmann's odd response to charges lodged against him (he pleaded "guilty, but not in the sense of the indictment").[58] While the prosecution (and the judges) thought he was falling back on a variation of the excuse given by Nazi war criminals at Nuremberg – namely, that he was "only following orders" – Eichmann sensed that something very important hinged on the distinction between obedience to orders and obedience to the law. He found the significance of this distinction – the distinction between the duties of a "law abiding citizen" and blind soldierly obedience – difficult to articulate, however. As a matter of practice, he had always acted cautiously, making sure he was always "covered" by orders and avoiding initiative and responsibility wherever and whenever he could. Thus, as Arendt notes, Eichmann became "completely muddled, and ended up stressing alternately the virtues and the vices of blind obedience."[59]

Why does this distinction matter, and why does Arendt harp on it? Simply because Eichmann's deep internalization of the idea of the "duties of a law-abiding citizen" reveals the way his conscience worked to support and justify the performance of his genocidal duties. If one part of Eichmann wanted to evade responsibility and claim, like the bigger fish at Nuremberg, that he "was only following orders," the other part of him – the conscientious, moralizing part – wanted to assert precisely that non-performance of his duties would have been a crime. We see here how the assumptions of criminal law, and a good deal of moral philosophy and theology, are turned topsy-turvy by a "formal" conscience which equates morality with obedience to duties given by law. Such an equation may promote (in the words of the psychiatrists) "very positive ideas," so long as the individual making it is lucky enough *not* to be a citizen of a criminal state, operating under criminal laws. In the latter case, however, the avoidance of "crime" and the conscientious fulfilment of one's civic or professional obligations leads to active complicity in horror.

What evidence does Arendt give that Eichmann was led to commit his horrendous crimes precisely out of a desire to avoid the taint of "lawlessness" and criminality? First there was his repeated insistence, both to the Israeli police interrogators and the courts, that "he had not only obeyed orders, he also obeyed the law."[60] Although he was muddled about the exact nature of this distinction, his intuitive grasp of the issues involved came out when the court asked him about a peculiar moment in the transcript of his interrogation, where Eichmann had "suddenly declared with great emphasis that he had lived his whole life according to Kant's moral precepts, and especially according to a Kantian definition of duty."[61] Asked by Judge Raveh to clarify what he had meant, Eichmann replied, "I meant by my remark about Kant that the principle of my will must always be such that it can become the principle of general laws."[62]

That a man such as Eichmann could give a generally correct formulation of the categorical imperative was, in itself, disconcerting. Even more disconcerting was his statement that he had read Kant's *Critique of Practical Reason*, and his explanation that he realized that he had ceased to live according to Kantian moral principles from the moment he was charged with carrying out the Final Solution.[63] He claimed to have been distressed by this, but consoled himself with the fact that he no longer was "the master of his own deeds," and (therefore) that he "was unable to change anything."[64]

But – as Arendt points out – during the period of what he himself called "crimes legalized by the state," Eichmann hadn't really abandoned the Kantian formula at all. Rather, he had "distorted it to read: Act as if the principle of your actions were the same as that of the legislator of the law of the land."[65] Or, in Hans Frank's formulation of "the categorical imperative of the Third Reich," "Act in such a way that the Führer, if he knew your action, would approve it."[66] Needless to say, both these formulations go against the spirit of Kant, who had insisted that every man, as the possessor of "practical reason," is a moral legislator, and not merely a subject of pre-given duties. Nevertheless, Eichmann's "distortion" of the categorical imperative did agree with what he himself called the version of Kant "for the household use of the little man."[67] As Arendt points out, "in this household use, all that is left of Kant's spirit is the demand that a man do more than obey the law, that he go beyond the mere call of obedience and identify his own will with the principles behind the law – the source from which the law sprung. In Kant's philosophy, that source was practical reason; in Eichmann's household use of him, it was the will of the Führer."[68] The result of this identification was a high degree of conscientiousness in carrying out all duties related to the Final Solution; a conscientiousness which, as Arendt notes, people wrongly see as typically German or else as the mark of the "perfect bureaucrat." Eichmann's "uncompromising attitude toward the performance of his duties" flowed from neither of these sources, nor from ant-Semitic zealotry, but rather from an identification with his lawful duties and the will behind them.

This "Kantian" identification of conscientiousness with duty under law was also on display in Hungary in 1944, during what Arendt describes as Eichmann's "last crisis of conscience." Hungary had joined the war on Germany's side in 1941, largely in order to gain territory from its neighbours Slovakia, Romania, and Yugoslavia. There was no question, however, that the government was strongly anti-Semitic, as shown by its immediate expulsion of all stateless Jews from its newly acquired territory. This expulsion hardly meshed with the German plan to "comb Europe from West to East." Matters were further complicated when the Hungarians merely pushed the expelled Jews into German-occupied Russia. The German authorities protested, and the Hungarians were forced to take back thousands of the able-bodied for forced-labour purposes and to have the others shot by Hungarian troops under German supervision.[69] Yet for the next three years, probably due to the "moderating" influence of Italian Fascism, Hungary nevertheless became a haven for Jewish refugees from Poland and Slovakia – so much so that 300,000 Jews were added to the native Jewish population of about half a million.

All this changed dramatically in March 1944, when the German Army occupied the country and Hitler demanded that Admiral Horthy's government take "the steps necessary to settle the Jewish question."[70] The new Reich plenipotentiary, Dr Edmund Veesenmeyer (whom Arendt describes as "Himmler's agent") arrived, along with SS Obergruppenführer Otto Winkelmann (a member of the Higher SS and the Police Leader Corps, under the direct command of Himmler). Finally, Eichmann, in his capacity as "expert" on Jewish evacuation and deportation also arrived on the scene, although he remained under the command of his superiors in the RSHA (Head Office for Reich Security), Muller and Kaltenbrunner. Despite this typically Nazi multiplication of functions and chains of command, things went smoothly for Eichmann, who, over the next two months, arranged for 147 trains carrying 434,351 people to Auschwitz.[71] He encountered no difficulties in carrying out his duties until the arrival of yet another representative of Himmler, Kurt Becher, whose "special mission" consisted in gaining control of major

Jewish businesses in exchange for guaranteed emigration – all behind the back of the Hungarian government, which, under Nazi policy, had the "right" to all confiscated property.

Eichmann strongly objected to Becher's "corrupt" activity – the Final Solution as business opportunity – even though it had the approval of Himmler. Indeed, as Germany's defeat clearly approached, Himmler decided, in the fall of 1944, to call off the entire Final Solution – the better to present himself as leader of the so-called moderate wing of the SS and (thus) a potential leader of the defeated Germany. As Arendt tells it, Eichmann was stunned by this total disregard for the Führer's orders, and began to systematically sabotage Himmler's directives for dismantling the deportation and extermination apparatus – much to the astonishment of Dr Robert Kastner, a prominent leader of the Budapest Jewish community who had been directly negotiating with Becher.[72]

What at first appears to be solid evidence of Eichmann's fanaticism on the Jewish question – his adamant sticking to the "radical" solution when even Himmler himself had (for pragmatic reasons) abandoned it – is, in fact, his last "crisis of conscience." He waged a futile struggle against Himmler and the "moderate wing" of the SS out of loyalty to Hitler (to be sure), but also because of what he clearly perceived to be the criminal nature of Becher and Himmler's activity. It was his conscience that forbade him from joining Himmler's unilateral change of policy on the Jewish question, since this change of policy went against Hitler's orders and, in the Third Reich, "the Führer's words had the force of law."[73] Deeply imbued with the need to respect the law – to uphold lawfulness against any and all "criminal" activity – Eichmann did his best to cleave to the original "radical" program, even when all around him this program was being abandoned. His final "crisis of conscience" led him to take on Himmler himself – no small risk for a man who avoided all initiative.

Arendt devotes a good deal of attention to this incident because it reveals not simply the strange functioning of Eichmann's conscience, but also the most troubling moral and legal problems raised by the trial. Her concern is not "how can the law appropriately respond to crimes in the light of absence of motive," but (rather) how can moral and legal thought come to grips with the fact that many perpetrators did what they did out of an obedience to law and conscience? How can moral and legal thought come to grips with the fact that the "ordinary experience of lawfulness" which enables a soldier to clearly recognize a criminal order can – in the case of a legal framework like that of the Third

Reich – actually work in favour of the greatest evil? For Eichmann, the "black flag" which read "Prohibited!" flew not over Hitler's commands, but over Himmler's reversal. We are dealing, in other words, with the paradoxes posed by a regime which establishes a criminal legal order, one which depends on precisely those attributes which are supposed to preserve us from complicity in atrocity – namely, a firm sense of lawfulness, moral duty, and conscientiousness. To quote Arendt: "To fall back on an unequivocal voice of conscience or … on a 'general sentiment of humanity'" when dealing with crimes committed by a man like Eichmann under such circumstances "not only begs the question, it signifies a deliberate refusal to take notice of the central moral, legal, and political phenomena of our century."[74]

Viewed from this angle, Eichmann's apparent lack of motive appears as only one aspect (and by no means the most important one) of the "banality of evil." What is far more central to this notion is the fact that for Eichmann, and untold thousands like him, evil had lost the quality of temptation that usually attends criminality. Strangely and disturbingly, it now spoke with the voice of conscience, of moral obligation. As Arendt concludes her chapter on "The Duties of a Law-Abiding Citizen":

> And just as the law in civilized countries assumes that the voice of conscience tells everybody "Thou shalt not kill," even though man's natural desires and inclinations may at times be murderous, so the law of Hitler's land demanded that the voice of conscience tell everybody: "Thou shalt kill," although the organizers of the massacres knew full well that murder is against the normal desires of most people. Evil in the Third Reich had lost the quality by which most people recognize it – the quality of temptation. Many Germans and many Nazis, probably an overwhelming majority of them, must have been tempted *not* to murder, *not* to rob, *not* to let their neighbors go off to their doom … and not to become accomplices in all these crimes by benefitting from them. But, God knows, they had learned how to resist temptation.[75]

Here, as elsewhere, we have to pay strict attention to what Arendt is saying. She is *not* denying the presence of fanatics, sadists, anti-Semites, and ideologues in the upper echelons of the Nazi apparatus or among the "foot soldiers" of the Holocaust. What she is pointing out is that this policy of evil could hardly have worked as well as it did had not countless normal – law-abiding, and generally "moral" individuals – not seen it as their obligation to fight their inclinations and perform their specific duties as long as the law of the land required it. Eichmann is a "representative perpetrator" for Arendt, not because he was a "desk murderer," or because he lacked motives, but because – at least in Arendt's eyes – he stands for all those non-fanatical "good Germans" who became willing instruments of horror because their conscience demanded it.

This is a disorienting and counter-intuitive thought. Indeed, perhaps it is not surprising that, in all the debate and controversy surrounding *Eichmann in Jerusalem*, this Arendtian point has hardly, if ever, been discussed. Considered as a serious possibility, it forces us to abandon not only our stereotypes concerning "Hitler's willing executioners," but also the comforting idea that human beings have a built-in moral sense or feeling which generally enables them to recognize crime as crime (unless they have been blinded by hatred, wickedness, or ideological conditioning). Arendt does not deny the existence of conscience – in Eichmann or anyone else. What she questions is how this voice speaks to people whose legal and moral reality has been turned upside down by a criminal regime. Her answer, as I have already indicated, is not reassuring. But to ignore the possibility she presents in her "report on Eichmann's conscience" is to delude ourselves that the Holocaust can be explained by the virulent anti-Semitism of one nation, or by reference to entrapment in ideological fiction. Such explanations make *our* lives easier by leaving most of our moral-cognitive assumptions about the nature and sources of state-sponsored evil intact. But the price of such comfort is to actively ignore "the central moral, legal, and political phenomena" of the previous century – and, possibly, of our own.

It should be clear that I do not think *Eichmann in Jerusalem* is a narrowly legalistic book, animated by a conservative philosophy of law. Like Felman, Arendt is primarily concerned with the "broader historical significance" of the Eichmann trial. Unlike Felman, she does not delineate this significance in terms of the trial's therapeutic value in a society where – despite the fact that one in five Israelis were survivors – the Holocaust had been a source of embarrassment more than anything else. By giving public voice to the survivors, the Eichmann trial permanently altered the Israeli perception of the Holocaust. This is an important historical and sociological fact. But it hardly exhausts the "broader significance" of the trial, nor does it really touch upon the most disturbing moral issues raised by Eichmann's character and role in the Final Solution.

Today, the most thought-provoking question about the Holocaust is not what the victims suffered – a question to which there is a richly documented and horrific answer, in the works of historians, filmmakers, and survivors like Primo Levi. Nor is it how we can best fulfil our duty to the memory of the victims. Rather, the most thought-provoking question remains how it was that so many apparently normal people, in one of the most civilized nations in Europe, were able to lend their best, most conscientious efforts to the manufacture of horror. In a world where political evil – evil as policy – shows no signs of abating, this question – Arendt's question – retains its priority as a stimulus to moral and psychological reflection on the worst evils of our time.

NOTES

1 Shoshana Felman, "Theaters of Justice: Arendt in Jerusalem, the Eichmann Trial, and the Redefinition of Legal Meaning in the Wake of the Holocaust," *Critical Inquiry* 27, no. 2 (Winter 2001): 201–38.

2 For the outlines of the controversy surrounding Arendt's *Eichmann in Jerusalem*, see Elisabeth Young-Bruehl, *Hannah Arendt: For Love of the World* (New Haven, CT: Yale University Press, 1982), ch. 8.

3 Daniel Jonah Goldhagen, *Hitler's Willing Executioners: Ordinary Germans and the Holocaust* (New York: Vintage, 1997), 379. The publication of Bettina Stangneth's *Eichmann vor Jerusalem: das unbehelligte Leben eines Massenmörders* (Hamburg: Rowolt Verlag, 2014), has reignited the controversy over the extent of Eichmann's own anti-Semitism, which Stangneth documents as extreme if not fanatical. Stangneth has indeed uncovered a lot of material that was unavailable to Arendt, all of which helps to round out our picture of Eichmann and modify, perhaps, Arendt's overall assessment of him. However, Stangneth's book by no means reveals that Arendt was "wrong" about Eichmann all down the line. As Seyla Benhabib has noted (in an op-ed piece in the *New York Times*, 21 September 2014), ideology and banality are by no means mutually exclusive. Moreover, Arendt never said that Eichmann wasn't an anti-Semite, only that the carrying out of his duties was not primarily a function of a *fanatical* anti-Semitism. Throughout *Eichmann in Jerusalem* Arendt evinces a healthy scepticism at Eichmann's own explanations of his behaviour, making them a choice target of her much-criticized sarcasm and irony. Contrary to what Stangneth and some other critics believe, she was not taken in by what would have been the most masterful self-disguising

performance of the century (if it was, indeed, wholly a performance). She knew when Eichmann lied, when he disguised his motives, when he mitigated his involvement, and so forth. This, I think, is the Achilles heel of Stangneth's presentation, namely, the idea that Eichmann possessed an extraordinary capacity for appearing other than what he was – for acting. One might say that if Arendt's presentation of Eichmann underestimates the role ideology played in the performance of his actions, Stangneth's presentation overestimates his chameleon-like acting abilities, abilities which supposedly fooled even the most sceptical of observers. Another weakness is Stangneth's assumption that Arendt presents him primarily as a bureaucrat, the archetypal "desk murderer." In fact, while aspects of Eichmann's behaviour and language at the trial gave clear evidence of a bureaucratic mindset, Arendt never actually characterized him in these terms. For Arendt, it was Eichmann's ordinariness, his capacity for self-deception, and his utter lack of moral imagination (what she somewhat misleadingly termed his "thoughtlessness) that made him an exemplar of the "banality of evil." These – not a "bureaucratic mind-set" – are the things she thought he shared with many other Germans who were "just doing their jobs," whether on the frontline or in the ministries in Berlin.

4 See, for example, Lawrence Douglas, *The Memory of Judgment* (New Haven, CT: Yale University Press, 2001), which is framed in terms of the same "law as narrative" paradigm that Felman adopts, and which makes fundamentally the same critique of Arendt.

5 David Ben-Gurion, article in the *New York Times* magazine, cited by Young-Bruehl, *Hannah Arendt*, 341.

6 As Arendt points out, the Israeli judges were compelled to "re-write" the prosecution's case, since much of it – particularly the assertion of Eichmann's all-embracing authority in implementing the Final Solution – simply couldn't be sustained by the evidence. See Arendt, *Eichmann in Jerusalem: A Report on the Banality of Evil* (New York: Viking Penguin, 1963), chapter 15.

7 Ibid., 6–9.

8 Ibid., 8.

9 Ibid., 223. As Tom Segev notes in the chapter on the Eichmann trial in his book *The Seventh Million: The Israelis and the Holocaust* (New York: Henry Holt and Company, 1991), "the proceedings were designed as an emotional experience more than an informative one" (348). Thus, what Hausner described as "the parade of Holocaust witnesses" – more than a hundred – were called mostly as "background witnesses" (a fact Arendt notes in *Eichmann in Jerusalem*). As Segev observes, "the judges more than once evinced discomfort with the weak connection between the testimony

and the defendant standing before them. Time after time they demanded that the prosecution concentrate on the deeds of the defendant himself, yet Hausner continued to call up witnesses he had chosen, one after the other … Once the witnesses were on the stand, it was almost impossible to stop them or demand that they be brief. For it was not the mass murder policy that was at the center of their stories, not the general organization or the timetables of the trains for which Eichmann was responsible, but the terrors of death itself … In encouraging them to unlock what had been sealed within their memories and to relate their personal stories, he [Hausner] redeemed them and an entire generation of survivors: Thus the trial served as a sort of national group therapy" (350–1).

10 Ibid., 267.

11 Felman, "Theaters of Justice," 224.

12 Arendt, *Eichmann in Jerusalem*, 274–7.

13 Felman, "Theaters of Justice," 207. Felman does not dismiss Arendt's concern with the "unprecedented" character of the crime, nor her emphasis on the paradoxical task of coming to terms with it through a legal vocabulary rooted in precedent; rather, she sees it as one intriguing dimension of the trial, which pales in comparison with its status as *the* event which finally broke the (relative) silence surrounding the Holocaust.

14 Ibid., 211; emphasis in original.

15 Ibid., 224.

16 Friedrich Nietzsche, "The Utility and Liability of History for Life," in Nietzsche, *Unfashionable Observations*, trans. Richard T. Gray (Stanford, CA: Stanford University Press, 1995), 106.

17 Ibid., 97.

18 Felman, "Theaters of Justice," 225.

19 Ibid., 226–7.

20 Ibid., 230.

21 Ibid.

22 It is, of course, an uncomfortable fact (which Felman notes and Arendt underlines) that the silence surrounding the Holocaust in Israel had much to do with feelings of shame and denial prompted by the Zionist/Sabra idea of the "strong Jew" – an idea that did much to frame surviving European Jews as unmanly and sheep-like.

23 Ibid., 232–3.

24 Ibid., 226.

25 Ibid.; emphasis in original.

26 Ibid.

27 Ibid., 215, 233, 234.

28 Cf. Douglas, *Memory of Judgment*.
29 See Arendt, *Eichmann in Jerusalem*, 252: "The purpose of a trial is to render justice, and nothing else; even the noblest of ulterior purposes … can only detract from the law's main business: to weigh the charges brought against the accused, to render judgment, and to mete out due punishment."
30 Ibid., 91; emphasis added.
31 Ibid.
32 Arendt to Jaspers, quoted in Young-Bruehl, *Hannah Arendt*, 330.
33 Arendt, *Eichmann in Jerusalem*, 86–91.
34 Ibid., 26. See Segev, *The Seventh Million*, 345: Hausner claimed that, on the stand, Eichmann had "disconcerting eyes" that "burned with a bottomless hatred."
35 Arendt, *Eichmann in Jerusalem*, 25–6.
36 See Segev, *The Seventh Million*, 355.
37 Arendt, *Eichmann in Jerusalem*, 25; emphasis added.
38 Ibid., 26; emphasis added.
39 Friedrich Nietzsche, *Beyond Good and Evil*, trans. Walter Kaufmann (New York: Vintage, 1989), section 198.
40 Arendt, *Eichmann in Jerusalem*, 95.
41 Felman, "Theaters of Justice," 205.
42 See, in this regard, the very important introductory paragraphs to Arendt's 1971 essay, "Thinking and Moral Considerations," *Social Research* 38, no. 3 (Fall 1971): 417–46.
43 Arendt, *Eichmann in Jerusalem*, 113.
44 Ibid., 94.
45 Ibid.
46 Eichmann, quoted in ibid.
47 Ibid., 95.
48 Ibid.
49 Ibid, ch. 7. It is in this chapter that Arendt also makes her controversial claims about the importance of the *Judenrate* in facilitating the implementation of the Final Solution.
50 Ibid., 113.
51 Ibid., 114; emphasis in original.
52 Ibid., 116.
53 Ibid., 130.
54 Ibid., 131.
55 Ibid., 126; emphasis added.
56 Again, Nietzsche is apposite here. In addition to *Beyond Good and Evil*, sec. 199, see *The Gay Science*, sec. 335.

57 Arendt cites "one of the best known experts on constitutional law in the Third Reich, Theodor Maunz," who, in 1943 wrote that "The command of the Führer … is the absolute center of the present legal order." See Arendt, *Eichmann in Jerusalem*, 24.
58 Ibid., 23–5.
59 Ibid., 135.
60 Ibid.
61 Ibid., 135–6.
62 Ibid., 136.
63 Ibid.
64 Ibid.
65 Ibid.
66 Ibid.
67 Ibid.
68 Ibid., 136–7.
69 Ibid., 138–9.
70 Ibid., 140.
71 Ibid.
72 Ibid., 145.
73 Ibid., 148.
74 Ibid.
75 Ibid., 150; emphasis in original.

Chapter Three

Banality, Again

DANIEL CONWAY

That such remoteness from reality and such thoughtlessness can wreak more havoc than all the evil instincts taken together which, perhaps, are inherent in man – that was, in fact, the lesson one could learn in Jerusalem.

– Hannah Arendt, 1963[1]

Fifty years on, Arendt's reference to the *banality of evil* remains both controversial and misunderstood. What she regarded as a "strictly factual" matter,[2] pertaining to the monstrous evils unleashed by agents supposedly devoid of malevolence, remains a flashpoint of critical attention, scepticism, and outright enmity.

While some aspects of the ongoing controversy appear to involve wilful misunderstandings of Arendt's aims, a stubborn point of genuine concern is her apparent claim that Eichmann was representative, and perhaps ideally so, of the phenomenon she proposed to disclose. Indeed, even some critics who are generally receptive to her diagnosis of the banality of evil insist that it is not particularly helpful in coming to grips with Eichmann's seminal contributions to the administration of the Final Solution. According to Deborah Lipstadt, for example,

> In Eichmann's case [Arendt's] analysis seems strangely out of touch with the reality of his historical record. Though he may not have started out as a virulent anti-Semite, he absorbed this ideology early in his career and let it motivate him to such an extent that even well after the war he described ... the joy he had felt at moving Hungarian Jews to their death at an unprecedented clip and his pleasure at having the death of millions of Jews on his record.[3]

If Eichmann is meant to be the poster boy for the banality of evil, or so sounds a familiar refrain, then Arendt's understanding of evil is deeply (and perhaps irreparably) flawed. David Cesarini, who similarly describes Eichmann as having been "educated to genocide,"[4] judges "[Arendt's] depiction of Eichmann" to be "self-serving, prejudiced and ultimately wrong."[5] In a similar vein, Bettina Stangneth portrays Arendt as the victim of a clever ruse, perpetrated by a master manipulator: "[Arendt] fell into his trap: Eichmann-in-Jerusalem was little more than a mask. She didn't recognize it, although she was acutely aware that she had not understood the phenomenon as well as she had hoped."[6]

More recently, Richard Wolin has distilled this general line of criticism into a stark *reductio*: "It is at this point that the ultimate stakes of the debate of Eichmann's 'banality' emerge most clearly. For if Eichmann was 'banal,' then the Holocaust itself was banal. There is no avoiding the fact that these two claims are inextricably intertwined."[7] To be sure, claims such as these are rhetorically powerful. If Arendt's profile of Eichmann obliges us to entertain, even for a moment, the possibility that "the Holocaust itself was banal," as Wolin puts it, then her assertion of the banality of evil would appear to compel our summary dismissal.

Part of the problem here, as many scholars have noted, is that Arendt does not clarify for her readers what she actually meant by the "banality of evil." Her sole reference to this phenomenon in the body of her report appears in her concluding sentence, where she attributes to the deathbound Eichmann an unwitting performance of "the lesson that this long course in human wickedness had taught us."[8] And although she revisits this theme in her Epilogue and Postscript, and again in her subsequent reflections on the Eichmann trial, her critics are surely within their rights to complain that her scattered references to the banality of evil are simply not sufficient, even in their totality, to support such a provocative, counter-intuitive, and potentially offensive thesis.

I nevertheless wish to present this essay as an attempt to render a sympathetic reconstruction of what Arendt had in mind when she referred to the "banality of evil." As we shall see, she deems the production of evil to be *banal* in the event that the criminals in question fail to attain the minimum threshold for criminal intent; hence her growing, avowed interest in the emergence of the "new type of criminal" suggested to her by Eichmann's appearance in Jerusalem.[9] These criminals fail, she furthermore believes, in a very particular way – namely, owing to their inability, often through no fault or choice of their own,[10] to achieve a sympathetic identification with those others, both internal and external, from whom they otherwise might expect to receive an instructive rebuke. Whereas traditional villains produce evil by exploiting their intimate associations with the proposed targets of their villainy, this "new type of criminal" visits evil upon unsuspecting victims toward whom he feels no genuine malice. For the most part, that is, this criminal's victims are unknown to him, unheard by him, and unrepresented by him before the bar of conscience.[11] Evil counts as *banal*, in short, in the event that its thoughtless perpetrators are either ignorant of or indifferent to the fate of its victims.[12]

Finally, as we shall see, Arendt locates the banality of evil in those individuals who are unusually responsive to the circumstances of their contexts and the expectations of their audiences. Unable to project themselves beyond the settings and situations in which they find themselves, they are involuntarily reliant on the roles and personas – not to mention the "language rules"[13] – made available to them. In order to gain the recognition and approval they crave, these individuals appear to be – but never actually become – whatever their audiences expect or need them to be at the moment. Their motives thus remain ever banal, even when they are engaged, like Eichmann, in the planning and commission of crimes against humanity.

Banal Motives

What did Arendt mean to convey when she described Eichmann as *banal*? First of all, the banality of evil pertains only to the motives (or intentions) of the criminals in question, and not to the magnitude or audacity or horror of the crimes they commit. Rather than suppose or claim that the evil perpetrated by Eichmann was "commonplace,"[14] as her critics often allege, Arendt insists that his intentions were unremarkable. According to her analysis, nothing about his motives would remotely suggest the catastrophic consequences for which she holds him criminally responsible.[15] The familiar rejoinder that Arendt's attention to the banality of evil somehow trivializes the brutality of the Nazi regime is thus misplaced (or perhaps exaggerated). Indeed, the deeper irony of this rejoinder is that Arendt *meant* for her report to direct her readers' attention to an incarnation of evil that she regarded as pervasive, devastating, previously undetected, and unique to European modernity. In other words, she meant to introduce her readers to a manifestation of evil that had gone largely unnoticed, despite its central role in producing horrific crimes against humanity.

According to Arendt, the historical emergence of the banality of evil means that we may no longer draw with confidence the familiar moral inference from *maleficence* (i.e., evil deeds) to *malevolence* (i.e., evil intentions). Formerly, she observes, evil was generally understood to involve the *intentional* or *deliberate* destruction of life, liberty, property, dreams, possibilities, hopes, or aspirations. Instances of great evil both required and implied the malevolent activity of larger-than-life villains and criminal masterminds. What we now know, however, is that evil on the grand scale does not require a world-historical villain at the helm, for the destruction in question need not be meaningfully deliberate (or informed) on the part of those who are tasked with its fruition.[16] While reflecting on the reception of *Eichmann in Jerusalem*, Arendt explains that her appeal to the banality of evil was meant to account for "the phenomenon of evil deeds, committed on a gigantic scale, which could not be traced to any particularity of wickedness, pathology, or ideological conviction in the doer, whose only personal distinction was a perhaps extraordinary shallowness."[17] As we now know, moreover, a qualitatively greater scale of destruction may be caused by the actions of thoughtless, banal agents like Eichmann. If we continue to ignore the banality of evil, in short, we do so at our own peril.

So as to capture Arendt's guiding insight, we might say on her behalf that the banality of evil refers to the *subjective* expression of evil, pertaining to the guiding motives of the evildoer(s) in question. Evil is banal, she means to claim, when it is produced by agents whose motives are ordinary, normal, common, or benign, i.e., those who have no personal, intimate stake in the devastation of those against whom this evil is directed. As we shall see in the next section, these agents differ from traditional evildoers in that they neither knowingly nor willingly commit a crime. Owing in large part to the rise of totalitarianism in the twentieth century, Arendt believes, the subjective expression of evil has been permanently altered. It is no longer useful to assume that the production of evil may be traced to a diabolical genius or criminal mastermind. The face of modern evil is the face of everyman, of Zarathustra's "last man," a face as blank as it is bland. As we shall see, it is *this* change that obliges us in turn to revisit the rudiments of our legal systems and the principles of moral psychology on which these systems rest.[18]

This is not to suggest, however, that Arendt was unconcerned with what might be called the *objective* expression of modern evil. As she explains in the passage extracted above, in fact, she was particularly concerned to link the "extraordinary shallowness" of criminals like

Eichmann to the "gigantic scale" on which their evil has been objectively realized.[19] Indeed, it is precisely because the objective expression of evil now includes acts of genocide, administrative massacre, and ethnic cleansing that we would do well to acknowledge the "new type of criminal" who is indispensable, or so she insists, to the commission of these crimes.[20]

According to Arendt, the rise of totalitarianism has also occasioned a permanent alteration of the objective expression of evil. It has done so, moreover, not simply *quantitatively* – i.e., with respect to "the gigantic scale" of the deeds that are uniquely representative of modern evil – but also *qualitatively* – i.e., with respect to the unique character of the newly recognized crimes against humanity. The Nazis were able to displace and exterminate so many innocent victims because the agents they recruited, like Eichmann, were, by virtue of their affective detachment, coldly efficient in the performance of their duties. These agents were effective, in large part, because they held no personal stake in the extermination of the Jews, and they were neither motivated nor distracted by merely personal animosities.

Arendt thus regards the mobilization of Eichmann and his ilk as crucial to the emergence of genocide as the defining crime of European modernity.[21] Whereas genocide takes proximate aim at a particular people or nation, she understood, its ultimate target is the worldly character of the human condition. Genocide qualifies as a crime against humanity, not simply because it threatens a disturbingly large number of victims, but also because it places at risk the plurality of the world that all peoples (and all human beings) share in common.[22] A world "cleansed" of the Jews, for example, would be a world permanently depleted for all peoples and nations. It is in this respect, Arendt believed, that the Final Solution constituted an assault not only on European Jewry, but also on human plurality itself.[23] Thus we might say, though Arendt does not,[24] that modern evil is *radical*, for it strikes at the worldly roots of our political existence. Having identified plurality as constitutive of the human condition, as the *sine qua non* of political speech and action,[25] Arendt was uniquely positioned to understand the Final Solution as a campaign to diminish the political freedom available to *all* peoples and nations.[26]

Arendt thus meant for the "banality of evil" to designate the "strictly factual" (and, so, not merely theoretical or hypothetical) production of evil "on a gigantic scale" by agents who are thoughtlessly engaged in maintaining a sprawling program of genocidal violence.[27] While the motives of these agents are only ever banal, the evil they produce is both quantitatively and qualitatively unprecedented.

As this disparity between doer and deed is meant to indicate, Arendt wished to contribute to the inauguration of nothing short of a fundamental change in our understanding of the nature of evil.[28] Although she never put it this way, her encounter with Eichmann prompted her to identify the need for a new paradigm in moral psychology, which, she apparently hoped, legal theorists eventually would adopt in their efforts to reshape the modern practice of jurisprudence.[29] The aim of this new paradigm would be to accommodate the emergence of the "new type of criminal" suggested to her by Eichmann – i.e., a criminal devoid of criminal intent.[30] Within the new paradigm, presumably, evil would be understood to be the product of individuals acting only (or chiefly) on banal motives, even as they facilitated the commission of horrific crimes, including crimes against humanity.[31]

The magnitude of the change she wished to initiate was not lost on her. Nothing is more distinctive or more praiseworthy about "civilized jurisprudence," she allowed, than the universal consensus that has coalesced around "the assumption ... that intent to do wrong is necessary for the commission of a crime."[32] At the same time, however, she realized that criminals like Eichmann do (or may) not satisfy the minimal threshold conditions of mens rea.[33] What to do? The first step, Arendt decided, and the only step she trusted herself to take in this new direction, was to alert the civilized world to the limitations, perhaps even the obsolescence, of its current understanding of the nature of evil. The traditional paradigm of moral psychology may be a reliable generator of clarity, certainty, and justified moral outrage, but it is not particularly useful, or so she claimed, in furthering our understanding of the species of evil exemplified by Eichmann.[34] In reliably providing us with clarity, certainty, and outrage, moreover, the traditional paradigm actually may be seen to distract us from the uniquely modern evil that is produced and mobilized by totalitarian regimes. As Arendt explained her aims, "When I wrote my *Eichmann in Jerusalem*, one of my main intentions was to destroy the legend of the greatness of evil, of the demonic force, to take away from people the admiration they have for the great evildoers like Richard III or et cetera."[35]

As far as I can tell, Arendt's own contribution to the consolidation of the new paradigm was meant to extend no further than her efforts to draw attention to the "strictly factual" matter of the banality of evil,[36] for which the new paradigm eventually would provide an adequate explanation. She did not believe, for example, that she had succeeded in creating the new paradigm or that it was available somehow to the judges presiding over the Eichmann trial.[37] The construction of the new paradigm, I take it, was to be a task she bequeathed to the post-Eichmann generation of philosophers, political theorists, and legal scholars who shared her concerns about the limitations of the traditional paradigm. In declaring the traditional paradigm to be fatally flawed, in fact, she became a lightning rod for criticism, thereby freeing others to devote themselves to the urgent business of fashioning a new paradigm.[38]

Disproving a Villain: What the Banality of Evil Is Not

Despite describing the banality of evil as "word- and thought-defying,"[39] Arendt resisted the conclusion that nothing of interest can be said about it. In particular, she insisted, the banality of Eichmann's motives becomes apparent when he is regarded in juxtaposition to more traditional villains. As we shall see, in fact, she believed that a serious investigation of the banality of evil will oblige us, eventually, to set aside much of what we think we know about evildoers and their motivations:

> When I speak of the banality of evil, I do so only on the strictly factual level, pointing to a phenomenon which stared one in the face at the trial. Eichmann was not Iago and was not Macbeth, and nothing would have been farther from his mind than to determine with Richard III "to prove a villain." Except for an extraordinary diligence in looking out for his personal advancement, he had no motives at all. And this diligence in itself was in no way criminal; he certainly would never have murdered his superior in order to inherit his post. He *merely*, to put the matter colloquially, *never realized what he was doing* ... [He suffered from a] lack of imagination.[40]

Before turning to an explication of the extracted passage, let us note its context: Having mentioned "the banality of evil" only once in the body of her report, and only then in a concluding flourish, Arendt devotes this section of her Postscript to a clarification of the "phenomenon" to which she referred. In other words, it is her wish at this point in her Postscript to elaborate on her oft-misunderstood reference to the banality of evil.[41]

As she often does, Arendt presents her basic insight as both relative and privative: Eichmann is *not* to be confused with Iago, Macbeth, or

Richard III. Whereas these villains were thoughtful, imaginative, diabolical, malevolent, *and*, therefore, ripe subjects for further study and contemplation, Eichmann displayed none of these qualities. For this reason, Arendt insists, it is simply a mistake to address the evil attributed to Eichmann as if it were commensurate with the malevolence of a traditional villain.

As we know, Shakespeare regarded evil as the province and prerogative of superior, albeit flawed, human beings. His villains fascinate by virtue of their psychological and affective complexity. They not only host a rich internal chorus of opposing voices, but also tolerate (for a time) the dissonance that ensues between and among these voices. In particular, the Shakespearean villains named by Arendt weigh the merit of the crimes they have planned to commit and then implement their plans in full anticipatory awareness of the evil they will produce. As their nefarious plans unfold, moreover, these villains stage and accommodate the harrowing "two-in-one" experience of internal dialogue that Arendt, following Shakespeare, associated with the dark midnight of genuine solitude.[42]

As Arendt says of Socrates, the moral imperative to pursue justice, to do the right thing for the right reasons, emanates from the primal concern (or fear) that one eventually must answer to "the other fellow," i.e., one's internal dialogical partner and critic, with whom one is obliged to share a single soul and self.[43] Shakespeare's point, of course, is that the villain's tolerance for this internal conflict, his capacity to live in close quarters with his evil, is as unsustainable in the long run as it is fascinating in the short term. Under the unrelenting scrutiny of their obtrusive partners in cohabitation, Shakespeare's villains eventually pay for their misdeeds with their lives, souls, and/or sanity.

Compared to these villains, Arendt insists, Eichmann had no motives at all, save the banal motive to further his position, standing, and career. According to Arendt, moreover, Eichmann's banality was no accident: He lacked the imagination needed to "prove a villain," which ensured that he never would become one. Arendt explicitly links his lack of imagination to his failure to realize "what he was doing," even, apparently, as he was immersed in the logistical details of his official business. On the world-stage envisioned by Shakespeare, Eichmann might be cast as a knave, stooge, or fool, but he would not qualify as a genuinely evil villain.

Shakespearean evildoers, Arendt thus implies, are distinguished by their ability to project themselves imaginatively into their crimes and into the resulting suffering of their prospective victims. Having done so, moreover, they affirm their wish to proceed as planned and to wreak the havoc they have imaginatively surveyed. In short, Shakespeare villains are *agents* in the full, robust sense of that term: They know exactly what they are doing; they understand the immorality of what they intend to do; and they implement their plans in full appreciation of the criminal intent they bear. As such, these villains may be (and often are) regarded as both great and admirable, which are elements of the "legend" of evil that Arendt is particularly keen to discredit.[44]

When Gloucester (Richard III) announces his plan to "prove a villain," he also evinces his aspiration to an existence beyond what his present lot – unable to "prove a lover" – will allow him. He is in fact proud of his determination to make of himself, and not simply appear to be, something he currently is not. Ingredient to this expression of pride is his recognition that what he proposes to do is both wrong and contrary to the dictates of conscience, over which he means to assert his mastery.[45] Regardless of what we may think of his determination to tread a darker path, the strength of his resolve sets him apart from those ordinary, lesser men, who, like Eichmann, harbour no such aspiration or ambition.[46] Unable to imagine himself as a villain, Eichmann was, as a result, unlikely to "prove" anything. Ever responsive to the shifting circumstances he serially encountered, he was only concerned to appear to be whatever the situation demanded of him.

In setting out to "prove a villain," Gloucester availed himself of the opportunities and advantages that are incident to the treachery of betrayal. Turning on those closest to him, most notably his brother (Clarence), he schemed to gain the throne and win the queen (Anne) of his choice, whom he later sought to replace. Macbeth too had recourse to betrayal in pursuit of a throne, stabbing his king (Duncan) and authorizing the murder of his best friend (Banquo), among others. An even more vivid example of the power of betrayal is that of the villain Iago, who schemed to pollute Othello's love for Desdemona and drive them apart. Succeeding undetected in this venture, "honest" Iago looked on as Othello killed Desdemona before taking his own life. As Iago's plan unfolded, others were drawn into his fatal vortex, including his wife (Emilia) and his benefactor (Roderigo). Once discovered and apprehended, Iago stubbornly refused to confess, explain himself, show remorse, or admit any wrongdoing.

This is an important clarification of the profile Arendt means to construct, for the evil that Shakespeare so vividly depicts is possible only for those would-be villains who have earned the trust and cultivated the intimacy of their intended victims. Iago, for example, was uniquely positioned to wound Othello. He was not only the Moor's "ancient," but also a trusted confidant. Privy to Othello's otherwise indiscernible weaknesses and vulnerabilities,[47] Iago was able to engineer the fall of Othello and Desdemona through a seemingly blameless whispering campaign of innuendo, conjecture, and insinuation.[48] As the case of Iago indicates, moreover, Shakespeare's villains enjoy access to an enlarged faculty of imagination because they are or have been intimate with others; as a result, they already know what it is like to feel the suffering of another. As such, they are accustomed to considering the points of view, feelings, and objections of others as if they were their own. In order to "prove a villain," in other words, one must at one time have been something other than a villain, for example, a friend, comrade, benefactor, or confidant.[49] Only then is one poised to betray the trust one has earned. Only then must one endure the sleepless nights and spectral visitations that are likely to follow.

Arendt's point in contrasting Eichmann with these villains is to show that he was in no position either to contemplate or to perpetrate the intimate evil for which they are known. Never having made anything of himself, never having won the trust and loyalty of another person, never having gained access to the world (and its fragility) through the eyes of another, Eichmann was simply incapable of the evil apportioned by Shakespeare to his most notorious villains. What Arendt wishes to emphasize, of course, is that Eichmann was, as a result, especially well suited to the impersonal, indiscriminate evil for which, she insists, he was criminally responsible.[50]

When situated in the context of Shakespearean villainy, Arendt's reference to Eichmann's "lack of imagination" becomes particularly edifying. Iago, Macbeth, and Richard III not only imagined themselves as the villains they eventually became, which is presented here as prerequisite to the fruition of their respective misdeeds, but also imagined the suffering of the particular victims whom they marked for destruction.[51] This is in fact what makes them evil. As exemplified by these villains, the faculty of imagination is not simply abstract and representational, delivering merely conjectural insights and hypothetical points of view, but also embodied and personified, yielding affectively charged experiences of the harms intended. The Shakespearean villain thus knows what he is doing, tastes the evil of what he intends, and delights in both the anticipation and the execution – but not the aftermath – of his nefarious plan. In many cases, his imagination of the crimes he will commit is ingredient to the exhilaration he derives, temporarily, from his villainy.[52]

Arendt's attention to Shakespeare's villains thus suggests, again by way of contrast, that the banality of evil is predicated of agents who are *impersonally* invested in the maleficence they perpetrate. Whereas Iago targeted the great Othello, whom he personally resented and wished to destroy, Eichmann was neither personally nor particularly committed to the destruction of any (much less all) of the targets of the administrative massacre he supervised. And while Iago posed a danger only to those closest to him (and, ultimately, to himself), Eichmann imperilled everyone who had the misfortune of falling under the purview of his administrative jurisdiction. Precisely because he held no personal stake in the relocation and extermination of his victims, he was prepared to continue in these roles as long as his orders to do so remained viable and the prospect of recognition remained credible. As Arendt understood, in fact, the impersonal character of Eichmann's motives contributed to the unprecedented magnitude of the crimes he committed. She thus realized that crimes against humanity were likely to be carried out by those with no personal stake in the destruction of their victims.

Imagination and Thoughtlessness

Arendt's appeal to the projective properties of the faculty of imagination, as exemplified by Shakespeare's villains, thus sheds light on her widely disputed claim that the banality of Eichmann's motives was a function (and perhaps also a product) of his *thoughtlessness*. According to Arendt, the faculty of imagination funds the activity of thinking with the propulsive thrust she uniquely attributes to it.[53] Owing to his deficit in imagination, Eichmann was unable to project himself into the perspective and situation of another, unable to view and feel the world through the eyes and viscera of another. For this reason, he was largely unable to suspend his customary performance of his duty, for he was powerless to draw on the wisdom and perspectives of those others who would have exhorted him to ignore or challenge the dictates of his duty-bound conscience.[54]

The suggestion here is that moral awareness is not simply a matter of finding oneself in the company of others, making their acquaintance, and entertaining abstractly their different ideas and divergent points of view, especially if these others serve, in effect, as a kind of echo chamber.

Nor is it enough simply to consult one's conscience, especially if, like Eichmann's, one's conscience speaks with the "'respectable voice' ... of the respectable society around [oneself]."[55] Rather, one must project oneself fully into the life of another, taking on his or her point of view, owning the affective responses that fund it, and adjusting one's habits and practices accordingly.

In her Postscript, immediately following her assertion of Eichmann's "lack of imagination," Arendt offers an explanation of what she means:

> He was not stupid. It was sheer thoughtlessness – something by no means identical with stupidity – that predisposed him to become one of the greatest criminals of that period. And if this is "banal" and even funny, if with the best will in the world one cannot extract any diabolical or demonic profundity from Eichmann, that is still far from calling it commonplace.[56]

The context of this remark is important, for it confirms Arendt's intention to associate Eichmann's thoughtlessness with his inability to free himself from the context defined for him by his limited repertoire of clichés, stock phrases, and language rules. He was thoughtless, as we shall see, inasmuch as he could not project himself beyond or outside the context and setting in which he found himself, even when faced with the prospect of his own death.

While other observers in Jerusalem took note of Eichmann's unexpected linguistic limitations, Arendt detected a deeper, more basic deficit:

> Whether writing his memoirs in Argentina or in Jerusalem, whether speaking to the police examiner or the court, what he said was always the same, expressed in the same words. The longer one listened to him, the more obvious it became that his inability to speak was closely connected with an inability to *think*, namely to think *from the standpoint of someone else*.[57]

As this passage reveals, thoughtlessness implies (or designates) an inability to launch oneself, via imaginative identification, into the perspective and situation of specific others, especially those others whose claims on one's attention are (or should be) particularly compelling. Owing to this deficit, Eichmann was unable to enter and inhabit the standpoint of another person.[58] He was captive to the contexts and settings on which he was involuntarily reliant.

According to Arendt, Eichmann typically responded to novel situations and shifting settings by cycling through his limited repertoire of clichés and stock phrases, eventually settling on the banal expression that struck him as best suited to the situation at hand. As presented by Arendt, moreover, this repertoire of clichés and stock phrases served (and was meant to serve) as an ersatz fund of diverse experiences, from which Eichmann was able to draw in lieu of immersing himself in the experiences and standpoints of others.[59] Under such circumstances, Arendt believed, authentic expression was simply out of the question. Possessed of no relevant experience of genuine alterity, Eichmann lacked the projective thrust of imagination that was needed to occupy a standpoint from which a pointed rebuke might be meaningfully directed toward him.

When Eichmann engaged in (what passed for him as) introspection, or so Arendt suspected, he encountered nothing other than the familiar clockwork of his duty-bound conscience.[60] He was able to engage (formally) in self-reflection, but not in what we might call *self-contestation*. (As interpreted by him, after all, even the magisterial authority of Immanuel Kant confirmed the validity of his duty to obey "superior orders.")[61] His non-negotiable reliance on clichés, stock phrases, and language rules furthermore ensured that he was unlikely ever to attain escape velocity from the closed system of his thoughtless existence.

As far as I can tell, Arendt does not mean to brand Eichmann a solipsist. He knew very well that other individuals held divergent points of view and experienced the world very differently.[62] As she readily allows, in fact, "he knew quite well what it was all about and in his final statement to the court he spoke of the 'revaluation of values prescribed by the [Nazi] government.'"[63] Thus, as she repeats, his thoughtlessness cannot be considered a species of simple ignorance, inexperience, or stupidity. The key here, I take it, is his inability to try on, or sympathetically occupy, another standpoint *as if it were his own*. As a consequence, he was simply unable to view and experience the world from any standpoint other than his own, which, as we have seen, was structured in such a way as to assure him of the validity of his largely uncritical performance of his duty.[64] As a result, he was unlikely to be moved by any objections, whether real or hypothetical, that arose from alternative standpoints, including those of his victims or their witnesses. According to Arendt, in fact, "his conscience was indeed set at rest when he saw the zeal and eagerness with which 'good society' everywhere reacted as he did."[65] Unlike Shakespeare's villains, Eichmann was unlikely to be accosted in a lonely hour by the shades and spectres of those whom he had wronged.[66]

Eichmann was thoughtless, moreover, insofar as he had failed to develop within himself the kind of rich, heterogeneous plurality from which credible voices of dissent were likely to emerge. Presumably, the internal plurality that Arendt has in mind, the model for which she derives from the famous example of Socrates,[67] would have coalesced around the insistence that Eichmann refuse the "superior orders" on which he was prepared to act. Were he a different person, he eventually may have heeded such voices, if only because he would have been obliged to hear them every time he paused to think, i.e., to consult his inner plurality. Just as Socrates understood the existential need to appease "the other fellow" who joined him in his solitude and disrupted his introspective reveries,[68] so Eichmann, were he not thoughtless, would have understood himself to have been answerable to those voices of dissent that a properly constituted internal plurality would have accommodated. In this respect, what Arendt calls *thoughtlessness* also designates one's freedom from the adventitious intrusions into one's inner life of the objections of those others whose opinions one ought to respect. This too is a signal expression of the banality of evil.

For the sake of clarity, we might say that Eichmann certainly was capable of *thinking*, as this term and concept are generally understood. As his voluminous testimony proves, and as Arendt readily concedes, he thought about many (or several) things, including his career, his legacy, and his place in history.[69] What he could not do, however, was to think *imaginatively*, i.e., from the experience and point of view of those who were most likely to raise a credible objection to his present or proposed course of action.[70] This he could not do, we know, because he was unable to project himself into – and, so, to try on – the experiences and points of view of relevant others. Although he played many roles and apparently performed them convincingly, he could play no role that required him to inhabit the lived experiences of anyone else.[71]

Finally, Arendt's habit of referring to Shakespeare's villains indicates that an education in the great books and leading ideas of Western letters, i.e., an education that places Shakespeare at or near its moral centre, has ill prepared European modernity for an encounter with the banality of evil. Alert to the diabolical evil that is perpetrated by criminal masterminds, we late moderns have been slow to acknowledge (and slower to detect) evil in its banal manifestations. According to Arendt, in fact, the education that would prepare us to address Eichmann and his ilk as the criminals they actually are has yet to take shape. The same may be said of the laws and legal institutions that would allow us to prosecute, judge, and punish this "new type of criminal": they do not yet exist.[72]

Eichmann in Context

Eichmann's motives also qualify as banal inasmuch as his modest aims were unusually context- and audience-dependent. Seeking above all to fit in, Eichmann took his cues from the situations and settings in which he found himself. Eager to impress, and keen to reap the personal and professional rewards of making a favourable impression, he was inclined to say and do whatever he believed would elicit a positive response from his audience. As profiled by Arendt, Eichmann was a seasoned con man, a shape-shifting Zelig who manipulated others by anticipating and fulfilling their expectations of him.

Although he diligently pursued the tasks assigned to him, his motives in doing so were altogether unremarkable. According to Arendt, in fact, Eichmann became and remained dangerous only when placed in roles and offices in which his naturally banal motives led him to undertake acts of prescribed villainy that he otherwise would not have thought to perform. While he very well may have expressed the kind of ideological rigidity that recent contributions to the scholarship have attributed to him, his aims were guided by the typically normal motives associated with personal and professional advancement.[73] When Arendt claimed that "[Eichmann] had no motives at all,"[74] what she meant was that he possessed no motives that could not be readily adapted to his setting and audience du jour – i.e., no context-independent motives that might have led him to contest or refuse the setting in which he found himself.

This particular element of Arendt's profile of Eichmann poses a potentially formidable challenge to the interpretation advanced recently by Bettina Stangneth.[75] Relying extensively on her careful analysis of the "Argentina Papers," and the transcripts of the Sassen interviews, Stangneth delivers a comprehensive account of Eichmann's life prior to his trial in Jerusalem. Focusing her attention on his seemingly peaceful life in Argentina, Stangneth presents an Eichmann who was in fact the hardened Nazi whom the spectators assembled in Jerusalem fully expected to behold: "For [Eichmann], the war – his war – had never ended. The SS *Obersturmbahnführer* might have been retired from active service, but the fanatical National Socialist was on active duty ... his fighting spirit was unbroken. The ideological warrior had not been defeated, and he was by no means alone."[76] Stangneth thus describes in strong, unambiguous terms the extent and fervour of Eichmann's investments in the guiding ideology of National Socialism. What is especially important for our present purposes is the certitude of her conviction that Eichmann, who, she agrees, possessed a "talent for self-dramatization,"[77] was nevertheless discernibly authentic when espousing his fanatical allegiance to the ideology of National Socialism. In Jerusalem, she allows, Eichmann played to the crowd, "doing his best to stay alive and to justify his actions."[78] Prior to his arrest and trial, however, he displayed a "firm, ideological conviction" that his various masks and performances could not hide from view.[79]

In light of Stangneth's thesis, it is interesting to note how closely her interpretation accords with Arendt's account of Eichmann's penchant for theatricality:

> Eichmann acted out a new role for every stage of his life, for each new audience and every new aim. As subordinate, superior officer, perpetrator, fugitive, exile, and defendant, Eichmann kept a close eye on the impact he was having at all times, and he tried to make every situation work in his favor. And there was a method to his behavior, as a comparison of the many roles he played will reveal.[80]

As we know, Arendt arrived at a similar conclusion,[81] which is why she so quickly shifted her focus to the "new type of criminal" suggested to her by Eichmann.[82] As far as Arendt was concerned, of course, the "method" in question was shaped and directed by banal motives that warranted no further comment or attention.

Despite this initial point of agreement with Arendt, however, Stangneth draws a very different conclusion. While Arendt regarded Eichmann's habitual showmanship as symptomatic of the banality of his motives and of his thoughtlessness more generally, Stangneth treats the very same condition as indicative of a robust, villainous self, possessed of a wilful capacity to use and exploit others. Whereas Arendt spied a craven and shallow manipulator of images, à la the Wizard of Oz, Stangneth discloses a Machiavellian schemer – a master manipulator of audiences and settings. According to Stangneth, in fact, Eichmann employed his keen attunement to the expectations of his audience to pursue his authentic aims, which she identifies as audience- and context-independent. Although he sought and received recognition, just as Arendt had observed, he was not content simply to fit in and impress. In particular, Stangneth insists, he wanted to further the ideological agenda of National Socialism, with which, she claims, he proudly and openly aligned himself.[83] Apparently, Eichmann "proved a villain" after all, even as he played one for the appreciative audiences he found in Argentina.

Thus we arrive at the deepest point of disagreement between Stangneth and Arendt: Although both regard Eichmann as an inveterate performer, Stangneth ascribes to him, and Arendt fails to detect in him, a measure of agency that both funds and exceeds his various performances.[84] Stangneth portrays Eichmann as the master of his audiences and the willing author of the various personas he enacted,[85] while Arendt presents him as captive to his context, involuntarily responsive to the expectations of his audience.[86] Whereas Arendt points to Eichmann as indicative of the emergence of a "new type of criminal," i.e., a criminal devoid of criminal intent, Stangneth treats him like a traditional villain, possessed of malevolence and wilfully invested in the maleficence he actually caused. As we have seen, finally, Arendt regards Eichmann as representative of the "banality of evil," while Stangneth treats him as the canny manipulator of this condition in others: "Eichmann himself understood that the 'inability to think' was something very useful ... [He also] understood that he had to instrumentalize normal men and women. You could say Eichmann himself understood the 'banality of evil' too well."[87]

A notable product of this disagreement is its contribution to a refinement of our appreciation of what Arendt meant when she invoked *the banality of evil*. As we have seen, her attention to Eichmann's "thoughtlessness" apparently was meant to suggest that Eichmann failed to achieve, and did not possess, an identity or self that might be judged to be genuine or authentic.[88] For Arendt, the question of the *real* Eichmann, the actor behind the masks, the schemer behind the schemes, was simply a non-starter. On her view, he was utterly incapable of forming the kind of inflexible ideological commitments that would remain intact and undiluted as he entered new roles and encountered potentially unsympathetic audiences.[89] The oft-rehearsed contrast with Shakespeare's villains was apt, she believed, precisely because Iago, Macbeth, Richard III, et al., were all master manipulators who remained in control (at least initially) of the deceptions they sowed. The same cannot be said of Eichmann, who became aware of his performances, if at all, only as he enacted them.[90]

What Arendt realized, in short, was that Eichmann was a creature of his context, dependent on the recognition of his audience and captive to its expectations. Her reference to "the banality of evil" was meant to explain not who Eichmann really was, but why he was (and always would be) no one in particular.[91] As she confirmed while reflecting on the Eichmann trial, the banality of his motives was indicative of a more basic failure to exceed the confines of the roles to which he was assigned:

> [Eichmann] functioned in the role of prominent war criminal as well as he had under the Nazi regime; he had not the slightest difficulty in accepting an entirely different set of rules. He knew that what he had once considered his duty was now called a crime, and he accepted this new code of judgment as though it were nothing but another language rule. To his rather limited supply of stock phrases he had added a few new ones, and he was utterly helpless only when he was confronted with a situation [viz., the occasion of his own death] to which none of them would apply.[92]

What Eichmann could not do, Arendt believed, was to refuse the "different set of rules" that was thrust upon him as he embarked upon a new role or entered a new setting. Indeed, he was generally unable to assert himself in defiance or independence of the context in which he found himself.

According to Arendt, we might say, Eichmann was only ever a performer. He possessed no context-independent identity or core convictions that directed his various performances. Lacking the imagination to set his own course,[93] he achieved full potentiation only within schemes and networks devised for him by others. Although she would not have put it in quite this way, she apparently viewed Eichmann as a simple product (or expression) of his situation, possessing little or no agency independent of his efforts to fulfil the expectations he associated with the role in which he found himself. Borrowing a distinction introduced by Arendt in *The Human Condition*, we might say on her behalf that Eichmann was content (and perhaps destined) to remain *what* he was, as determined and defined by others.[94] He simply never mustered the aspiration to discover *who* he might have become.[95]

Conclusion

This particular feature of the banality of evil – viz., its origination in the banal motives of an inauthentic, context-dependent self – may explain Arendt's macabre fascination with the clumsy, artless performance that elicited Eichmann's final words. Even in his final hour, Arendt notes, he reflexively reached for the appropriate slogan or cliché, which, unsurprisingly, utterly failed to capture the circumstances of his impending death:

> He began by stating emphatically that he was a *Gottgläubiger*, to express in common Nazi fashion that he was no Christian and did not believe in life after death. He then proceeded: "After a short while, gentlemen, *we shall all meet again*. Such is the fate of all men. Long live Germany, long live Argentina, long live Austria. *I shall not forget them.*" In the face of death, he had found the cliché used in funeral oratory. His memory played him the last trick; he was "elated" and he forgot that this was his own funeral.[96]

Arendt's point here, expressed as an enthymeme and couched in her familiar irony, is that Eichmann died a captive of his own charade, tricked by his faulty memory into playing one last role for which he was, once again, ill suited.[97] Even in his final moment, the moment wherein most mortals hope to lay claim to some kernel of authentic expression, Eichmann once again mouthed the words that were scripted for him by another. According to Arendt, Eichmann died as he had lived, unknown to himself, uncurious about himself, forever the instrument of plans, orders, and language rules devised for him by others.

It thus bears noting that it was Eichmann's final misadventure, wherein he managed to mischaracterize his own death, which inspired the coinage that would cause Arendt so much consternation in the years to follow: "It was as though in those last minutes [before his death] he was summing up the lesson that this long course in human wickedness had taught us – the lesson of the fearsome, word-and-thought defying *banality of evil*."[98] This lesson, as Arendt believed she had made abundantly clear, pertains to the relatively recent emergence of a type of person – and, so, a type of criminal – whose motives would only ever be banal. The exemplars of this emergent type may look and sound and act like traditional villains, she cautioned, but they are in fact far more dangerous than we are currently prepared to acknowledge.[99] The "terrifying" normality of their existence and the banality of their motives uniquely qualify them, she warned, to participate in the defining crime of the modern epoch: *genocide*, which, as we have seen, she regarded as involving an assault on the worldly plurality of the human condition.[100]

NOTES

I am grateful to Stefan Dolgert, Claire Katz, John Seery, and an anonymous referee for their generous comments on an earlier draft of this essay.

1 Hannah Arendt, *Eichmann in Jerusalem: A Report on the Banality of Evil* (New York: Viking Penguin, 1963), 288.

2 Arendt, *Eichmann in Jerusalem*, 287.

3 Deborah E. Lipstadt, *The Eichmann Trial* (New York: Schocken Books, 2011), 169–70. Berkowitz attributes a similar position to David Owen: "While Arendt's thesis concerning the banality of evil is a fundamental insight for moral philosophy, she is almost certainly wrong about Eichmann." According to Berkowitz, Christopher Browning similarly maintains that "Arendt grasped an important concept, but not the right example." Roger Berkowitz, "Misreading 'Eichmann in Jerusalem,'" *New York Times*, last modified 7 July 2013, http://opinionator.blogs.nytimes.com/2013/07/07/misreading-hannah-arendts-eichmann-in-jerusalem/.

4 David Cesarini, *Becoming Eichmann: Rethinking the Life, Crimes, and Trial of a "Desk Murderer"* (Cambridge: Da Capo Press, 2004), 16.

5 Ibid., 15.

6 Bettina Stangneth, *Eichmann before Jerusalem: The Unexamined Life of a Mass Murderer*, trans. Ruth Martin (New York: Alfred A. Knopf, 2014), xxiii.

7 Richard Wolin, "Thoughtlessness Revisited: A Response to Seyla Benhabib," *Jewish Review of Books*, 30 September 2014.

8 Arendt, *Eichmann in Jerusalem*, 252.

9 Here I follow Susan Neiman, "Theodicy in Jerusalem," in *Hannah Arendt in Jerusalem*, ed. Steven E. Aschheim (Berkeley: University of California Press, 2001), 73–81. See also Shoshana Felman, *The Juridical Unconscious: Trials and Traumas in the Twentieth Century* (Cambridge, MA: Harvard University Press, 2002), 107–10.

10 In her revised version of the verdict, Arendt writes, "Let us assume, for the sake of argument, that it was nothing more than misfortune that made you a willing instrument in the organization of mass murder; there still remains the fact that you have carried out, and therefore actively supported, a policy of mass murder. For politics is not like the nursery; in politics obedience and support are the same" (Arendt, *Eichmann in Jerusalem*, 279).

11 Ibid., 126.

12 As Neiman, "Theodicy in Jerusalem," puts it, "Arendt is hardly attempting to mitigate the guilt of Eichmann or of anyone like him. On the contrary:

she is insisting on the need for a moral theory that locates guilt and responsibility in something other than intention" (77–8).

13 Arendt, *Eichmann in Jerusalem*, 85–6.

14 Ibid., 287–8.

15 At one point in her Postscript, Arendt claims that "except for an extraordinary diligence in looking out for his personal advancement, [Eichmann] had no motives at all" (Arendt, *Eichmann in Jerusalem*, 287).

16 Here I follow Neiman, *Evil in Modern Thought: An Alternative History of Philosophy* (Princeton, NJ: Princeton University Press, 2004), 274–81.

17 Hannah Arendt, "Thinking and Moral Considerations," in *Responsibility and Judgment*, ed. Jerome Kohn (New York: Random House/Schocken Books, 2003), 417.

18 Arendt, *Eichmann in Jerusalem*, 276. See Neiman, *Evil in Modern Thought*, 270–77; and Gottlieb, 49–51.

19 Arendt, "Thinking and Moral Considerations," 417.

20 Arendt, *Eichmann in Jerusalem*, 276.

21 Here I follow Hans Mommsen, "Hannah Arendt's Interpretation of the Holocaust as a Challenge to Human Existence: The Intellectual Background," in *Hannah Arendt in Jerusalem*, ed. Steven E. Aschheim (Berkeley: University of California Press, 2001), 226–31.

22 I am indebted here to Leora Bilsky, *Transformative Justice: Israeli Identity on Trial* (Ann Arbor: University of Michigan Press, 2004), 130–2; and Seyla Benhabib, "International Law and Human Plurality in the Shadow of Totalitarianism: Hannah Arendt and Raphael Lemkin," *Constellations* 16, no. 2 (2009): 239–44.

23 See Seyla Benhabib, *The Reluctant Modernism of Hannah Arendt* (London: Sage, 1996), 184–5; Mary G. Dietz, *Turning Operations: Feminism, Arendt, and Politics* (London: Routledge, 2002), 183–96; and Benhabib, "International Law and Human Plurality," 342–4.

24 In her famous reply to Gershom Sholem, Arendt explains, "It is indeed my opinion now that evil is never 'radical,' that it is only extreme, and that it possesses neither depth nor any demonic dimension. It can overgrow and lay waste the whole world precisely because it spreads like a fungus on the surface. It is 'thought-defying,' as I said, because thought tries to reach some depth, to go to the roots, and the moment it concerns itself with evil, it is frustrated because there is nothing." Hannah Arendt, "The Eichmann Controversy: A Letter to Gershom Scholem," in *The Jewish Writings*, ed. Jerome Kohn (New York: Random House/Schocken Books, 2007), 471. For an instructive analysis of Arendt's letter to Scholem, see Richard J. Bernstein, *Hannah Arendt and the Jewish Question* (Cambridge,

MA: MIT Press, 1996), 160–8; Neiman, *Evil in Modern Thought*, 300–4; and Peter Baehr, "Banality and Cleverness: *Eichmann in Jerusalem* Revisited," in *Thinking in Dark Times: Hannah Arendt on Ethics and Politics*, ed. Roger Berkowitz, Jeffrey Katz, and Thomas Keenan (New York: Fordham University Press, 2010), 139–42.

25 Hannah Arendt, *The Human Condition* (Chicago: University of Chicago Press, 1958), 7–11, 175–6. See also Benhabib's critical discussion of Arendt's "anthropological universalism," *Reluctant Modernism*, 195–8.

26 Arendt, *Eichmann in Jerusalem*, 276–9.

27 Arendt, "Thinking and Moral Considerations," 417.

28 Here I follow Susan Neiman, "Theodicy in Jerusalem," 76–80.

29 See Susannah Young-ah Gottlieb, "Beyond Tragedy: Arendt, Rogat, and the Judges in Jerusalem," *College Literature* 38, no. 1 (Winter 2011): 48–50.

30 Arendt, *Eichmann in Jerusalem*, 276–7.

31 Seyla Benhabib, "Who's on Trial, Eichmann or Arendt?" *New York Times*, "Opinionator," 21 September 2014, makes a similar point. See also Corey Robin, "The Trials of Hannah Arendt," *The Nation*, 1 June 2015, http://www.thenation.com/article/trials-hannah-arendt/.

32 Arendt, *Eichmann in Jerusalem*, 277.

33 Here I follow Felman, *The Juridical Unconscious*, 107–9; and Neiman, *Evil in Modern Thought*, 272–6.

34 See Leora Bilsky, *Transformative Justice*, 242–6.

35 Roger Errera, "Interviewing Hannah Arendt," in *Hannah Arendt: The Last Interview and Other Conversations* (New York: Melville House, 2013), 60.

36 Arendt, *Eichmann in Jerusalem*, 287.

37 She concedes, in fact, that the verdict and penalty in the Eichmann trial, with which she voiced no disagreement, were motivated by "propositions" of justice that, according to her, "we refuse and consider as barbaric" (Arendt, *Eichmann in Jerusalem*, 277). See also Bilsky, *Transformative Justice*, 143–4; and Gottlieb, "Beyond Tragedy," 48–50.

38 I would thus suggest that Arendt's report of the trial was meant, to borrow Felman's words, "to create a space, a language that is not yet in existence" (*Juridical Unconscious*, 123). In this respect, Arendt may not have been as "jurisprudentially conservative" as Felman maintains (122).

39 Arendt, *Eichmann in Jerusalem*, 252.

40 Arendt, *Eichmann in Jerusalem*, 287.

41 See Peter Sinclair, "Drama and Narrative in Hannah Arendt's *Eichmann in Jerusalem*," *Journal of Narrative Theory* 43, no. 1 (Winter 2013): 46–8.

42 Arendt, "Thinking and Moral Considerations," 186.

43 Ibid., 186.

44 Errera, "Interviewing Hannah Arendt," 60.
45 See Marjorie Garber, *Shakespeare After All* (New York: Random House/Anchor Books, 2005), 136–40.
46 In acknowledging her intention "to destroy the legend of the greatness of evil, of the demonic force," Arendt explicitly mentions her wish "to take away from people the admiration they have for the great evildoers like Richard III" (Errera, "Interviewing Hannah Arendt," 60).
47 Here I follow Garber, *Shakespeare After All*, 597–603. See also Stanley Cavell, *Disavowing Knowledge in Seven Plays of Shakespeare* (Cambridge: Cambridge University Press, 2003), 132–7.
48 See Garber, *Shakespeare After All*, 604–9.
49 I am influenced here by the thesis advanced by Elaine Pagels in *The Origin of Satan* (New York: Random House/Vintage Books, 1995), chapter 2.
50 Here I follow Neiman, *Evil in Modern Thought*, 271–7.
51 Of the three villains mentioned by Arendt, Macbeth is perhaps least faithfully representative of the anticipatory tendencies I describe here. In Macbeth, we might say, the "demonic force" of the imagination is more clearly evident in the guilt that clouds his reign and the visions and visitations that hasten his downfall. See Garber, *Shakespeare After All*, 712–19.
52 Ibid., 135–8.
53 See Arendt, "Thinking and Moral Considerations," 159. See also Bernstein, *Hannah Arendt and the Jewish Question*, 168–75.
54 I take my cue here from the research conducted by Dana Villa, who has shed welcome light on Arendt's concern with Eichmann's conscience. As Villa instructively demonstrates, the question of Eichmann's conscience is central to her investigation in *Eichmann in Jerusalem*. See Villa's contribution to this volume, "*Eichmann in Jerusalem*: Conscience, Normativity, and the 'Rule of Narrative.'"
55 Arendt, *Eichmann in Jerusalem* 126. See Lipstadt, *The Eichmann Trial*, 87–91.
56 Arendt, *Eichmann in Jerusalem*, 287–8.
57 Arendt, *Eichmann in Jerusalem*, 49; emphasis added.
58 See Benhabib, "Who's on Trial?"; and Robin, "The Trials of Hannah Arendt."
59 Arendt, *Eichmann in Jerusalem*, 85–6. See Bilsky, *Transformative Justice*, 122–6.
60 Arendt, *Eichmann in Jerusalem*, 95. Here too I am indebted to Villa, "*Eichmann in Jerusalem*: Conscience, Normativity, and the 'Rule of Narrative,'" in this volume.
61 Arendt, *Eichmann in Jerusalem*, 136. See Lipstadt, *The Eichmann Trial*, 131–4.

62 As Arendt allows, in fact, "he knew quite well what it was all about and in his final statement to the court he spoke of the 'revaluation of values prescribed by the [Nazi] government' " (Arendt, *Eichmann in Jerusalem*, 287).
63 Ibid.
64 As Villa points out in this volume, "for Eichmann, and untold thousands like him, evil *had lost the quality of temptation* that usually attends criminality. Strangely and disturbingly, it now spoke with the voice of conscience, of *moral obligation*." See also Bilsky, *Transformative Justice*, 128–30.
65 Arendt, *Eichmann in Jerusalem*, 126.
66 See Garber, *Shakespeare After All*, 716–23; and Cavell, *Disavowing Knowledge*, 242–4.
67 Arendt, "Thinking and Moral Considerations," 168–89.
68 Ibid., 185.
69 Stangneth, *Eichmann before Jerusalem*, xx.
70 See George Kateb, *Hannah Arendt: Politics, Conscience, Evil* (Totowa, NJ: Rowman and Allanheld, 1983), 194–6.
71 I am indebted here to Disch's elaboration on Arendt's metaphor of preparing "one's imagination to go visiting," Lisa Jane Disch, *Hannah Arendt and the Limits of Philosophy* (Ithaca, NY: Cornell University Press, 1994), 157–71.
72 Arendt, *Eichmann in Jerusalem*, 287–8. Here I follow Felman, *Juridical Unconscious*, 137–40.
73 Arendt, *Eichmann in Jerusalem*, 287.
74 Ibid.
75 Stangneth, *Eichmann before Jerusalem*.
76 Ibid., xix–xx. See also Lipstadt, *The Eichmann Trial*, 169–73.
77 Stangneth, *Eichmann before Jerusalem*, xvii.
78 Ibid., xviii. See also Lipstadt, *The Eichmann Trial*, 122–7.
79 Stangneth interview with Gal Beckerman, "Taking the Banality Out of Evil: A New Book on Eichmann Reveals His True Face," *Jewish Daily Forward*, 19 September 2014.
80 Stangneth, *Eichmann before Jerusalem*, xvii.
81 Arendt, "Thinking and Moral Considerations," 159–60.
82 Arendt, *Eichmann in Jerusalem*, 276.
83 Stangneth, *Eichmann before Jerusalem*, xix–xxi.
84 Ibid., xix–xx). In her interview with Gal Beckerman, moreover, Stangneth confirms that "Eichmann had, without any doubts, a firm ideological conviction and criminal motives."
85 Stangneth believes that Eichmann's manipulative mastery extends even to his effect on Arendt herself: "And one of the most significant insights to be gained from studying Adolf Eichmann is reflected in Arendt: even someone of average intelligence [presumably, Eichmann] can induce a

highly intelligent person [presumably, Arendt] to defeat herself with her own weapon: her desire to see her expectations fulfilled. We will be able to recognize this mechanism only if thinkers deal bravely enough with their expectations and judgments to see their own failures" (ibid., xxv).

86 Reflecting on her report of the Eichmann trial, Arendt elaborates on the limitations she associates with the banality of evil: "Clichés, stock phrases, adherence to conventional, standardized codes of expression and conduct have the socially recognized function of protecting us against reality, that is, against the claim on our thinking attention which all events and facts arouse by virtue of their existence. If we were responsive to this claim all the time, we would soon be exhausted; the difference in Eichmann was only that he knew no such claim at all" (Arendt, "Thinking and Moral Considerations," 160).

87 Stangneth interview with Gal Beckerman.

88 "Thinking and Moral Considerations," 159. See also Judith Butler, *Parting Ways: Jewishness and the Critique of Zionism* (New York: Columbia University Press, 2012), 170–1; and Robin, "The Trials of Hannah Arendt."

89 See Lipstadt, *Eichmann Trial*, 168–72.

90 See Butler, *Parting Ways*, 169–71.

91 Here I follow Butler, who remarks that "[Eichmann] failed to call upon himself. To be called upon, someone must be home. And Arendt concluded that, with Eichmann, no one was at home" (ibid., 170).

92 Arendt, "Thinking and Moral Considerations," 159–60.

93 Arendt, *Eichmann in Jerusalem*, 287.

94 This is not to suggest, of course, that Eichmann had access to a political space in which he might have appeared and been fully disclosed. In the "dark times" of late modern totalitarian rule, Arendt understood, individuals like Eichmann had no or little occasion for self-disclosure and furthermore possessed no will to speak and act in a genuinely political space. See Kateb, *Hannah Arendt*, 74–82.

95 Arendt, *The Human Condition*, 175–81. I am grateful to Annabel Herzog for impressing upon me the importance of this distinction.

96 Arendt, *Eichmann in Jerusalem*, 252.

97 As Arendt explains in another context, Eichmann "was forced to rely on clichés ... which were inapplicable in his case because he was not the survivor" (Arendt, "Thinking and Moral Considerations," 160). See Sinclair, "Drama and Narrative," 58–9.

98 Arendt, *Eichmann in Jerusalem*, 252.

99 Ibid., 288.

100 Arendt, *Eichmann in Jerusalem*, 276.

Chapter Four

Eichmann on the Stand: Self-Recognition and the Problem of Truth

VALERIE HARTOUNI

If we forget that we are related to those we condemn, even those we **must** condemn, then we lose the chance to be ethically educated or "addressed" by a consideration of who they are and what their personhood says about the range of human possibility that exists, even to prepare ourselves for or against such possibilities.

Judith Butler, 2005[1]

In 1961, Adolf Eichmann stood trial in Jerusalem for his central role in the genocide of European Jewry.[2] A mid-level bureaucrat in the regime's political hierarchy, Eichmann was one of only a handful of officials in the Nazi SS whose sole job, at least initially, was to implement the regime's various political and, after 1941, physical solutions for what it identified as its "Jewish problem." Originally, this entailed putting in place a system of registration in order to more efficiently locate, more accurately categorize, and more precisely track the concentration and movement of bodies, wealth, and resources both within and across borders. But, as Germany's imperialist war and thus empire expanded and the brutal conditions of mass expulsions and "resettlement" deteriorated (further), Eichmann came to oversee the mobilization of primarily Jewish populations for rapid transport, first to the ghettos and then to the camps, where, as it is known, large numbers were systematically murdered.

While Eichmann never denied his role in helping solve Germany's Jewish problem – he claimed to have been an "expert" in Jewish affairs, a champion of Zionist aspirations no less – he insisted repeatedly that he harboured no ill will towards the Jews. He acted, he claimed, not from base or perverse motives but out of a sense of responsibility and duty, honouring faithfully to the end the oath of allegiance he had taken to Germany and Hitler both. Unlike many of his colleagues who, in his view, lacked "the courage of their convictions," he had remained true to his oath when tested and thus true to his highest moral obligation: obedience was demanded and he complied fully. It was only with respect to such compliance that he now saw, in hindsight, any possible basis for guilt, although it was a guilt mitigated by the fact that he too was a victim of superiors who had abused and exploited his trust and fidelity: in his words, "I was a tool in the hands of forces stronger than myself."[3] If the annihilation of the Jews was "one of the greatest crimes in the history of humanity" – and this Eichmann was at pains to stress throughout the trial – it was a crime initiated and perpetrated by Germany's political leaders, and thus a crime for which he could not be made to assume personal responsibility. While he was culpable for reasons of rank and function and quite prepared to atone for his complicity in facilitating the state's murderous agenda, his hands were nevertheless clean: his job had been to organize and coordinate moving stock. That the trains were transporting human beings for "labor service" or death was something over which, he insisted, he had no control: some might live, others might perish and not knowing what specific fate awaited whom was his foothold, how he lived with himself. Moreover, this "not knowing" was also proof of a sort, or so he maintained, that he had murdered no one and thus did not bear what he called "blood guilt."[4]

Eichmann's testimony alternately frustrated and puzzled the court. The evidence before it, not to mention the testimony of some of the major war criminals at the original military tribunal at Nuremberg, seemed overwhelming to place him at the epicentre of genocide. Given this evidence and under the threat of the gallows, there appeared to be nothing left for him to do but to shed his claims of innocence and proffer a truthful account of his central role in the regime's murderous, decade-long drive against the Jews. In the final month of the proceedings, then, the judges bypassed the translators and took to questioning the defendant directly in his native tongue in an effort to wrest from him the story they appeared certain he knew but was withholding. However, with each query, an earnest, if also sometimes confused or annoyed, Eichmann appeared only to confound, deflect, qualify, or deny what the court took to be the program, facts, and trajectory of Germany's genocide. Although he claimed, repeatedly, that he was now facing the truth and indeed telling it, from the perspective of the bench it was all empty talk and great subterfuge.

If a wide chasm exists between what the court understood to be the nature of Eichmann's involvement in facilitating the genocide of Europe's Jews and Eichmann's own account of his involvement, certainly an ever-expanding scholarship has emerged since the trial to fill the gulf. Scholars have combed the historical record, ransacked the archives, and reassessed the evidence – facts known to the court in Jerusalem or pieced together subsequently– to establish the full measure, meaning, and significance of Eichmann's place in the Nazi machinery of power, with the aim, in some cases, of further cementing his status as an icon of evil and, in other cases, of simply refining it.[5] Bracketing for the moment what is now and was originally in Jerusalem the foregone conclusion of Eichmann's "objective guilt," what interests me and what I want to explore in this chapter is the apparent standoff in the courtroom between Eichmann and his judges, specifically the urgency they conveyed about extracting from him a set of utterances that would clearly establish – but then this is precisely the question – clearly establish what?

The facts in this case were plain – indeed, apparently so plain that three months before the trial began the state sought to amend a law that permitted the court to debate only the sentence of a defendant whose conviction was made automatic with a guilty plea. Anticipating that Eichmann might opt to plead guilty, the new law – which was unofficially called "the Eichmann law" and which was rescinded once the trial was over – allowed the court to proceed with trial regardless of Eichmann's response to the charges against him.[6] Clearly at stake was more than a conviction – and in this regard, certainly a considerable amount has been written about Ben-Gurion's behind-the-scene efforts to ensure that the trial staged a spectacle of lasting national import and redemption. For Ben-Gurion, the goal, in his words, was "not so much the punishment of a particularly odious criminal, as the exposure of a sacred experience in this history of Israel."[7] That said, the political and politically instructive ends which Ben-Gurion may have sought to realize by means of the trial – inspiring (or consolidating) an unapologetic Jewish national pride, exposing a world still awash in murderous anti-Semitism, legitimating thereby an unquestioned and unquestionable need for expansive state power and military might – were not necessarily the court's. Nevertheless, a trial "staged in a public auditorium, with evidence presented not to prove the guilt of a man presumed innocent but, rather, to commit events to memory and thereby restore the 'correct historical perspective'" on matters foundational to national identity – such a trial certainly presented unusual challenges for those called upon to hear the case.[8]

For his part, by all accounts, presiding Judge Moshe Landau struggled to maintain a procedurally fair, uncompromised process – a process immune so far as this was possible to the violent, but for the most part legally irrelevant, cross-currents of historical revelation and political imperative ever present in the state's case against the accused. It was not enough for justice to be done in this case, as Landau understood clearly. To satisfy the scepticism of an international community, piqued by Israel's ostensibly flagrant disregard for international norms in abducting Eichmann from Argentina and then prosecuting him for crimes committed beyond its borders, justice had also to appear to have been done.[9] We might then ask whether, in the context of a judgment whose conclusion was already foregone, this was what moved the bench to interrogate Eichmann directly. What stories were the justices waiting to hear that hadn't already been revealed over the course of the trial and how could these stories be known to exist, indeed already known to all, and remain a mystery which only Eichmann was in a position to disclose? What is the truth the court required from Eichmann that he in turn refused or clearly demonstrated he could not possibly speak?

Alongside and clearly related to this issue of truth telling is also the question of Eichmann's affect, specifically the form, quality, and manner of his shame, guilt, and contrition. Eichmann's studied indifference throughout the proceedings stood in stark contrast to the emotional logic and spectacle of the trial, and while the judges repeatedly attempted to contain the latter, their questions to an unflinching, disturbingly removed Eichmann by contrast appealed to and aggressively aimed to provoke the accused towards some sort of emotional display – to bring him to a dramatic breaking point or at least to the edge of sentiment by forcing him to confront and accept in Jerusalem all he seemed to refuse and elude.[10] But here as well we might ask to what end? What was the quality of shame or guilt the three judges sought in Eichmann and insisted he not simply convey but unambiguously perform – or perhaps more to the point, what form or expression of shame or guilt would they have found credible or been able in the end to hear, tolerate, witness, or understand as such?

In the discussion that follows, I begin first by turning to the trial transcripts to set out the exchanges between Eichmann and the three judges that oversaw the proceedings: Yitzhak Revah, Benjamin Halevi, and Moshe Landau. Described as both lengthy and methodical, their examination of the former Nazi official is considered by scholars to have been exemplary, and I take no issue with this depiction.[11] More significant for my purposes, and it is to this that the paper's discussion then moves, is the way the impasse between Eichmann and the court is produced by a yearning for truth whose possibility is on the one side narrowly circumscribed by the legal norms set out at Nuremberg and, on the other, rigidly conditioned by the extralegal national need to shore up Israel's legitimate place and power as a nation among nations. The judges demand from Eichmann a response to the *why* of genocide – even while the very event of the trial presupposes and is designed to stage a historically grim indeed ancient answer. In this respect, there was no great riddle to be solved. Still, in the context of the trial, Eichmann continuously went off-script, and although this in some sense hardly mattered – he had a role to play and his apparent refusal to play it, despite his insistence that he was willing, was generally dismissed as part of a "horrible and ridiculous" but transparent ruse[12] – it revealed for Hannah Arendt at least something about the *how* of genocide. For Arendt, the "empty talk" of the accused that seemed at times to so confound the judges – Eichmann's apparent "thoughtlessness" as she put it – represented a certain logos. And while it may have escaped legal resonance and the understanding of the court, in this logos she found the beginnings of an answer to a set of political questions about genocide's preconditions. It is then to Arendt's reading of Eichmann that I turn in the concluding section of this paper.

1

To set the stage: Attorney General Gideon Hausner presented the state's case against Eichmann which had been exhaustive in constructing a wrenching montage of terror and death. Hausner tracked Germany's exploitive advance across the Continent and set out, largely through survivor testimony over the course of sixty-five sessions, the disastrous and ever more deadly impact of that advance on Europe's Jewish population, country by country – all to expose Eichmann's unique, aggressively proactive and thus monstrous role at the centre of a murderous apparatus.[13] Hausner sought to establish that it was Eichmann and Eichmann alone whose business had been the European-wide genocide: he had been the zealous architect of Nazi terror against the Jews, the driving force behind the Wannsee Conference, "the central pillar of the whole wicked system" – personally selecting the sites of the gas chambers, choosing the kind of poisoned gas that was to be used in these chambers, and specifying the number of people to be killed in them daily.[14] A consummate liar and "savage sociopath," his hatred of the Jews, as Hausner presented it, was relentless in its pursuits, deadly in its expression, and riddled with sadistic impulse.

For its part, and following an initial failed effort to challenge the legal basis of the trial as well as Israel's authority to conduct it, the defence countered with an anemic rebuttal of the state's case.[15] It aimed to blunt the impact of survivor testimony by drawing an elaborate portrait of the regime's complex, redundantly tiered bureaucratic organization and internal command structure while featuring Eichmann's subordinate place within both. A mid-level administrator responsible for "transport matters," Eichmann was in a position only to serve, transmit, and implement the will of those of higher rank in the regime's hierarchy. Within the framework of the order to carry out the Final Solution, he was not, indeed could not have been, an initiator of action or deviser of plans. Professionally, his designs or intentions were irrelevant: others drafted the legal regulations, handled finances and property, oversaw the ghettos and concentration camps, and dealt with "the actual technical side of things."[16] To be sure, this line of reasoning more or less mirrored the arguments advanced by at least some of the original defendants at Nuremberg – and just as the strategy was thwarted at Nuremberg, disallowed in fact, so it was as well in Jerusalem. Nevertheless, it constituted the core of Eichmann's response to the charges against him. He acted solely in service to his nation: being a recipient of orders authored by the state and/or issued by his superiors, he had no alternative but to obey. Yet, and this was central to his defence, he had obeyed these orders only with the greatest reluctance, and this fact was made evident, he argued, by his repeated requests for reassignment and transfer.[17]

Once the prosecution and defence finished presenting their cases, cross-examining, re-examining, and rebutting, the bench turned to questioning Eichmann directly, challenging the sense he proffered throughout that he was merely a tool of the state and calling upon him to assume his proper place in the unfolding legal narrative. Judge Revah led the examination clearly in search of a moral agent, a subject more directly aligned with and legible in terms of what the judge understood the Nazi project of annihilation to have entailed. According to writer Haim Gouri,

Revah was emotional but soft-spoken as he began his interrogation of the accused. And with his first questions, Gouri reports, there was a shift in the tenor and pace of the proceedings, leading the writer and others in the courtroom that day to sense that something momentous was about to unfold.[18]

Judge Revah referred Eichmann to the police interrogation to which he had been subject in the months preceding the trial and asked if he could explain to the court an account he had given at that time about having tried throughout his life to live in accordance with Kant's categorical imperative: Did he understand the Kantian imperative, Revah queried? And how precisely had it informed or corresponded to his genocidal activities, deporting Jews, and even, apparently, taking pride and pleasure in their slaughter? Hadn't he after all written and intended to deliver a self-congratulatory speech to his subordinates once the regime collapsed, exulting in the death of Germany's enemies, five million Jews – a job well done? What did this have to do with Kant? And turning to the Wannsee Conference: surely a mere stenographer – because such was the function Eichmann claimed to have performed at this pivotal meeting and moment in the formulation of policy with respect to the final solution – would not have joined the head of the Gestapo, Henrich Müller, and the head of the Reich Main Security Office, Reinhard Heydrich, following this formal rendezvous of highly placed government administrators for a bit of cognac, a smoke, a round of song, and a little fellowship by the fireside.

Eichmann conceded that Kant's imperative might indeed seem an ill-fitting framework for a life lived under compulsion, as his was especially after 1940; and he acknowledged further that killing people violently could not normally be considered a maxim for universal action consistent with the spirit of Kant's directive. In fact, he had experienced a crisis of sorts when he was "sent to the East and compelled to watch people being shot to death," especially when his coat was splattered with brain matter.[19] But he had come to understand that the time in which he lived was one of war and unprecedented destruction, and further upon reflection, much to his relief, that even within this unusual, highly constrained historical moment he could reinflect Kant's understanding of moral duty to accommodate the conditions then circumscribing his life.[20] As he described it to the judge, this version of Kant, the one he came to adapt and adopt, was "the categorical imperative for the small man's domestic use." It required foremost personal discipline so as to create an orderly life, unquestioned service to the law, and obedience to authorities – conducting oneself so as not to come into conflict with either. This adaptation more or less provided a universalizable maxim, and although it was not exactly what Kant had in mind, it was, in Eichmann's view, at least a workable iteration of the philosopher's program for ethical action.[21]

As for Wannsee, he was as he had insisted throughout the trial a minor official at this all-important meeting of state secretaries, a mere recipient of orders. Various possibilities for centralizing and more efficiently routinizing the killing process had indeed been discussed at this gathering of the regime's "top brass" but, as Eichmann viewed it, the official part of the meeting was largely symbolic. Its function was to underscore Heydrich's authority and control over all matters related to the deportation and resettlement of Jews in the territories occupied by Germany in order to end the petty rivalries and tumultuous intrigues between departments, sections, and ministries with respect to Jewish affairs.[22] For his part, Eichmann was present only to supply data as needed and craft the minutes in a way that best reflected the account Heydrich wanted placed in the administrative record.[23] Still, being in the presence of such leaders and listening to their lively deliberations over how best to exploit the labour power of those among Europe's remaining eleven million now or soon-to-be stateless Jewish refuges still fit for work while also discussing "various possible solutions" for dealing with the superfluous rest – this had convinced Eichmann that neither the conference nor what was clearly to follow from it had anything to do with him and that he could, therefore, in good conscience, wash his hands of responsibility. Gouri reports that Judge Revah's eyes widened in amazement as Eichmann proffered this account of the conference.[24] An exasperated Judge Halevi beseeched the accused: "Will you at least shoulder the burden of the facts in order not to be suspected of wishing to evade things?"[25]

Although Eichmann had assured the court that he welcomed the opportunity to set the record straight, he appeared to the bench not to have fully "wrestle[d] with himself towards an acknowledgment of the whole truth."[26] Judge Halevi pressed on in the wake of Revah's frustration. He appealed to Eichmann's conscience, pride, and duty to answer for his action; he appealed to his masculine conceits; and he appealed to his responsibilities as a father: didn't his sons deserve to hear from him the truth about where he stood and what he did? Hadn't he wanted generations to come, especially young Germans, to hear in his testimony and see in his bearing a model of expiation that might answer their questions and alleviate their historical burden and future guilt?

Eichmann insisted that he had spoken throughout the trial with courage and candour and that he was satisfied that the record would reflect both. He had been a Nazi, it is true. He had believed in the Reich and the political vision of its leaders. But he had not been anti-Semitic. While he joined the party wilfully and with enthusiasm, in the early years he had not much concerned himself with an anti-Semitism that he and many others regarded as merely party propaganda: what interested him was work and bread, freedom, and an end to the servitude imposed by (the Treaty of) Versailles.[27] Others were responsible for instilling fear and inciting terror: he had had no part in the legal and economic dispossession of Jews nor in the harassment and oppression they suffered.

When a policy of forced emigration was adopted, he had seen this as a positive thing, a mutually beneficial arrangement, something Jews desired as much as Germans. And recognizing this shared interest and goal, he had dealt with Jewish functionaries on equal footing and worked with them to find solutions that would best accommodate the distinct needs of each party. Had the court compelled them, witnesses could have been called to attest to his equanimity and candour during these initial years.[28] But, once the war began, indeed once the Zionist representatives of the Jewish people declared war against the German people, the context and terms of his negotiation with Jewish officials, by necessity, did change: forced emigration gave way to expulsion, deportation, ghettoization, and resettlement, but, even so, this shift was not the result of his own initiative.[29] Personally, he harboured no blood lust and had never endorsed a physical solution to the Jewish question. And although the leadership had mandated that members of the Jewish nation be dealt with harshly as conquering forces drove east, he had not devised the policy or been involved in setting out the ever-evolving strategic and tactical plans for its implementation or ever taken part in any executions, least of all mass murder. Laws were made, commands were issued, and he faithfully gave himself over to both. This was not easy – because he did his duties at the expense of his own inclinations, he sometimes experienced a form of splitting between what he described as the demands of office and his human impulses – but his oath of allegiance constituted his highest moral duty. As such, and regardless of what he personally might have preferred, it prevailed.[30]

He acknowledged that in the aftermath of defeat and from the historical vantage point of fifteen years as well as less turbulent times, blind devotion to the state and unconditional obedience to orders regardless of their nature were hard to comprehend and had become little-admired virtues. And certainly even he, Eichmann, had realized in the years since the war, although this shift had taken time, that unchecked nationalism, "the dislike of the unlike," led to brute egoism and potentially abhorrent consequences.[31] But all of this was evident only in hindsight and even then, divorced from the political mood and milieu of the age, hindsight could provide at best only a partial portrait: in the aftermath of the First World War and then, of course, during the Second World War, the life and death of the nation had been at stake, and for Eichmann as for others loyalty and duty were paramount. Indeed, the now apparently commonplace notion that it was possible under such circumstances to shirk one's oath, to oppose or even question one's orders, was in Eichmann's view, a fairy tale propagated by victors and traitors alike only after defeat.[32]

When finally the presiding judge, Judge Landau, moved to interrogate the accused, his questions returned the courtroom's focus to Eichmann's anti-Semitism: surely when he joined the National Socialist Party he had been aware of its intended program against the Jews, its propaganda linking the economic plight of Germany, the unemployment and food shortages, to world Jewry, its intention from the beginning to forcibly remove Jews from the German national body?[33] Surely he would not have been drafted into the head office for Reich Security and tasked with the logistical aspects of the annihilation process had he not been reliably, indeed fanatically, anti-Semitic and demonstrated, moreover, avid initiative and single-minded determination in identifying and delivering Jews to the killing sites. Hadn't his job as a highly placed official in what was in effect the Gestapo required drive and a certain tough resolve: to be tough, especially with respect to others? Wasn't this required of every SS man?[34] And wasn't his toughness something one could measure by or see manifested in the suffering and persecution of Jews whose paths crossed his as he crossed Europe?

Here again, Eichmann was at pains to stress that the bench had misunderstood. Toughness was not primarily about one's dealings with others, although certainly there were some in the SS fraternity who were brutal and conducted themselves in this way – "there was [in the SS] all sorts of species."[35] Rather, it was more accurate to see in this requirement, said Eichmann, a call for discipline and self-control: one was required to be tough on oneself, to subordinate one's self to the immediate demands and circumstances at hand. And the anti-Semitism? He had tried throughout the trial to distinguish himself from prominent anti-Semitic figures like Julius Streicher – whom he claimed most of his compatriots found offensive – and to impress upon the court as well that he had found the rabid racism of Streicher's publication, *Der Stürmer*, crude and revolting.[36] An incredulous Landau interrupted, "most of his compatriots?" But Eichmann pressed on. Animus against the Jews had never inspired him; indeed, what the court failed to understand is that it was nothing so personal with him. In the beginning, when there existed what he thought of as a mutually shared set of interests between Germans and Jews, facilitating their departure from German territory filled him with a sense of inner satisfaction – in the final years, not so much. But in either case he had been driven not by ideology as by a job to do, and he did not have to hate the Jews to do it in the meticulous way demanded, by the book and according to regulation. Tasked with organizing populations for transfer, Eichmann was first and last a transport officer concerned only with logistics. As he told the court, he was willing now to atone for the regime's monstrous excesses by hanging – these excesses overwhelmed him with shame – but he was not himself a monster: he had not authored or overseen the implementation of the policies or acts that inspired such excesses and could not, indeed would not, be made therefore to assume responsibility for them in the way and degree insisted on by those now judging him.

2

For the judges – and this they went to great lengths to impress upon Eichmann – whether the truth or rather the "whole truth" was finally revealed depended entirely on him having the courage to tell it, although, they added, they were not naive enough to believe all they were told and it was, in the end, their prerogative to determine whether he had been faithful to the facts.[37] And of course, they concluded well in advance of their subsequent final judgment that he had sought throughout the proceedings only to deceive and confuse the record by disavowing the racial animus they were certain had driven him to become the principal force behind the regime's "Final Solution." A cold and calculating anti-Semitism was the component, in some respects the most important component, that was missing from the account the accused gave of himself. A fierce will to achieve the criminal object of the destruction of Europe's Jews: this was the confession that he refused to make and that could not be extracted from him, much to the disappointment of spectators and court personnel as well. In fact, Eichmann himself was a disappointing figure both in demeanour and appearance, certainly not the imagined, diabolical Gestapo leader whose mere presence could project the chilling aura of one the prosecution called "Prince of Darkness."[38] Rather, he appeared in court to be "Mr. Average," indeed, "everyone's next-door neighbor."[39] Stripped of his boots and parabellum, according to Gouri, he looked pathetic, and it was for this reason that some argued he should be forced to take the stand in an SS uniform.[40]

In the end, such theatrics were unnecessary. What was essential to the proceedings but nevertheless missing from what the court characterized as Eichmann's glib and cunning testimony was the Zionist metanarrative that circulated freely throughout the trial and across discursive arenas. It was produced as part of the fabric of fact which was culturally resonant in the aftermath of his capture, faithfully sustained by the prosecution through witness testimony, and painstakingly set out in the court's subsequent judgment. As Shoshana Felman argues, Eichmann was brought to trial as an emblem of a long history of persecution culminating in legalized genocide; the story he rehearsed following his capture and expected others to find credible could only be told by one who felt if not excused by this history than certainly protected by it. But his capture and trial changed everything. In Felman's words:

> Th[e] whole insidious framework of legal persecution and of legalized abuse c[ould] now for the first time be dismantled legally, since Zionism ha[d] provided a tribunal (a state justice) in which the Jew's victimization c[ould] be for the first time legally articulated. In doing justice and exercising sovereign Israeli jurisdiction, the Eichmann trial ... legally reverse[d] the long tradition of traumatization of the Jew by means of law. The voiceless Jew or the perennial accused c[ould] for the first time speak, say "I" and voice his own "J'accuse."[41]

Of the trial's 121 sessions, 65 were devoted to the testimony of, what the prosecution called, "background witnesses" called to the stand to describe in vivid detail the conditions of life in diasporic communities both before and during the catastrophe. These witnesses were strategically chosen to "shock the heart" of spectators both in and beyond

Israel; and taken together, their testimony provided not only a massive living recreation of the odious, sadistic, inescapable cruelty visited upon Europe's Jews by Nazi Germany, but a striking tableau of both rebellion and heroism amid atrocity and tragedy. They were considered the "bearers of truth" during this trial, painstakingly describing what perpetrators, including Eichmann, never expected would be told, certainly not in a court of law, because they had devoted themselves to destroying anyone or thing that could tell it. Speaking for themselves, to be sure, these witnesses also spoke in a collective voice on behalf of innumerable others – friends, family, children, neighbours – who, as Hausner insisted on their behalf, had been "await[ing] the Jewish state but were not privileged to see it."[42] And, if the case for the prosecution was, as Gouri described it, "a memorial service for the dead," memorialized as well, and for the living, were hard-won victories and acts of glory, miraculous deeds in the service of life amid immeasurable suffering under conditions of terror.[43]

For Felman, the Eichman trial set out to perform what she calls, after Nietzsche, "monumental history," a form of history as Nietzsche explained it that captures the world-altering, seemingly other-worldly quality of the singular deed and typically provides models of rare courage, strength, ingenuity, and greatness for subsequent generations to emulate but, more importantly, surpass. Felman retains the awe-inspiring sensibility that animates this form of history for Nietzsche, but also fundamentally refigures it: in her iteration the history monumentalized by the trial was not driven by remembrance of the rare and the classic or the greatness of one who has changed the course of human events. It was, rather, remembrance through law of those, the six million, who did not make history but suffered or "*were subject* to it" – abandoned by the world, hunted, deceived, cast into an inferno, and silenced. They were now able to give voice to their anguish and through the state hold their murderers accountable. In Ben-Gurion's words, "Here for the first time in Jewish history, historical justice is being done by the sovereign Jewish people. For many generations it was we who suffered, who were tortured, were killed – and we who were judged … For the first time Israel is judging the murderers of the Jewish people."[44] Although these people had been forever cut off from the land of the living, their blood could be avenged: and it was their claim, according to Felman, that Gideon Hausner invoked in his opening address to the court and by their authority that he had been tasked with making the extent of the great and otherwise unacknowledged national tragedy – their story – fully known:

> When I stand before you, oh judges of Israel, to lead the prosecution of Adolf Eichmann, I do not stand alone. With me here are six million accusers. But they cannot rise to their feet and point their finger at the man in the dock with the cry "J'accuse!" on their lips. For they are now only ashes – ashes piled high on the hills of Auschwitz and the fields of Treblinka and strewn in the forests of Poland. Their graves are scattered throughout Europe. Their blood cries out, but their voice is stilled. Therefore will I be their spokesman. In their name will I unfold this terrible indictment?

For Felman, the trial was a revolutionary moment, a singular, transformative event of law out of which emerged a sacred narrative that was "at once a tale of jurisprudence and collective mourning": "a Jewish past that formerly had meant only a crippling disability was now being reclaimed as an empowering and proudly shared political and moral identity."[45] And while the judges in their final ruling explicitly dismissed as historically significant but for the most part legally irrelevant the very testimony that Felman argues actually constituted the trial's monumental character – its creation through the testimony of the persecuted of a legal narrative, language, and culture, indeed a national narrative, language, and culture not yet or not fully in existence – their final judgment nevertheless institutionalized, through established law, a resonant founding (and foundational) story. Addressing the contention of the defence that the court lacked jurisdiction to try the accused, the judges appealed to international jurisprudence and history, identifying in the Holocaust the roots from which the sovereign state of Jews, what they described as a state of survivors, had first emerged and now acted with international sanction to bring to justice those who had sought the annihilation of the Jewish people. It was not Belgian Jews, or Romanian Jews, or Hungarian Jews, each group separately, that National Socialism had targeted, but the annihilation of an entire people regardless of the country in whose territory they resided, including the Jewish "Yishuv" in Palestine. And it was the prerogative, the sovereign and historical right as well as duty of the State of Israel, through its judiciary, to extend a "protective wing" over the whole of Jewry and punish those who had assailed or threatened to destroy it.[46] The judges continued:

> The massacre of millions of Jews by the Nazi criminals that very nearly led to the extinction of the Jewish People in Europe, was one of the tremendous causes for the establishment of the State of survivors ... The people and the crime are one ... The very existence of a people who can be murdered with impunity is in danger to say nothing of the danger to its "honor and authority." This has been the curse of the diaspora and the want of sovereignty of the Jewish People, upon whom any criminal could commit his outrages without fear of being punished by the people outraged. Hitler and his associates exploited the defenseless position of the Jewish People in its dispersion, in order to perpetrate the total murder of that People in cold blood. It was in order to provide some measure of redress for the terrible injustice of the Holocaust that the sovereign state of the Jews, which enables survivors of the Holocaust to defend its existence by the means at the disposal of the state, was established.[47]

So what then was the story the justices were waiting to hear from Eichmann that hadn't already been revealed over the course of the trial? And how was this story known to exist, indeed already known to all, but a mystery all the same which only Eichmann was in a position to disclose? One of the problems with "monumental history," according to Nietzsche, is that it tends towards generalizations and approximations; it ignores or neglects historical contingency and specificity and shakes off the incongruent for the sake of correspondence, what he calls "the archetypal truth." This form of history is susceptible to seeing the past in mythical terms and of treating events primarily as re-enactments of the same fundamental plot, the same catastrophe, repeated at different intervals.[48] The accused, like others in ages past, had viciously and without mercy gone to every extreme to bring about the speedy and complete extermination of all Jews: this had been the well-known project of National Socialism from the beginning. And although the court determined that the idea of the Final Solution was not Eichmann's own, without his zeal, genuine devotion, fanatical enthusiasm, and insatiable bloodthirstiness, that idea, they insisted, might never have assumed so satanic an expression.[49] He killed the Jews because he hated the Jews. But for this was a trial really required?

3

What emerged during the Eichmann trial and acquired a certain momentum in its aftermath was a sweeping simplification of the meaning of the Nazi genocide with radical anti-Semitic evil on one side and radical (Jewish) innocence and bravery on the other. This morally reductive discourse would become more or less institutionalized by the 1970s, the basis for what historian Peter Novick refers to, less enthusiastically than Felman, as the "sacralization" of the Holocaust[50] – its transformation from a historical event to a mythic, metaphysically framed one, unique(ly evil) and therefore outside of history, incomprehensible and therefore beyond interpretation, inexplicable and unimaginable and therefore beyond representation.[51] But even in its nascent form, in the context of the trial and its immediate aftermath, this materially reductive discourse worked against ambiguity or the unsettled and unsettling questions that political theorist Hannah Arendt claimed were now given features of contemporary life. As Arendt saw it, the Nazi genocide, and Eichmann's part in it, were not just the most recent chapters of a much larger and longer story detailing the natural and inevitable destruction wreaked by anti-Semitism; the Nazi genocide was not, as the prosecution and judges alike appeared to consider it, simply the "most horrible pogrom in Jewish history." For Arendt, it represented something unprecedented: it entailed an attack first and foremost on human plurality or what, she argued, constituted not only the cornerstone or precondition for shared human life in the world, but a fundamental source of its meaning. Given the organization and logic of the Nazis' extermination policies, she suggested in a letter to Mary McCarthy at the time of the trial, the death factories would not have shut down once the Jews – or the Poles, or the Gypsies – had been annihilated in their entirety. Retreating from a position she had advanced a decade earlier in *The Origins of Totalitarianism*, Arendt had come to believe that "extermination per se," the elimination of those deemed superfluous to the ongoing life of the nation, "was more important than anti-Semitism or racism" – more important, in other words, than the particular ideologies that ostensibly rationalized it and could be (as they were) amended, reformed, and rescripted to accommodate the changing needs and vision of the regime.[52] As Arendt understood it, then, "the crime against the Jewish people was *first of all a crime against the human status*," although most commentators failed, in her view, to fully see or appreciate the implications of this significant if nuanced difference. As a crime against humanity, it was a matter that vitally concerned and inescapably involved not just the Jews and not only Israel, but the international community as well.[53]

> Had the court in Jerusalem understood that there were distinctions between discrimination, expulsion, and genocide, it would immediately have become clear that the supreme crime it was confronted with, the physical extermination of the Jewish people, was a crime against humanity, perpetrated upon the body of the Jewish people, and that only the choice of victims, not the nature of the crime, could be derived from the long history of Jew-hatred and anti-Semitism. Insofar as the victims were Jews, it was right and proper that a Jewish Court should sit in judgment; but insofar as the crime was a crime against humanity, it needed an international tribunal to do justice to it … If genocide is an actual possibility of the future, then no people on earth – least of all, of course, the Jewish people, in Israel or elsewhere – can feel reasonably sure of its continued existence without the help and the protection of international law.[54]

For Arendt, the Eichmann trial squandered the opportunity to initiate an internationally compelling and binding means for addressing a special type of crime – administrative massacre – that threatened human plurality and thus exceeded the scope of any one state's jurisdiction: "State-employed mass murderers must be prosecuted because they violat[e] the order of mankind, not because they kill millions of people." But significantly, the trial also failed to make judicial sense of what she insisted was "a special type of criminal" – one who has no intent to do wrong, does not act from base motives, and "who commits his crimes under circumstances that make it well-nigh impossible for him to know or to feel that he is doing wrong."[55] In Eichmann, Arendt saw what she characterized as "*sheer thoughtlessness*" and in this *thoughtlessness*, she argued, lay a story about the banality of evil.

As Arendt frames it, the issue with Eichmann is not – as it seems to have routinely become in studies of the Nazi leadership or the regime's mid-level administrators – what precisely he (or Albert Speer, Joseph Strangl, and countless other prominent officials) knew and when he (they) knew it; or what animus he felt and didn't feel.[56] Nor is it a question of Eichmann's intelligence as some critics have understood her argument and gone to great lengths to counter: as she explains it, "Thinking in its non-cognitive, non-specialized sense … is not a prerogative of the few but an ever-present faculty in everybody; the inability to think is not a failing of the many who lack brain power but an ever present possibility for everybody – scientists, scholars, and other specialists in mental enterprises not excluded – to shun that intercourse with oneself whose possibility and importance Socrates first discovered."[57]

Sheer thoughtlessness in the case of Eichmann had rather to do with his refusal at any number of significant junctures over the course of his career – and some eighteen years afterwards – to engage the entangled world of living and dying as it was, to track the arc of his actions, and to say *no* even as he described for the court, as we have seen, any number of instances that threw into painfully sharp relief the broader meaning and unmistakably dreadful consequences of his job as a "transportation" officer for dispossessed populations across Europe.

The Wannsee Conference is, of course, one such instance. Arendt draws our attention to another story that she found especially striking which Eichmann told his interrogators prior to the trial. As Eichmann described it, he was called to Auschwitz by the camp's commandant, Rudolf Höss, on behalf of Bernard Storfer. Storfer was an international banker and prominent member of the Jewish leadership in Vienna who had also collaborated with Eichmann to organize the illegal emigration to Palestine of some 2,200 Jews from Prague (in December 1939). Arrested late in the war (1944), deported to Auschwitz, and assigned to a labour gang, Storfer sent an appeal for help to Eichmann through Höss. And Eichmann agreed to meet with him:

> I said to myself, O.K., this man has always behaved well, that is worth my while … I'll go there myself and see what is the matter with him … With Storfer afterward, well, it was normal and human, we had a normal, human encounter. He told me all his grief and sorrow: I said: "Well, my dear old friend [*Ja, mein lieber guter Storfer*], we certainly got it! What rotten luck!" And I also said: "Look, I really cannot help you, because according to orders from the Reichsführer nobody can get out. I can't get you out. Dr. Ebner [chief of the Gestapo in Vienna] can't get you out. I hear you made a mistake, that you went into hiding or wanted to bolt, which, after all, you did not need to do." [Eichmann meant that Storfer, as a Jewish functionary, had immunity from deportation.] I forget what his reply to this was. And then I asked him how he was. And he said, yes, he wondered if he couldn't be let off work, it was heavy work. And then I said to Höss: "Work – Storfer won't have to work!" But Höss said "Everyone works here." So I said: "O.K.," I said, "I'll make a chit to the effect that Storfer has to keep the gravel paths in order with a broom," there were little gravel paths there, "and that he had the right to sit down with his broom on one of the benches." [To Storfer] I said: "Will that be all right, Mr Storfer? Will that suit you?" Whereupon he was very pleased and we shook hands, and then he was given the broom and sat down on his bench. It was a great

> inner joy to me that I could at least see the man with whom I had worked for so many long years, and that we could speak with each other.[58]

Characterizing this episode as one "filled with macabre humor *surpassing that of any Surrealist invention*" – for within six weeks of Eichmann's joyful reunion, Storfer had been shot – Arendt was compelled to wonder whether Eichmann's narrative wasn't simply "a textbook case of bad faith, of lying self-deception combined with outrageous stupidity?"[59] That he could so fail to grasp the circumstances of this meeting, the larger or even more immediate context that brought *his dear old friend* Storfer to be pleading for help on a gravel path in Auschwitz; that he could not see the desperate and degrading situation that was hardly a matter of happenstance or simple misfortune, as Eichmann intimated (*what rotten luck! … I hear you made a mistake!*); and that he could not understand even some eighteen years after the encounter – for this was a story he told his captors – the ways in which his actions and Storfer's fate were linked or the ways in which Storfer's situation at the time of the meeting implicated the operation he, Eichmann, had overseen throughout the war suggested, in Arendt's view, an utter dearth of imagination. And by characterizing it as such, she meant to underscore Eichmann's inability to "bridge certain abysses of remoteness," to understand what was happening as though it were his own affair or to think from a point of view other than his own – even after having years during which he might have figured it out. In the absence of imagination, Arendt argues, we cannot "take our bearings in the world"; it is what provides, in the end, "the only inner compass we have."[60]

The story with Eichmann, therefore, as Arendt tells it, is that he refused to engage in the kind of thinking activity that she insists would have allowed him to tolerate the doubt he claimed to have experienced at Wannsee or the ditches in Minsk where he was splattered with brain matter and, moreover, use this doubt as the disruptive opening it presented for (re)considering the meaning of the business-as-usual functions, the bureaucratic formulas, rules, codes, and directives that together organized and continued to organize his sense of who he was and what he was doing. That Eichmann's identity was so constituted was clearly evidenced for Arendt in his insistence throughout the trial, as we have seen, that "he would have had a bad conscience only if he had not done what he had been told to do," that is, only if he had broken with the formulas, rules, codes of expression, and directives that had come to comprise his sense of self.[61] Along these same lines and equally as telling was the fact that some two decades after the regime's collapse, Eichmann still insisted that officialese was his only language and still could not give a coherent account of himself – of what he said and did – that was not riddled with clichés or stock phrases or rendered in terms of the ever-present pile of documents that accompanied him in prison and court as if these papers provided definitive points of reference to some unfamiliar story that was supposedly his own. Indeed, when considered through the lens that Arendt provides, there was, in the end, no personal story to be told, in part, because there was no thinking subject to tell it.

> What causes a man to fear [conscience] is the anticipation of the presence of a witness who awaits him only if and when he goes home. Shakespeare's murderer says: "Every man that means to live well endeavors … to live without it," and success in that comes easy because all he has to do is never start the soundless solitary dialogue we call "thinking," never go home and examine things. This is not a matter of wickedness or goodness, as it is not a matter of intelligence or stupidity. A person who does not know that silent intercourse (in which we examine what we say and what we do) will not mind contradicting himself, and this means he will never be either able or willing to account for what he says or does; nor will he mind committing any crime, since he can count on its being forgotten the next moment.[62]

Eichmann held tenaciously to an empty oath and rules of conduct that together worked to insulate him from encountering his own witness, the ever-present, observant other. Indeed, as Arendt puts it, "he and the world he [had] lived in [were] in perfect harmony."[63] Thus, he could arrange for the displacement, deportation, and eventual death of hundreds of thousands across Europe and still maintain in all sincerity, without duplicity, that he was innocent of the charges brought against him. As he told the court: "Officially I had nothing to do with [the gassing] and, unofficially, I wasn't interested … I am responsible for the things my orders obliged me to do … I have no desire to evade that responsibility. But, I refuse to take responsibility for things I had no orders for and which were not in my department"[64] In contrast to Eichmann, there emerges in Arendt's report another figure, Anton Schmidt, whose story was first told during the trial in the context of survivor testimony and whom she takes as an example of someone clearly guided by his own judgment against what were the nearly unanimous opinions and inclinations of the world around him. Schmidt was an army sergeant overseeing a patrol in Poland whose task it was to recover German soldiers who had been separated from their units. In the course of sweeping for soldiers, Schmidt was said to have encountered members of the Jewish underground; and rather than turning these partisans in, he opted instead to help them by supplying forged papers and trucks. This he did successfully without extracting or accepting payment for some five months until he was arrested and executed.[65] "How utterly different everything would be today in the courtroom," Arendt reflects, "if only more such stories could have been told."[66]

Where Eichmann could not have imagined acting in any other way than he did – "I obeyed my orders without thinking; I just did what I was told … What would I have gained by disobedience? And whom would it have served?"[67] – Schmidt obviously could and did take his bearings from elsewhere. Indeed, in a context that aimed to level difference, silence speech, and extinguish spontaneity and in contrast to Eichmann and all the many others who argued that opposition to the Nazi regime was virtually impossible and when possible "practically useless," Schmidt became, to use Arendt's language, his own witness. In times of political emergency this in itself can become an opening and act of resistance. But it was only the first of such acts for Schmidt. For while the character of his action suggests that he began what Arendt infers was a silent, solitary dialogue with himself, he seems to have also extended the conversation in ways and directions others at the time may have considered morally meaningful, but also dismissed as politically pointless: he joined his life to and died in solidarity with marked others to counter a regime that sought "to abolish the most basic material conditions for thought, identity, and agency."[68] For Arendt, the political lesson to be drawn from his example is clear and establishes a starting point for understanding the nature of Eichmann's culpability that was and remains obscured by the trial's imperatives and messianic purpose: "Under conditions of terror most people will comply but *some people will not* … Humanly speaking, no more is required, and no more can be reasonably asked, for this planet to remain a place fit for human habitation."[69]

NOTES

1 Judith Butler, *Giving an Account of Oneself* (Bronx, NY: Fordham University Press, 2005), 46.

2 For a detailed discussion of Eichmann's abduction by one of the men who engineered it, see Zvi Aharoni and William Dietl, *Operation Eichmann: The Truth about the Pursuit, Capture and Trial* (New York: Wiley, 1996).
3 *The Trial of Adolf Eichmann: Record of Proceedings in the District Court*, (hereafter *TAE*), vol. 4 (Jerusalem, 1993), 1811.
4 Jochen von Lang with Claus Sibyll, *Eichmann Interrogated: Transcripts from the Archives of the Israeli Secret Police* (New York: Da Capo Press, 1999), 104, 113, 291.
5 The field on this front is dense, but for two very different recent examples see: Deborah E. Lipstadt, *The Eichmann Trial* (New York: Schocken, 2011); and David Cesarani, *Eichmann: His Life and Crimes* (New York: Vintage, 2004).
6 Idith Zertal, *Israel's Holocaust and the Politics of Nationhood* (New York: Cambridge University Press, 2012), 107.
7 Cited in ibid., 106.
8 Pnina Lahav, *Judgment in Jerusalem: Chief Justice Simon Agranat and the Zionist Century* (Berkeley: University of California Press, 1997), 158.
9 "The widest possible publicity given to the legal process, which makes the court accessible to public evaluation, is the best possible means of ensuring that justice and judgment are done without any bias or prejudice." Cited in Hannah Yablonka, *The State of Israel vs. Adolf Eichmann* (New York: Schocken, 2004), 57.
10 For speculation about this strategy see Haim Gouri, *Facing the Glass Booth: The Jerusalem Trial of Adolf Eichmann* (Detroit: Wayne State University Press, 2004), 233–7.
11 Cesarani, *Eichmann*, 299.
12 Gouri, *Facing the Glass Booth*, 192.
13 Cesarani *Eichmann*, 282.
14 Gideon Hausner, *Justice in Jerusalem* (New York: Herzl Press, 1977), 300, 90–7; Gouri, *Facing the Glass Booth*, 247–8.
15 The defence challenged the authority of the court on four fronts: 1) the impartiality of the judges and state; 2) the illegality of Eichmann's capture in Argentina; 3) the jurisdiction of the Israeli court to try Eichmann for crimes not committed on Israeli territory; and 4) the retroactive nature of the 1950 Nazi and Nazi Collaborators (Punishment) Law.
16 *TAE*, 4:1827.
17 Cesarani, *Eichmann*, 281.
18 Gouri, *Facing the Glass Booth*, 226.
19 Cesarani, *Eichmann*, 106.
20 *TAE*, 4:1803.

21 *TAE*, 4:1804. Hans Frank, who was governor general of occupied Poland's "General Government" territory and who was tried at the International Military Tribunal at Nuremberg, invoked a version of Kant as well that diverged only slightly from Eichmann's: "Act in such a way that the Führer, if he knew your action, would approve."

22 Von Lang and Sibyll, *Eichmann Interrogated*, 93.

23 *TAE*, 4:1810.

24 Gouri, *Facing the Glass Booth*, 228.

25 Ibid., 233.

26 *TAE*, 4:1813.

27 Von Lang and Sibyll, *Eichmann Interrogated*, pp. 36, 41.

28 Yablonka, *The State of Israel vs Adolf Eichmann*, 91.

29 *TAE*, 4:1576, 1584–5.

30 Ibid., 4:1820.

31 Ibid., 1:187; 4:1821.

32 Eichmann's Final Appeal: http://remember.org/eichmann/ownwords.

33 *TAE*, 4:1828–9.

34 Ibid., 4:1830–1

35 Ibid., 4:1830.

36 Julius Streicher was tried at the International Military Tribunal at Nuremberg and convicted for inciting atrocity through racist speech (he was a newspaper editor).

37 *TAE*, 4:1813

38 Gideon Hausner, cited in Tom Segev, *Simon Wiesenthal: The Life and Legends* (New York: Schocken, 2012), 151.

39 Cesarani, *Eichmann*, 257.

40 Gouri, *Facing the Glass Booth*, 156; Cesarani, *Eichmann*, 257.

41 Shoshana Felman, *The Juridical Unconscious: Trials and Traumas in the Twentieth Century* (Cambridge, MA: Harvard University Press, 2002), 119.

42 Cited in Tom Segev, *The Seventh Million* (New York: Picador, 2000), 349.

43 Gouri, *Facing the Glass Booth*, 157; Segev, *The Seventh Million*, 429.

44 David Ben-Gurion, *Israel: A Personal History* (New York: Funk and Wagnalls, 1971), 599.

45 Felman, *The Juridical Unconscious*, 129, 127.

46 Hausner, *Justice in Jerusalem*, 413; Final judgment, section 38.

47 *TAE*, Final Judgment, section 36.

48 Friedrich Nietzsche, *The Use and Abuse of History*, trans. Adrian Collins (New York: Bobs-Merrill, 1957), 15.

49 Finding of the Israeli Supreme Court, Judge Moshe Silberg, cited in Hausner, *Justice in Jerusalem*, 443.

50 Peter Novick, *The Holocaust in American Life* (New York: Houghton Mifflin, 1999), 141.

51 Elie Wiesel is most often identified as the exemplar of such claims.

52 Carol Brightman, ed., *Between Friends: The Correspondence of Hannah Arendt and Mary McCarthy 1949–1975* (New York: Harcourt Brace 1995), 148.

53 For a discussion of the ways in which the category "crimes against the human status" has been repeatedly redefined, sentimentalized, and trivialized see Alain Finkielkraut, *Remembering in Vain: The Klaus Barbie Trial and Crimes against Humanity* (New York: Columbia University Press, 1992); emphasis in original.

54 Arendt, *Eichmann in Jerusalem: A Report on the Banality of Evil* (New York: Viking Press, 1963), 269, 272.

55 Arendt, *Eichmann in Jerusalem*, 276.

56 An example here would be the approach of journalist Gitta Sereny, who has interviewed numerous highly placed former Nazis in an attempt to determine, in her words, "some new truth which would contribute to the understanding of things that have never yet been understood." *Into That Darkness: An Examination of Conscience* (New York: Vintage, 1974), 23. See also Sereny, *Albert Speer: His Battle with Truth* (New York: Vintage, 1996).

57 Arendt, *Life of the Mind*, vol. 1 (New York: Harcourt Brace Jovanovich, 1971), 191.

58 Arendt, *Eichmann in Jerusalem*, 51.

59 Ibid., 51–2; emphasis in original.

60 Arendt, "Understanding and Politics (The Difficulties of Understanding)," in *Essays in Understanding* (New York: Harcourt Brace, 1994), 323.

61 Arendt, *Eichmann in Jerusalem*, 25.

62 Arendt, *Life of the Mind*, 1:190–1.

63 Arendt, *Eichmann in Jerusalem*, 52.

64 Lang and Sibyll, *Eichmann Interrogated*, 197, 199–200.

65 Ibid., 230.

66 Arendt, *Eichmann in Jerusalem*, 231.

67 Lang and Sibyll, *Eichmann Interrogated*, 157, 291.

68 Norma Moruzzi, *Speaking through the Mask: Hannah Arendt and the Politics of Social Identity* (Ithica, NY: Cornell University Press, 2000), 133.

69 Arendt, *Eichmann in Jerusalem*, 233; emphasis in original.

Chapter Five

Arendt's Conservatism and the Eichmann Judgment

RUSSELL A. BERMAN

The 1963 publication of Hannah Arendt's *Eichmann in Jerusalem* elicited enormous controversy in the intellectual public sphere; Irvine Howe characterized the ensuing debate as "violent," while Mary McCarthy described the attacks on Arendt as assuming "the proportions of a pogrom."[1] Half a century later the discussion of the book has moved into narrower academic quarters, but it still provokes deep disagreements. The point of these disputes, however, is rarely Eichmann himself: no serious arguments have been mounted to question his culpability. Rather the debates involve the substantive arguments and rhetorical choices made by Arendt, especially subtexts in her account of the trial that have led it to be read as a statement on the Shoah more broadly, on anti-Semitism or on Zionism and the character of the State of Israel. *Eichmann in Jerusalem* attracts so much debate not because of Eichmann but because of these several other issues embedded in the narrative.

Readers who pursue these lines of interpretation – asking about Arendt's view on the Shoah, on Zionism or on Israel, rather than specifically on Eichmann – stand on firm textual grounds, since the book does speak, if sometimes indirectly, to all these issues, no matter that Arendt herself, as author and narrator of the text, frequently appears to wish to narrow the focus of the account onto the single defendant on trial. Indeed, a key refrain involves her criticism that the Jerusalem trial should have focused solely on Eichmann, but instead succumbed to the prosecutor's efforts to pursue a larger inquiry into Nazi genocidal policies. Her own text, with all its side roads and interlinear suggestions, is therefore more expansive than her primary legalistic argument. This tension inherent in the book itself between Arendt's appeal for a narrow judgment and the much broader and heterogeneous implications of the text contributes to the many controversies, the focus of which, moreover, has shifted over time. Initial criticisms of *Eichmann in Jerusalem* objected to its account of the Shoah and the killings and the reading (or misreading) that Arendt associated them with banality. As we will see, Saul Bellow – one example for many – makes this case in his response in *Mr. Sammler's Planet* (1969). Yet recently, *Eichmann in Jerusalem* has been appropriated for the academic debate over Zionism, especially in Elhanan Yakira's *Post-Zionism, Post-Holocaust* (2009) and in Judith Butler's *Parting Ways* (2013). These varying perspectives will be discussed below. (Of course the question of Zionism also played a role in the initial reception of the book. Yet challenged by the accusation that the book was anti-Zionist, Arendt endorsed the contrary view that the book supports Israel.[2] As we will see, Butler nonetheless draws on *Eichmann in Jerusalem* as evidence to make her own case against Israeli statehood.)

Beyond this already complex hermeneutic situation, evaluating *Eichmann in Jerusalem* becomes an even greater challenge because of the ambiguities endemic to Arendt's political thought more broadly. Parsing her politics is a challenging task, to say the least. Her predisposition to anchor her theoretical claims in particular historical material (especially in *Origins of Totalitarianism* but equally in *Eichmann in Jerusalem*) rather than exclusively in systematic expositions (such as in *The Human Condition*) can make her work simultaneously intriguing and frustrating. She did not hesitate to make her own lack of ideology a badge of honour. Asked whether she inclined towards liberal or conservative views, she replied, "I don't know. I really don't know and I've never known. And I suppose I never had such a position. You know the left think that I am conservative, and the conservatives think I am left or I am a maverick or God knows what. And I must say that I couldn't care less. I don't think the real questions of this century will get any kind of illumination by this kind of thing."[3]

The complexity of her thinking, its variation over time, as well as a capacity to tolerate her own inconsistencies all contribute to explaining this resistance to pigeonholing. One should not fault her for refusing one-dimensional political allegiances. On the contrary, reading Arendt can be productive precisely because she refuses to leave us with simplistic answers. However, her rejection of the conventional left-right spectrum of political ideas with the implication of its inherent insufficiency is itself identifiable as an arguably conservative habit. The rejection of a political framework in which a set of left-wing ideas mirrors a symmetrical set on the right is an indicator of that European conservatism that rarely embraced the project of theoretical thinking with the same fervour as did the left, a distinction familiar since Edmund Burke's *Reflections on the Revolution in France* (1790) and its critique of the enlightened philosophical advocates of upheaval. The more apt context for Arendt however is the early twentieth-century conservative German criticism of modernity with its disdain for politics as a necessarily degraded sphere of activity. In that sense, the young Thomas Mann entitled his wartime memoirs *Reflections of an Unpolitical Man* (1918). Similarly the political theorist Arendt, who came of age in that same world of German cultural conservatism, would shun explicitly partisan political allegiances in order to stand above the fray. The one exception was her committed Zionism, briefly during the 1940s, and, as we will see below, *Eichmann in Jerusalem* has come to be read now, by supporters and detractors, as an expression of her break with that past. Hence its pertinence to contemporary debates over Israel and Palestine.

Arendt's conservatism involves a set of intellectual allegiances, cultural values, and political-theoretical predispositions, including this allergy against emphatic political partisanship, as well as her scepticism towards the experience of modernity, a critique of the notion of progress, and an apprehension concerning centralized state power (and this last point particularly undergirds her concerns about the Israeli state). In what follows, the texture of this conservatism will be explored in some detail, particularly as it emerged in the controversial essay "Reflections on Little Rock" of 1959. Although she would eventually retract the positions articulated there, a critique of school desegregation, they nonetheless shed light on issues that would emerge in the Eichmann controversy only a few years later. Underneath the evaluation of the Holocaust and the State of Israel that readers found in *Eichmann in Jerusalem*, it was likely also her conservative political-theoretical assumptions that fuelled the controversial reception.

In addition, it will be important to ask how the conservative thinker Arendt could be appropriated by Butler for an explicitly progressive formulation of anti-Zionism. This migration across the right-left spectrum deserves scrutiny. How does the conservative Arendt become a crown witness for the left? How does the Weimar conservative criticized by Bellow turn into an important resource for Butler? To be sure, the path from the Weimar right to the New Left is well trodden; the case of Herbert Marcuse comes to mind, and Richard Wolin has discussed this terrain in detail.[4] At stake in this chapter is the specific implication of the Eichmann discussion in the itinerary across political loyalties, to understand which requires some further investigation of Arendt's conservatism.

Arendt's Conservatism

The significance of the anti-Zionist overtones in *Eichmann in Jerusalem* becomes clear only against the backdrop of Arendt's enthusiastic engagement with Zionism during the 1940s. This is not the place to trace the complexities of the competing Zionist political programs that were debated during the darkest days of the war and genocide. Suffice it to say that Arendt, during her first years in the United States, appeared to live up to a primary tenet of her philosophy, an advocacy for politics as public action. She participated in and identified with the Zionist movement, thus, for example insisting on the importance of raising a Jewish army to fight the Germans, and she celebrated the Warsaw uprising by placing it in the context of a long Jewish national history: "Honor and glory are new words in the political vocabulary of our people. We should perhaps have to go back to the days of the Maccabees to hear such language."[5] Referring to the novelty of the terminology, Arendt implies the emergence of a new Jew, akin to the "new man" of modernism and socialism, now casting off the subaltern degradation of the past and achieving a genuine political nationality: "To the extent that *the* Jew is disappearing, Jews have come to life: organizing, fighting, proud of their flag and deeds, suffering and hoping for a better future – a nationality like the other nationalities who sprang from the fostering soil of Western history."[6] It is important to parse the political language here. The terminology of Jews as "a nationality like the other nationalities" reveals her core Zionism. The shift from the disappearance of "the Jew," in the singular, to the plurality of "Jews" is consistent with her emphasis on politics as action in concert with others, and resonates with the Heideggerean notion of *Mitsein.* No doubt the birth of the "new Jew" can be read as a progressive vision, but her values and points of reference – honour, glory, the legacy of antiquity – echo a conservative rhetoric, as does the invocation of "Western history."[7]

Despite this enthusiasm for the political ambitions of the Jewish nation, Arendt rapidly distanced herself from the Zionist movement after the 1942 Biltmore Conference, which established the focus on state formation in line with David Ben-Gurion's agenda. As committed as she was, in theory, to the public sphere and political action, she developed an animosity towards popular nationhood and nationalism, combined with a general disdain for party politics, especially when politics merged with variants of ethnic identity. While her Zionist moment might be read as, at least in part, modernist and progressive although simultaneously heroic and conservative, her leanings moved increasingly away from the former and towards the latter. Modernity became a suspect site of decline.

A key feature of Arendt's conservatism is her adamant rejection of the very foundational idea of progressive thought, the notion of progress itself. Far from a guarantor of ameliorated conditions for human life, the rhetoric of progress takes on an ominous character in her writings, a source of a destructive capacity in the unfolding of the modernity of which she is so deeply suspicious. Thus in response to the social change and turmoil of the 1960s, she wrote in *On Violence* in 1969: "Not only has the progress of science ceased to coincide with the progress of mankind (whatever that may mean), but it could even spell mankind's end, just as the further progress of scholarship may well end with the destruction of everything that made scholarship worth our while. Progress, in other words, can no longer serve as a standard by which to evaluate the disastrously rapid change-processes we have let loose."[8] Arendt's complaint here is not that progress has somehow stalled and needs reinvigoration (e.g., through the then contemporary agenda of the Great Society of the Johnson administration), nor does she merely invert the progressive paradigm with a dystopic vision of an ever-increasing, progressive repression, as did Max Horkheimer and Theodor W. Adorno in their *Dialectic of Enlightenment* (1944). Instead she rejects the concept of progress as such, in some ways anticipating Jean-François Lyotard's rejection of the grand narratives of progress, but without his postmodern celebration of multiple plot lines. For Arendt, by way of contrast, a fundamental existential stability in the human condition necessarily collides with the illusory and deceptive claims of any illusion of linear progress. Implicit in this estimation is a profoundly conservative perspective in which the core features of human existence remain constant and never changing, except in the case of totalitarianism, which she views as a unique effort to change human nature and the foundational conditions of human life. This core thesis of *Origins of Totalitarianism* rejects the conventional interpretations of Nazism as an indication of German backwardness, a throwback to pre-modernity, or as eruptions of archaic strata of human life but instead treats totalitarianism itself as cut from the same cloth of the progressive aspiration to remake the world: totalitarianism is nothing if not modern.

In addition to her critique of progress, Arendt's conservatism is evident in several other enduring aspects of her thought: her anxiety about the rise of the social (elaborated especially in *The Human Condition*), the valorization of political authority over economic needs, the hostile critique of bureaucracy (which figures prominently in her characterization of Adolf Eichmann as the ultimate bureaucratic perpetrator), and, perhaps most obviously, her consistent hostility towards Marxism.[9] In the depths of the Cold War and the McCarthy era, *Origins of Totalitarianism*, which appeared in 1951, treated Stalinism and Nazism as twin evils, two manifestations of the same political principle. For decades after, the left would begrudge Arendt that "totalitarianism thesis." Her treatment of Stalinism and Nazism as comparable dictatorships – despite the conventional wisdom that they represented profoundly disparate agendas and despite the world war history after 1941 that pitted them against each other – echoes her self-description cited earlier regarding the insufficiency of the traditional categories of right and left. Yet to fully understand Arendt's conservatism and its consequences for political judgment, it is important to look in some detail at another essay that led to its own controversy immediately prior to the Eichmann debate.

Conservatism in Little Rock and the Problem of Ethnic Politics

Only four years before *Eichmann in Jerusalem*, Arendt stumbled into a conflict with another variant of identity politics: her controversial comments on the Supreme Court's school desegregation decision, "Reflections on Little Rock." Several of her arguments there, especially her assertions concerning the role of the state, are germane to the positions staked out in *Eichmann in Jerusalem* regarding the Israeli state. Written initially for *Commentary*, the piece was withheld from publication, only appearing later in *Dissent* in 1959. The essay puts forth a critique of the desegregation agenda, with all of Arendt's unnerving mixture of acute insight and stunning obtuseness. Not surprisingly, it elicited considerable criticism, and Arendt eventually distanced herself from it. While it is therefore certainly not appropriate to hold her to the positions expressed in Little Rock, nor should the piece be ignored, since it does provide important insights into her intellectual profile. At the very least, one can say that the political theorist Arendt could suffer from a tin ear to political circumstances. In addition, given a continuity between her position here against desegregation and her similar comments in 1969 in *On Violence*, one should be wary of making too much of her public distancing from the essay.[10]

"Reflections on Little Rock" displays some of Arendt's signature conservative political-theoretical predispositions, a review which is important for an understanding of the reception of the Eichmann book. A hierarchical prioritization of principles over empirical experience leads her, in the discussion of the desegregation policy, to concede the desideratum of equality, in the abstract, but to diminish the significance of the case at hand: "The American Republic is based on the equality of all citizens …The point at stake … is not the well-being of the Negro population alone, but, at least in the long run, the survival of the Republic."[11] The alternative she presents evidently sets up a conflict between the higher principle of "the Republic," placed at odds with the social condition of a particular group. While there is a long, and largely conservative, tradition of interrogating the consequences of equality, the contrastive demotion of the "well-being" of the African-American community seems gratuitous at best. It is reasonable to see her harsh phrasing here as a premonition of the lack of compassion of which she would be accused in the Eichmann controversy, when Gershom Scholem would attack her lack of love for Israel.[12] In "Reflections on Little Rock" she invokes a norm of equality in contrast to empirically lived inequality, giving short shrift to the latter, while in *Eichmann in Jerusalem* she focuses on the question of abstractly procedural justice for the defendant while appearing to diminish the importance of the lived suffering of the victims (more on this below).

The two cases display a further parallel insofar as each involves a modality of ethnic or identity politics, a phenomenon towards which she directed harsh criticism in *Origins of Totalitarianism*, in her discussions of ethno-nationalist movements, which she regards as undermining liberal civil order and therefore contributing to the rise of totalitarianism[13] This suspicion of ethnic or identity politics came into play both in the Little Rock and the Eichmann controversies. Given this animus, those readers of Arendt inclined to invoke her authority to support anti-Zionism, should understand that her aversion against ethno-nationalism also formed the basis for her rejection of desegregation. More generally, the juxtaposition of the two examples points to the wider question of whether the critique of Zionism derived from Arendt involves a rejection exclusively of an agenda for a Jewish nation-state or (as we will see in Butler) a rejection of all nation-states. That conclusion however would also jeopardize any advocacy for a project for a Palestinian nation-state. Surely the Arendtian critique of the nation-state, inherent in the interlinear discussion of the Israeli state in *Eichmann in Jerusalem*, ought to apply to other national or ethnic communities as well: that is the significance of "Reflections on Little Rock" for current debates. Intellectual honesty demands that proponents of appropriating the author of *Eichmann in Jerusalem* for support of an anti-Zionist agenda recognize and explain how the same author with similar arguments opposed desegregation. The weight of her authority is welded to both political judgments (leaving aside the fact that, as we have seen, she herself regarded the book as pro-Israel, her critics notwithstanding).

"Reflections on Little Rock" should not be dismissed merely as an early misstep. On the contrary, in the prefatory note to the *Dissent* publication Arendt indicates that she understands quite well how her remarks may provoke distress and underscores "that as a Jew [she] take[s her] sympathy for the cause of the Negroes as for all oppressed or underprivileged peoples for granted."[14] Yet she undercuts her own attempt at an alibi through the unfortunate phrasing that she takes her sympathy "for granted," i.e., that she assumes it as a given and does not appear to give it further thought. However neither her argument nor her language provides evidence of the sympathy she claims. Despite her advertised denunciation of oppression, the essay in fact involves a much more extensive development of a critique of equality: "The more equal people have become in every respect, and the more equality permeates the whole texture of society, the more will differences be resented, the more conspicuous will those become who are visibly and by nature unlike the others. It is therefore quite possible that the achievement of social, economic, and educational equality for the Negro may sharpen the color problem in this country instead of assuaging it."[15] Even if one were to discount her judgment against desegregation of the schools as uninformed, Arendt's readers still have to confront her blunt and deeply conservative suspicion of equality. Her concern draws on traditional conservative anxieties about the social consequences of egalitarianism, which leads her logically to a criticism of federal desegregation programs: inheriting a suspicion of equality and a preference for hierarchy, she naturally questions the appropriateness of the emerging education policies. While she would eventually, under pressure, pull back from the claims in the Little Rock essay, her sceptical account of equality is fully consistent with her treatment elsewhere concerning the rise of the social and its deleterious impact on the public sphere. The text therefore does provide us with important insight into Arendt's philosophical and political personality. In fact, she later displays even stronger hostility to integration of the education sector in *On Violence*, which testifies to a long-term consistency in her view of desegregation in education.[16] Her self-criticism in the wake of Little Rock is, ultimately, overshadowed by clear continuities in her intellectual biography, which in turn demonstrates that her animosity towards ethnic identity communities represents at least one subtext of the Eichmann judgment as well as a pronounced feature of her political-theoretical persona.

A further aspect of "Reflections" that points towards the Eichmann discussion involves her insistence on the sharp distinction between the public sphere and the social realm. This is a familiar binary – and of course not only for Arendt – which she however deploys in a distinctive manner, locating the mandate for equality exclusively in the former, not the latter. "Segregation is discrimination enforced by law, and desegregation can do no more than abolish the laws enforcing discrimination; it cannot abolish discrimination and force equality upon society, but it can, and indeed must, enforce equality within the body politic. For equality not only has its origin in the body politic; its validity is clearly restricted to the political realm. Only there we are equals."[17] Arendt limits the zone of potential equality to a narrowly defined civic space while claiming its incongruity in the private realm. In addition she controversially locates education (including public schools) in the social realm of the private, as part of parental care for children, rather than as a public service. To reconstruct her argument: schooling does not belong to a public sphere, where a principle of equality must apply, but rather to a private or family sphere, where no such egalitarianism has standing. Because it is located outside of the body politic, in her view, education is therefore not subject to the principle of equal treatment, and this conclusion leads her to the critique of school desegregation, which she views as a public intrusion into the private sphere. This emphatic insistence on the private realm as outside the purview of the state and inimical to any principle of equality is further indication of her particular conservatism: by extension, this dichotomous account would shield private property from any redistributive claims and place the family similarly outside any legal norms.

Yet not only does Arendt propose rejecting state-enforced equality in education or elsewhere in the social sphere, she goes further by positively endorsing discrimination as the defining feature of social life: "What equality is to the body politic – its innermost principle – discrimination is to society ... Once we have entered [society], we become subject to the old adage of 'likes attracts like' which controls the whole realm of society in the innumerable variety of its groups and associations. What matters here is not personal distinction but the differences by which people belong to certain groups whose very identifiability demands that they discriminate against other groups in the same domain."[18] In society, for Arendt, principles of self-segregation apply and legitimately so, and because of her extensive definition of this realm – we have seen that she includes public education in it – she must logically endorse modalities of discrimination that were then embattled and today seem anachronistic, including the nasty practice of "restricted" hotels and resorts: "If as a Jew I wish to spend my vacations only in the company of Jews, I cannot see how anyone can reasonably prevent my doing so; just as I see no reason why other resorts should not cater to a clientele that wishes not to see Jews while on a holiday."[19] Arendt's stunning approval of discrimination would presumably also provide a justification for continued segregation practices in trains and restaurants, although she must have understood the precariousness of her argument, since she makes a parenthetical exception for "theaters and museums, where people obviously do not congregate for the purpose of associating with each other." Yet the same objection might be made with regard to hotels, as well: these are services for the convenience of travellers, not primarily venues for association with others.

Arendt shows herself to be doubly conservative here, with a peculiarly rigid distinction between the political and the social spheres, combined with significant anxiety about any expansive egalitarianism. The equality principle should, for her, be limited to a narrowly defined public sphere and excluded from the social realm in which idiosyncratic groupings or hierarchies properly prevail. She displays a pervasive fear of the masses, which might call into question the inherited hierarchies of order, and this anxiety will recur in her experience of the Jerusalem trial and her documented aversion to non-European Jews. Indeed the connection between her comments on school desegregation and the African-American experience, on the one hand, and Jewish politics, on the other, is itself spelled out in the Little Rock essay in her selection of examples of discrimination.

The final element in the Little Rock argument that anticipates the Eichmann book involves the question of states' rights, a centrepiece of the argument against federal enforcement of the Supreme Court decision. Arendt seizes on the peculiarities of American federalism, the dispersion of power between Washington and the states, in order to reiterate her argument against the European model of sovereignty marked by indivisible power. Checks and balances and the interplay between the different levels of government represent, for Arendt, the distinct advantage of the American model leading to greater power, a term that she distinguishes emphatically from mere force: force involves constraint, while power points to political cooperation and the capacity for action. "The point is that force can, indeed must, be centralized in order to be effective, but power cannot and must not. If the various sources from which it springs are dried up, the whole structure becomes impotent. And states' rights in this country are among the most authentic sources of power, not only for the promotion of regional interests and diversity, but for the Republic as a whole."[20] The federalist opposition to a unified sovereignty of the central state anticipates her dislike for the centralized Jewish state; her position here is largely consistent with later arguments in *On Violence* and *On Revolution*.[21] In addition, in the midst of the civil rights struggles, she displays little awareness of the contemporary political ramification of her advocacy for states' rights: a further example of her disregard for empirical political developments, a deficiency which may also explain her surprise at the Eichmann controversy that she herself ignited: "Arendt's feigned innocence was one of the strangest and most revealing aspects of this whole affair."[22] Again Arendt typically insists on the priority of a normative principle, which disallows any compassion for the real consequences of the states' rights discourse in that historical context.

"Reflections on Little Rock" is important for our discussion because it reveals Arendt's opposition to the intrusiveness of the centralized state as an agent of social change. This foreshadows her critical stance regarding the Israeli state, then still very much structured as a centralized quasi-socialist bureaucracy. (Indeed the reference in the opening paragraph of *Eichmann in Jerusalem* to "protection in government circles and the bureaucracy" in Israel clearly announces her discontent with the state at the outset.)[23] Just as one of Arendt's main targets in Little Rock is the expansive power of the federal government, in *Eichmann in Jerusalem*, she expressed her animosity to the bureaucratic and powerful labour-socialist state that developed under Ben-Gurion. This parallel helps us understand how her critique of the state, in both Little Rock and in Jerusalem, has a distinctly conservative character.

This genealogy should also make any anti-Zionist appeals to Arendt's authority in the debate over the legitimacy of the Israeli state at the very least problematic, since she mounted the same anti-statist arguments against desegregation. This is all the more the case when one turns to the political dimension of *Eichmann in Jerusalem,* which was not only about an examination of the trial or the controversial characterization of the culpability as "banal" – the key point in the early reception – it was also a judgment on the State of Israel, viewed by Arendt as the ultimate agent behind the trial, as well as on the assumptions underlying that state. The structure of power that Arendt identified and criticized in the State of Israel corresponded to the same European model of sovereignty towards which she saw the US government growing closer, for her unfortunately, through its interventionist desegregation efforts in the Little Rock essay and against which Arendt developed her endorsement of states' rights.

The Critique of Anti-Modern Conservatism

Yet prior to the focus on anti-Zionism in *Eichmann in Jerusalem,* during the early reception considerable attention was directed at the banality hypothesis. Arendt's claim was understood to diminish Eichmann's culpability and, more generally, to trivialize the experience of genocide. A telling, if somewhat belated, example of this response is found in Saul Bellow's *Mr. Sammler's Planet* (1969), a novel of intellectual life in New York, the perspectives of Shoah survivors, and broader reflections on the human condition on the planet. Early on, it incorporates a discussion of *Eichmann in Jerusalem* in which Bellow focuses specifically on Arendt's conservatism as a rejection of modernity. Thus he has the eponymous protagonist of the novel declare: "This woman professor's enemy is modern civilization itself. She is only using the Germans to attack the twentieth century – to denounce it in terms invented by Germans. Making use of a tragic history to promote the foolish ideas of Weimar intellectuals."[24] This rebuttal involves the assumption that the banality thesis depends on an implied contrast with a past, a former, non-banal time marked by possibilities of genuine grandeur and heroism (which we have seen Arendt claim eluded the Jews since antiquity), as well as on the accusation that the modern world of bureaucracy and technology renders human behaviour insignificant and human life trivial. For Bellow, speaking through Sammler, Arendt misinterprets Eichmann as well as the camps in the terms of the Nietzschean last man, caught in a universal degradation and loss of significance in a world where conformism reigns and ethics disappear. It follows that the individual guilt of the perpetrator is no longer at stake, but only the misery of the age. Thus the conservative Arendt effectively – at least in Bellow's reading – reduces Eichmann's guilt by discovering him as the icon, perhaps even himself the victim, of a modernity defined by a tendency to trivialize everything. This account however is, as we have read, for Bellow only a matter of "foolish ideas," a phrasing with which he rejects Arendt's Weimar conservatism. Indeed he mistrusts Arendt's motives to the extent that he sees her deploying the German philosophical tradition precisely in order to minimize German crimes.

Yet Bellow not only identifies the genealogy of Arendt's judgment on Eichmann; he also provides an alternative to the banality thesis. Anticipating arguments made more recently by Bettina Stangneth in her research on Eichmann's life in Argentina,[25] he claims that Eichmann's appearance as banal, as the bureaucrat, as the conformist following orders, was nothing other than an intentionally deceptive performance, not only by Eichmann individually but as part of the Nazi – he writes "German" – agenda altogether. "The idea of making the century's great crime look dull is not banal. Politically, psychologically, the Germans had an idea of genius. The banality was only camouflage. What better way to get the curse out of murder than to make it look ordinary, boring, or trite? With horrible political insight they found a way to disguise the thing."[26] Eichmann was no administrative bureaucrat; he was an actor, masking his criminal character in the appearance of banality. (As Stangneth comments in her conclusion: "Now the age of his ability to manipulate and distract people with his lies is over.")[27] For Bellow it was after all murder on a mass scale that was at stake, and murder of any sort is a desecration. "The best and purest human beings, from the beginning of time, have understood that life is sacred. To defy that old understanding is not banality. There was a conspiracy against the sacredness of life."[28] Yet Bellow sees Arendt succumbing to that conspiracy, deceived by Eichmann's act but also because of the flawed points of orientation she brings to the matter, precisely as an intellectual. "Intellectuals do not understand. They get their notions about matters like this from literature. They expect a wicked hero like Richard III. But do you think the Nazis didn't know what murder was? Everybody (except certain bluestockings) knows what murder is." Three distinct criticisms are combined in the extended passage: an insufficient perspicacity that prevents Arendt from seeing through the camouflage; an intellectualism that contributes to a lack of realism and therefore an inability to recognize genuine crimes; and finally the conservative critique of modernity that serves to contextualize and relativize Eichmann, hence minimizing his individual responsibility as banal. Of particular note is Bellow's accusation that Arendt instrumentalizes "a tragic history," the Shoah, in order to pursue her (so Bellow suggests) increasingly dated Weimar cultural conservatism.

That conservatism involves the vision that modern life has become trivial in a post-heroic age. From that perspective, Eichmann appears as the twentieth-century everyman. Arendt was certainly not the only observer who described Eichmann in denigrating terms, as David Cesarani has pointed out: For Lord Russell he was "a balding civil servant," and Telford Taylor called him a "myopic middle-aged clerk."[29] A stereotypical image must have been in circulation among the trial observers, and Eichmann likely fit the part, presumably an intentional element in his defence strategy. There was nothing original about Arendt's descriptor. In addition, the thesis of a "banality of evil" is never developed in the book to any significant extent, despite the intriguing contrast with the term "radical evil" that figured significantly in her earlier *Origins of Totalitarianism*.[30] It is difficult to scrape any clear philosophical statement out of *Eichmann in Jerusalem* beyond mid-twentieth-century clichés about bureaucratic conformism. There is however a certain element of intellectual elitism that informs the term; despite Arendt's specific understanding of "thinking" and "thoughtlessness," her characterization of Eichmann and his impoverished language and thought carries with it an implicit complaint that he is basically unintelligent, as Yakira observes: "Might we not then conclude that this whole grand theory of the banality of evil amounts to nothing more than the claim that Eichmann had no talent for empathy or that perhaps he was simply stupid?"[31] In any case, Arendt's word choice contributed significantly to the controversy, perhaps all the more so since she does not elaborate extensively on its significance in the book.

Eichmann in Jerusalem as Anti-Zionist Narrative

A decade and a half after her break with the Zionist movement, Arendt came to the Eichmann trial, and it was through the reception of *Eichmann in Jerusalem* that the conservative political theorist, anxious about modernity and hostile to the rise of social movements and the bureaucratic states they engender, would eventually be transformed into the avatar of progressive anti-Zionism. One cannot say that this appropriation of the conservative text does significant injustice to the book itself, at least in terms of the judgment on Jewish sovereignty. On the contrary, it is precisely because the main figure of the book is portrayed as so banal, so unworthy of attention, and so trivial that the author's presumed ulterior agenda – her coming to terms with Israeli statehood – emerges so powerfully, as if the real target of her prose were really Ben-Gurion, not Eichmann. While Arendt claims to be writing exclusively a report on the trial and therefore scolds the prosecutor for deviating from the question of Eichmann's culpability in order to paint a broad picture of the Nazi reign of terror, she too has an extensive agenda, judging the State of Israel broadly, rather than Eichmann or Nazi Germany narrowly. Yakira, who has described the anti-Zionist logic of the book in great detail, asserts that "the fact that she … used the occasion to settle accounts with Ben-Gurion and the Zionist movement he led explains much of the book's weakness," but it also explains Arendt's own transformation into a resource for anti-Zionism.[32] Both Yakira, who condemns Arendt's hostility to Israel, and Butler, who embraces it, view *Eichmann in Jerusalem* more as a judgment on the legitimacy of the State of Israel than as an inquiry into a Nazi war criminal. While the initial reception history revolved primarily (if not exclusively by any means) around the question of banality, with its cultural conservative implications, more recent attention, exemplified by Yakira and Butler, has shifted to the implications for Israeli statehood, against the backdrop of Arendt's doubts concerning nation-statehood altogether, i.e., not only Israel. Meanwhile the reception also illustrates the metamorphosis of the political contents of her thinking from her initially distinct, if idiosyncratic conservatism to her reappropriation for a self-designatedly progressive anti-Zionism.

There is a noteworthy resonance between Arendt's intratextual criticism of prosecutor Gideon Hausner's brief and her own expository strategy.[33] While she criticizes Hausner for casting too wide a net when he should have focused solely and precisely on the determination of Eichmann's individual guilt, Arendt generates a similarly decentred discourse, ostensibly describing the Nazi killing apparatus even though an underlying concern involves the trial as a symptom of the state that is conducting it. Both Hausner (as portrayed by Arendt) and Arendt herself take Eichmann's culpability as a pretext to pursue an alternative target: for Hausner, the larger topic is the experience of the Holocaust in general, and for Arendt it is the legitimacy of Israeli statehood. Hence certain displacements take place within the text itself that both serve Arendt's purpose and that make the book more available to an anti-Zionist reading.

Yakira points out how *Eichmann in Jerusalem* largely circumvents significant discussion of the extermination camps of the Final Solution. This framing is crucial since the Israeli state would come to invoke the Holocaust as part of its raison d'être. Instead of the mass killings, her narrative emphasizes the deportations of the Jewish populations as if the destination of the deportations were only of secondary importance. By presenting the history as one primarily of deportation rather than extermination, Arendt develops a narrative that appears to diminish the standing of the genocide in the Jewish experience while therefore also providing the basis for anti-Zionist analogies to the displacement of the Palestinian population: as if Eichmann only resettled Jews, as if Hitler's goal was only to move them and not to exterminate them. Because of Arendt's supplementary agenda, beyond Eichmann himself, to criticize the Israeli state, she offers an account in which deportation rather than extermination is the foundational historical experience.

For similar reasons, Arendt takes the question of anti-Semitism off the table.[34] In her account, Eichmann stands for the anodyne bureaucrat, not the ideological hater. The credibility of that paradigm was challenged at the latest in 1996 by Daniel Jonah Goldhagen in *Hitler's Willing Executioners*, but the scope of Eichmann's own ideological fanaticism has recently become a matter of record, thanks to Stangneth's *Eichmann before Jerusalem* (2014).[35] Arendt's minimizing Eichmann's anti-Semitic commitments can be attributed to her aspiration to present the image of the vacuous bureaucrat, but it also has the effect of eliminating the classic rationale for Zionism, the threat of anti-Semitism without which the historic justification for Zionist statehood begins to pale. Furthermore, in its reception, this omission of Eichmann's ideological Jew hatred can be seen as contributing to the contemporary anti-Zionist reception and its own complex relations to anti-Semitism, as discussed below.[36]

Because *Eichmann in Jerusalem* has become, thanks to Butler's reading, a foundational text for anti-Zionism, one should confront Arendt's own disturbing implication in certain forms of racism and anti-Semitism. A key piece of evidence on this point is her letter to Karl Jaspers of 13 April 1961 describing her initial impression of the courtroom and the mindset she brought to the trial and to Israel, combining an admiration for German Jews, side by side with a contempt for all that is "Oriental," whether Jewish or Arab: "My first impression [of the court room in Jerusalem]. On top, the judges, the best of German Jewry. Below them, the persecuting attorneys, Galicians, but still Europeans. Everything is organized by a police force that gives me the creeps, speaks only Hebrew and looks Arabic. Some downright brutal types among them. They would follow any order. And outside, the oriental mob, as if one were in Istanbul or some other half-Asiatic country. In addition, and very visible in Jerusalem, the peies and caftan Jews, who make life impossible for all reasonable people."[37] The description reads as a draft for the opening description of the courtroom in the book, and it provides us with important insights into the stereotypes Arendt brought with her to Jerusalem. In her own reading of the letter, Butler points out some aspects of Arendt's "racist typology," here and elsewhere, although her critique operates exclusively within a post-colonial framework of European contempt of the colonial subject: the Jew whom, for Butler, Arendt disdains is only the Arab Jew, but she turns a blind eye to Arendt's animosity for the Galician *Ostjuden* as somehow inferior to German Jews.[38] In other words, only certain biases are subject to critical scrutiny, not all.

However the passage in the letter to Jaspers is of further interest because, embedded in the topography of prejudice, one finds Arendt developing a trope that has become central to the anti-Zionist discourse. She describes the Israeli police force as the "brutal types" who either are or look Arabic – but only speak Hebrew – i.e., Jews from Arab countries, to whom she imputes, on the basis of their physiognomy, a willingness to "follow any order"; in other words, they are the functional equivalent of the defendant Eichmann, the bureaucratic killer, whose defence strategy was to claim that he had only followed orders. With that linkage, treating the presumably Mizrahi police officers as brutal, ignorant (speaking only Hebrew, i.e., no German), and willing to follow any order, Arendt not only participates in the Ashkenazi (i.e., European Jewish) discrimination against the immigrants from North Africa and Iraq, but effectively contributes to the poisonous rhetoric pervading contemporary anti-Zionism that portrays Israel as the successor of the Nazi state. Furthermore, this egregious claim is formulated in the passage not on the basis of any deeds but exclusively due to her assumptions about the appearances of the members of the police force. Yet in her discussion of Eichmann, Arendt avoids any significant inquiry into his anti-Semitism, which allows her to develop the phenotype of the thoughtless bureaucrat uncomplicated by any prejudices, consistent with her theoretical constructions. Had she chosen to interrogate Eichmann's ethnic stereotypes and his anti-Semitism, however, she might have been compelled to investigate her own.

Yakira's reading of *Eichmann in Jerusalem* identifies a second prohibition that operates within the book that makes it amenable to an anti-Zionist reception: a silencing of Jewish victims. This is no doubt a surprising feature of one of the most widely read books on the Shoah. Nonetheless, it is clear that *Eichmann in Jerusalem* turns out to focus on the organizational apparatus, the bureaucratic instruments for the organization of the destruction of the Jews, rather than on the experience of the victims. Arendt is fascinated by the organizational structure of the killing, which functions as a powerful foil to her theoretical paradigm of political power as action in concert. The emphasis on the administration of killing therefore appears to corroborate the critique of modernity, the violence wrought by the bureaucratic technological apparatus, rather than by individuals acting on the basis of ideological commitments. Her extensive description of bureaucracy left little room for discussions of survivors or resisters; indeed the presence of resisters would have undermined the integrity of her account of totalitarianism.

According to Yakira, this marginalization of victim experience in *Eichmann in Jerusalem* corresponds to Arendt's explicit animosity to victim testimony at the trial. She resented "this atmosphere, not of a show trial but of a mass meeting, at which speaker after speaker does his best to arouse the audience [which] was especially noticeable when the prosecution called witness after witness to testify to the rising in the Warsaw ghetto and to similar attempts in Vilna and Kovno – matters that had no connection whatever with the crimes of the accused."[39] Her repetitive phrasing "witness after witness" signals an annoyed impatience with the voices of the victims. Yet only the narrowest understanding of Eichmann's responsibility would declare the perspectives of the victims as irrelevant. There is more at stake here than a legalistic resistance to witness testimony.[40] Repeatedly Arendt's word choice conveys derision for the witnesses "who, country after country, told their tales of horrors."[41] It would, so the text suggests, have been better in her view if they had not spoken at all. This implicit aspiration to silence the victims and their suffering reflects her interest in focusing solely on what Eichmann, individually, did, rather than on his victims or the larger context. "Arendt was not a historian, and what she had to say about the trial, Eichmann, and the Holocaust was not based on scholarly research … she relies mainly on the works of Hilberg and Reitlinger, that is, on scholars who investigated the Holocaust from the point of view of the perpetrators."[42] Hence the emphasis on the perpetrators and the marginalization of the victims. She thereby missed the truly innovative aspect of the Jerusalem trial, the turn towards victim experience, a development which would eventually lead, decades later, to the process of the South African Truth and Reconciliation Commissions.

Despite Arendt's bemoaning the surfeit of victims who were invited to testify, she delays significant discussion of witnesses until the next to last chapter, as if their voices were largely an afterthought. Moreover, she only reports on four, and Yakira has shown in detail how her selections and her comments reveal her own biases and hostility.[43] She characterizes the first pejoratively, "as the author of several books on Auschwitz that dealt with brothels, homosexuals and other 'human interest stories,'' a designation presumably intended at that historical moment to elicit contempt with the reference to homosexuality but which, ironically, anticipates the more public discussion of the persecution of gays by the Nazis which would not gain widespread recognition until years later.[44] The second witness cited by Arendt was a member of the Jewish Brigade, and Arendt denounces his testimony as smacking of "propaganda."[45] She treats the third witness, Zyndel Grynszpan, better but only after dwelling on the story of his son, Herschel, known for the assassination of the German diplomat Ernst von Rath, which was used as a pretext for the *Kristallnacht* pogrom: Arendt emphasizes the pointlessness of the assassination as well as Herschel's mental illness. When she turns to Zyndel she does have some few exceptional words of praise for his "shining honesty," but his account involved only the expulsion from Germany into Poland in 1938 – a terrible experience, to be sure, "the senseless, needless destruction of twenty-seven years in less than twenty-four hours," – but as Yakira notes, the Grynszpan family survived the war and avoided the extermination camps.[46] In other words, Arendt's most compelling account of a Jewish victim is a narrative of displacement and dispossession, not mass killing. Her paradigm for the experience of the Shoah is ultimately the internment camp, such as the one from which she escaped at Gurs, rather than the factories of extermination. In Yakira's words: "It seems that 'the camp,' the hallmark of totalitarian regimes (and, according to Agamben, of the state as such) was, for Arendt, the Gurs detention camp, where the Vichy government held thousands of Jews and others prisoner, Arendt among them, rather than Auschwitz. Or, as M. Leibovici suggests with more nuance, seeing that Arendt's main sources were David Rousset, Bruno Bettelheim, and Eugene Kogon, all survivors of Nazi concentration camps but none of them of an *extermination* camp, it is in fact of the *universe concentrationnaire* (as Rousset called it) that she speaks, not of the extermination."[47]

The compassion that she fails to display for the other Jewish narratives is reserved for the fourth Jewish witness, Abba Kovner, whom she treats with icy disdain: he is described in ironic quotation marks as "a poet and author" – he was also a resistance leader in Lithuania. Yet she reports with uncharacteristic empathy Kovner's testimony regarding Anton Schmidt, a German sergeant, who provided support for the Jewish resistance until he was caught and executed. "And in those two minutes [when Kovner spoke about Schmidt], which were like a sudden burst of light in the midst of impenetrable, unfathomable darkness, a single thought stood out clearly, irrefutably, beyond question – how utterly different everything would be today in this courtroom, in Israel, in Germany, in all of Europe, and perhaps in all countries of the world, if only more such stories could have been told."[48] That is a rare moment of pathos in a book that otherwise censors any affect, and Schmidt deserves the glory and honour, but one can only offer the rejoinder to Arendt: how different would this book be if the author had displayed any similar admiration for a narrative of Jewish rather than exclusively German bravery, or any sympathy for any single victim among the many who apparently bored her when they "told their tales of horrors." Instead the logic of Arendt's *Eichmann in Jerusalem* is the suppression of victim suffering. Surely the four witness portraits corroborate Scholem's accusation that Arendt displayed a lack of sympathy for the Jewish experience: of the many she might have chosen, she links the first to brothels and the second to propaganda; the son of the third is a psychopath; and the fourth, Kovner, is dismissed as theatrical. "What made the Eichmann trial what it was was precisely what Arendt could not accept, to such an extent that she almost completely ignored it: the testimony."[49]

One further component contributes to the anti-Zionist value of *Eichmann in Jerusalem*. The provocation of the book involved not only the ambiguous connotation of banality but, perhaps with even greater incendiary power, the criticism of Jewish organizations for their complicity, especially how the Nazi apparatus enlisted Jews and organized structures of the Jewish community in the organization of the deportations.

Not only does Arendt denounce the historical role played by the Councils; she goes so far as to argue that the Jewish populations would have been better off without organizations, since apparently any Jewish organization would have been drawn into the genocidal apparatus: "Wherever Jews lived, there were recognized Jewish leaders, and this leadership, almost without exception, cooperated in one way or another, for one reason or another, with the Nazis. The whole truth was that if the Jewish people had really been unorganized and leaderless, there would have been chaos and plenty of misery but the total number of victims would hardly have been between four and a half and six million people."[50] She attempts to back up the comparative claim with statistics from Holland, where Jews who were able to hide survived at much greater rates than those deported via the organization of the Jewish Council and Dutch authorities. Yet that argument is misleading in its use of statistics: there was surely a selection bias with regard to Jews who were able to survive in hiding, just as there were undoubtedly limits on the size of the Dutch population willing to take the risk of hiding Jews. Her argument about the necessarily destructive role of the councils can therefore be questioned on empirical as well as statistical grounds.

However there is a further bias in her discussion of this topic, for while she underscores the deleterious role of the Jewish administration, she has next to nothing to say about the Jewish resistance. Yet in the immediately following passages, she turns to the question of those Germans who opted for "inner emigration" – i.e., participating outwardly in the Nazi apparatus – while claiming later to have harboured inward hesitations. The topic is relevant because it provides some context for Eichmann: he heard no one around him expressing doubts, so he could claim that his conscience was at rest. The strategy of inner emigration made any criticism of the regime invisible, which in turn excluded criticism from any communication with others and therefore eliminated the possibility of cooperation. "For opposition was indeed 'utterly pointless' in the absence of all organization."[51] That phrasing is of considerable significance, clearly stating that "organization" would have been productive for the political project of resistance.

Arendt's judgment on the Jewish councils contrasts significantly with her criticism of the German inner emigration. In the latter case, Arendt identifies how the silence of inner emigration prevented the development of organized resistance, which might have led to action, her privileged category for political praxis. In other words, in Arendt's account, for the Germans who might have resisted the regime, the absence of organization prevented action, and this evaluation is consistent with Arendt's general theory of political power: if only the Germans who might have opposed the regime had benefited from organization. Yet for the Jews, she argues that a complete absence of organization would have been preferable – that organized Jewish life was itself the problem. Nor can one frame this point as merely a specific judgment on the councils, since she offers no counter-model of Jewish organization, not even from the resistance, even though she saw resistance leader Kovner on the witness stand. The asymmetry in treatment contrasts the sort of political organization she would have liked to have seen among the Germans with her prescription for the Jews, for whom she can only recommend disorganization, even at the cost of "chaos and plenty of misery." The discrepancy demonstrates an explicit antipathy towards Jewish political organization that likely reflects, in part, a specific German-Jewish bias against activism, as measured against the histories of engagement of Jewish communities in France and England. Here Arendt indeed acts as the "unpolitical German," at least in her evaluation of the Jews. Of course, if her critique of Jewish organization in the form of the councils had led to a vision of an alternative organization – rather than no organization, which she recommends – she would have risked steering too close to the organized Zionist camp she wanted to avoid. Hence a further element of the objective anti-Zionism of the book: a diminishment of the capacity of Jews to act politically as Jews.[52]

Eichmann in Jerusalem provides an amalgam of several problematic constructs: the denigration of the Jews who are not from Germany, a trivialization of the suffering as if any victim narrative were a priori superfluous, and a rejection of Jewish political organization. This constellation rests upon a foundation of her conservative thinking with its particular German inflections: the anti-political suspicion of states and parties; a federalist fear of a unified sovereignty, especially a nation-state; and the harsh separation between the public sphere, the appropriate home for law, and the social and private spheres, the content of which she deems extraneous to the legal deliberation. That marginalization of private experience may explain the disregard for suffering, to which one can add the ethnic stereotypes that structure her view of the trial, and the biases with which she judges not only Eichmann but also Hausner and an array of other figures. Ultimately *Eichmann in Jerusalem* has come to be seen as conveying, as Yakira argues, a critique of Israeli statehood, framed by a minimization of Jewish victimhood in the Shoah and a similar diminishment of the role of anti-Semitism.

Given this analysis, it only makes sense that Butler turns to Arendt and to *Eichmann in Jerusalem* specifically to find what she calls "Jewish resources" to support a critique of Israel, and she does so explicitly in order to counter claims that anti-Zionism is anti-Semitic. If Arendt could be anti-Zionist, so Butler's argument goes, then anti-Zionism cannot be anti-Semitic. Yet in light of Arendt's hostility towards East European and Arabic Jews, replete with the biases historically associated with German Jews, she can hardly serve as a convincing witness: Arendt's prejudices were, at the very least, consistent with her anti-Zionism, and perhaps they even informed it on a deeper level. Butler does critique some of these prejudices; obviously this is nothing that she would endorse.[53] Yet the question remains as to whether the biases inherent in *Eichmann in Jerusalem* can ever be fully excised from the anti-Zionist argument extracted from it in order to achieve a credibly progressive program. If not, the problem of anti-Semitism in anti-Zionism remains open, to say the least, in particular for Butler, who recognizes the difficulty in locating Arendt on the left but nonetheless attempts to do so through a particular reading of the Eichmann book in ways that surprisingly draw on its conservative substrate.[54]

Whether a certain anti-Semitism implicit in Arendt's biases seeps into any anti-Zionist argument drawn out of *Eichmann in Jerusalem* raises the much larger problem of anti-Semitism and anti-Zionism in general. The logical separation between the two terms ought to be clear: on the one hand, a bigoted animus against Jews (whether as members of a religion, an ethnic group, or a nation); on the other, opposition to the political project of establishing a state for the Jewish people (I omit here the issue of cultural Zionism). As neat as the distinction appears, it comes under immediate pressure because Zionism developed historically as a response to anti-Semitism and, as Butler herself concedes, "some of those criticisms [of Israeli state violence] do employ anti-Semitic rhetoric and argument, and so must be opposed absolutely and unequivocally."[55] The holding of an anti-Zionist position – i.e., opposition to the legitimacy of the Israeli state – does not preclude anti-Semitic attitudes. Nor does it, according to Butler, necessarily imply them. On the contrary, her explicit agenda involves the demonstration that the anti-Zionist need not be anti-Semitic, despite her conceding empirical intersections of the two phenomena.

Yet once one leaves this high level of abstraction and considers historical developments, the polarity between the two terms becomes more difficult to maintain. Two specific moments make this clear. First, while anti-Zionism represented a widespread and plausible position within world Jewry prior to the Second World War, it is arguable that the Shoah radically transformed real possibilities, particularly for the displaced populations of survivors for whom neither return to demolished homes in Europe nor emigration to, for example, the United States represented credible options. Emigration to mandate Palestine provided an opportunity for these refugees, and the establishment of a state meant a political future that was moreover endorsed by the United Nations. To call the legitimacy of the Israeli state – the state as such, and not each of its policies – into question retrospectively implies denying the displaced Jewish population political rights and therefore might be seen as meeting the criteria for anti-Semitism. In the wake of the Holocaust, the separation between anti-Semitism and anti-Zionism has grown more difficult to maintain. Second, despite Butler's neat distinction between anti-Semitism and anti-Zionism, which certainly holds in theory, recent years, especially the summer of 2014, have witnessed significant demonstrations in Europe against Israel during the Gaza War, and in numerous instances those demonstrations included attacks on Jewish – not Israeli – sites, especially synagogues, as well as the use of specifically anti-Semitic slogans.[56] So if, in the abstract, anti-Semitism and anti-Zionism are distinct, at this particular historical moment what one might call really-existing anti-Zionism has taken on increasingly anti-Semitic tones.

Nonetheless, for Butler, Arendt provides a Jewish authorization of an anti-Zionist position. Yet in her reading of Arendt, both *Eichmann in Jerusalem* and other writings, Butler constructs a specific set of arguments against Israeli statehood that reveal aspects of the conservative thought of Weimar Germany. The first of these arguments insists on the diasporic condition as the essential feature of Judaism; it is, according to Butler, the exilic dispersion that generates the particular Jewish ethics that is necessarily lost when transplanted into a national homeland. "Jewishness can and must be understood as an anti-identitarian project insofar as we might even say that being a Jew implies taking up an ethical relation to the non-Jew, and this follows from the diasporic condition of Jewishness where living in a socially plural world under conditions of equality remains an ethical and political ideal … The point is not simply to scatter geographically, but to derive a set of principles from scattered existence that can serve a new conception of political justice."[57] The nature of such principles would necessarily include the recognition that "the embrace of heterogeneity is itself a certain diasporic condition."[58] Dispersion therefore stands as the positive alternative to the homogeneous and centralizing state, in turn echoing the federalist concerns we observed in "Reflections on Little Rock." In addition, the vision of a spiritual community that surpasses national territories and thereby escapes the constraints of a state structure viewed as parochial or mechanical incorporates elements of German romanticism since Novalis's *Christianity or Europe* (1799) as well as from aspects of the conservative revolutionary conceptualizations of the notion of *Reich* during the Weimar Republic.[59] Clearly an institutional model of diaspora does not provide an opportunity to build a political community that could afford rights for its citizens; in other words, the elevation of diaspora to program echoes the "unpolitical" agenda of Weimar conservatives and surely implies withholding political rights from the members of the "scattered" community.

Second, Butler places considerable weight on one particular ground for Eichmann's condemnation: his actions betrayed the belief that he could choose with whom to share the earth. "Eichmann thought that he and his superiors *might choose* with whom to cohabit the earth and failed to realize that the heterogeneity of the earth's population is an irreversible condition of social and political life itself. This accusation bespeaks a firm conviction that none of us should be in a position of making such a choice ... If Arendt is right, then it is not only that we may not choose with whom to cohabit, but that we must actively preserve and affirm the unchosen character of inclusive and plural cohabitation."[60] Butler expands the implication of cohabitation in a surely controversial manner. The court condemned Eichmann for an attempt to reduce the plurality of humanity through the genocide of a people. For Butler, that refusal of planetary cohabitation – the attempt to eradicate a people – becomes the obligation merely to cultivate heterogeneity ubiquitously. The egregious character of Eichmann's crime therefore disappears in a much broader field of diversity and minority rights, unless her implication is that every constraint on diversity is tantamount to genocide, which robs the term of its specific magnitude. In addition, her argument draws close to the equation of Eichmann's genocide (choosing with whom to cohabit) and the Zionist project of a Jewish state, a nation-state for a people. Her repeated insistence on the unchosen character of cohabitation – i.e., that one does not have the freedom to choose with whom to share the earth – introduces an element of compulsion and necessity into the centre of the account, another tip towards the tradition of German conservative thought. To that one should add her valorization of heterogeneity, which echoes a conservative anti-egalitarianism. While Butler may well intend the heterogeneity of cultural or ethnic diversity as it is understood today in the United States, it stands somewhat at odds with the legacy of equality and universalism; hence her preference for William Connolly's term "pluralization" that suggests an alternative to the homogenized and levelled world traditional conservatives have always feared: "The distinction between pluralization and universalization is important for thinking about unchosen cohabitation. Equal protection or, indeed, equality is not a principle that homogenizes those to whom it applies; rather, the commitment to equality is a commitment to the process of differentiation itself."[61] Butler is able to hold onto the progressive ideal of equality, but only through the conservative gesture of guaranteeing difference. Her anxiety concerning the threat of homogenization is structurally homologous to Arendt's fear of banality: two faces of bad modernity.

Arendt's suspicion of the sovereign state generates doubts about the court, its legitimacy, and its relationship to the Israeli government. Yet even more is at stake for Butler, not just Israeli law, which brings us to the third and final conservative stratum in her argument, a deep-seated suspicion of the state as such: "Arendt is not only taking issue with the way the Israeli courts arrived at the decision to sentence Eichmann to death. Her book finds fault with every existing legal code brought to bear upon the scene. And she is critical of Eichmann himself for formulating and obeying a noxious set of laws. So it is at some distance from positive law that she writes, exemplifying something of the prelegal, moral perspective that prefigures her later work on judgment."[62] Arendt's suspicion of state power – manifested in this example in the court, although it is the legitimacy of the state that is truly at stake – is transformed, in Butler's reading, into a supersession of positive law altogether. Obedience to the law is not only a fault in the extreme case of Eichmann; nor is the problem an obedience to a specifically wrong law. Rather, in Butler's reading of Arendt, it is always a moral failing to obey the law because that can mean acting without thinking, that is, to act in ways that fail to meet specific criteria including recognizing the consequences for others. Eichmann is not guilty, then, for the precise deeds he committed but for having committed them thoughtlessly, without empathy, which is, for Butler, the only way they could possibly be committed.[63] For Arendt, Eichmann's banality is a matter of this thoughtlessness in the commission of heinous acts. Butler amplifies this estimation by elevating the question of impaired moral reflection significantly above the deeds themselves. Thus, in Butler's words, "the failure to think is precisely the name of the crime that Eichmann commits."[64] For Arendt, thoughtlessness was one of the conditions of the crime, but not the crime itself.

Because for Butler thought replaces law, courts of law give way to a prelegal morality; hence her locating Arendt, as we have seen, "at some distance from positive law."[65] The impetus behind this conjecture was Arendt's hesitation about the state in general, but specifically about the State of Israel. In Butler's reading however the mandate against thoughtlessness – and therefore against the law – has general applicability: the verdict on Eichmann, with which she agrees, is not a narrow matter of Germans and Jews, but an instance of a universal principle with regard to empathetic thinking and a recognition of the plurality of humanity. This vision of a universalist, if pluralized and differentiated, morality unencumbered by the legal apparatus of the state should then necessarily hold everywhere: it is not only the court in Jerusalem whose standing is called into question, but the courts of law of any state anywhere. Thought through consistently, her critique of the Israeli state implies a critique of all states, certainly all nation-states, but in fact all political institutions that would ever generate positive law, since any such law elicits the unthinking obedience embodied in Eichmann. Her argument tends to push towards a principled anarchism and a generalized hostility to positive law on the basis of which one could oppose not only the State of Israel but every other state in the world as well, including a Palestinian state. The paradox that Butler leaves unresolved here then is the need to justify the particular political focus on Israel, or rather to explain why she limits her anti-statism only to the case of Israel.

A final difficulty in appropriating Arendt's conservatism for a progressive agenda becomes particularly salient in Butler's treatment of the closing passages of *Eichmann in Jerusalem*. It is impossible for her to finesse Arendt's approbation of the capital punishment, which Butler cannot accept and which therefore nearly disappears from her account. However this erasure of the deed, the fact of the execution, is consistent with a larger tendency in Butler's progressive reading of the conclusion to shift into a subjectivism, into the complexities of the textual construction in lieu of a concentration on the facts, the crimes, and the deeds, precisely where Arendt would have wished that court had directed its attention exclusively. This is particularly clear in her gloss on Arendt's conclusion. Agreeing with the verdict but not with the court's reasoning, Arendt introduces a final speech in which she fictively speaks with and for the judges: "And if it is true that 'justice must not only be done but must be seen to be done,' then the justice of what was done in Jerusalem would have emerged to be seen by all if the judges had dared to address their defendant in something like the following terms."[66] Butler provides a detailed exploration of the voice of the passage, trying to parse how Arendt sometimes writes for the judges and sometimes interpolates her own perspectives. "Something happens in this direct address to Eichmann that unleashes a greater emotional identification with those Jerusalem judges than her searing criticism of them would appear to allow. Her voice becomes entangled with theirs, nearly knotted up in that plurality. After all, the voice is and is not her own."[67] Identifying this formal structure of multi-vocality, Butler turns to an intense focus on the key element of Arendt's imaginary judgment which emphasizes the plurality of the human condition: "You supported and carried out a policy of not wanting to share the earth with the Jewish people and the people of a number of other nations – as though you and your superiors had any right to determine who should and who should not inhabit the earth."[68] For Butler, the crux of the matter is, as we have just seen, the plural cohabitation of the earth, which allows her to turn to the question of refugees and therefore the problem of the nation-state. Yet she lodges the problem of cohabitation in the plurality of the literary structure of the final passage as well as in her account of Arendt's insistence on the implicit recognition of a "we" whenever "I" think. The cohabitation, in other words, is located primarily in an interior or a literary space, not in a world of deeds.

Emphasizing deeds – or action – Arendt's text differs significantly from Butler's interiorized rendition, one last contrast that maps onto a distinction between Arendt's conservative realism and Butler's progressive subjectivism. What matters for Arendt is what Eichmann did, not what he thought or failed to think, although it was his thoughtlessness that enabled him to act. Thus Arendt, speaking through the judges, explicitly rejects contextual excuses as grounds to pardon this defendant: "Guilt and innocence before the law are of an objective nature, and even if eighty million Germans had done as you did, this would not have been an excuse for you."[69] There are no environmental excuses for deeds that have taken place, in the world, objectively between people. Eichmann is guilty for the crimes he committed, for which he is responsible, and which Arendt can name: "You have carried out, and therefore actively supported, a policy of mass murder." While Butler is eager to shift the account quickly away from mass murder and to the question of cohabitation, that is, by implication away from the Shoah and to the question of refugees in the Middle East, Arendt – despite her other agendas – insists in this final passage on the factuality of the crime, just as she concludes the judges' speech dramatically with the terse announcement of the verdict, another incontrovertible deed. Butler struggles with the capital punishment but can neither clearly reject nor endorse it, only suggesting that Arendt is resorting to a mode of sovereignty "that is closer to Schmitt than I would like," a reference that is certainly intended to mark a political difference between a conservative Arendt and Butler on the left. At the very least, on the question of capital punishment, Arendt's conservatism and Butler's progressivism have come to part ways.

NOTES

1 Michael Ezra "The Eichmann Polemics: Hannah Arendt and Her Critics," *Democratiya* no. 9 (Summer 2007): 142.

2 "'Eichmann in Jerusalem': An Exchange of Letters between Gershom Scholem and Hannah Arendt," in *The Jew as Pariah: Jewish Identity and Politics in the Modern Age*, ed. Ron H. Feldman (New York: Grove Press, 1978), 250.

3 "Hannah Arendt on Hannah Arendt," in *Hannah Arendt: The Recovery of the Public World*, ed. Melvyn A. Hill (New York: St Martin's Press, 1979), 333–4.

4 Richard Wolin, *Heidegger's Children: Hannah Arendt, Karl Lowith, Hans Jonas, and Herbert Marcuse* (Princeton, NJ: Princeton University Press, 2003).

5 Hannah Arendt, "The Political Organization of the Jewish People," in *The Jewish Writings*, ed. Jerome Kohn and Ron H. Feldman, (New York: Schocken, 2007), 199.

6 Ibid., 256; emphasis in original.

7 Ruth Starkman describes the transformation of Arendt's usage from this moment of militant Jewish patriotism to a still public but less assertive value in her later account of Greek antiquity. "In *The Human Condition* she asserts that *action* was always bound to ideas of 'honor' and 'glory,' since the Greeks and all the way to Machiavelli. Honor and glory derive from appearing publicly and participating in the theatrical nature of politics … That she includes the Jews in this human plurality with honor and glory is already apparent in her wartime writings. It seems, then, that for Arendt honor and glory shifted, after the War, to other kinds of experience besides

fighting under a people's flag and publically demonstrating national passions." Ruth Starkman, "'For the Honor and Glory of the Jewish People': Arendt's Ambivalent Jewish Nationhood," *European Legacy* 18, no. 2 (2013): 196; emphasis in original. This shift in significance of the terms suggests a reduced politicization, perhaps a return to the stance of the "unpolitical" German.

8 Hannah Arendt, *On Violence* (New York: Harcourt Brace Jovanovich, 1970), 30.

9 On the "rise of the social," see Hannah Arendt, *The Human Condition* (Chicago: University of Chicago Press, 1998), 38–49; regarding bureaucracy, consider her assertion: "Today we ought to add the latest and perhaps most formidable form of such dominion: bureaucracy or the rule of an intricate system of bureaus in which no men, neither one nor the best, neither the few nor the many, can be held responsible, and which could be properly called rule by Nobody." Arendt, *On Violence*, 38.

10 A recent defence of Arendt's essay is found in Daniel Cole, "A Defense of Hannah Arendt's 'Reflections on Little Rock," *Philosophical Topics* 39, no. 2 (Fall 2011): 21–40.

11 Hannah Arendt, "Reflections on Little Rock," *Dissent* 6 (1959): 47.

12 "'Eichmann in Jerusalem,'" in Feldman, *The Jew as Pariah*, 240–51.

13 See Hannah Arendt, *Origins of Totalitarianism* (New York: Harcourt, Brace and World, 1966), 227–43.

14 Arendt, "Reflections on Little Rock," 46.

15 Ibid., 48.

16 Arendt, *On Violence*, 18–19.

17 Arendt, "Reflections on Little Rock," 50.

18 Ibid., 51.

19 Ibid., 52.

20 Ibid., 54.

21 Cf. Hannah Arendt, *On Revolution* (New York: Viking Press, 1965), 139–53.

22 Elhanan Yakira, *Post-Zionism, Post-Holocaust: Three Essays on Denial, Forgetting and the Delegitimation of Israel* (Cambridge: Cambridge University Press, 2009), 260.

23 Hannah Arendt, *Eichmann in Jerusalem: A Report on the Banality of Evil* (New York: Penguin Books, 1977), 3.

24 Saul Bellow, *Mr. Sammler's Planet* (New York: Viking Press, 1970), 18–19.

25 Bettina Stangneth, *Eichmann before Jerusalem* (New York: Alfred Knopf, 2014), esp. 234–310.

26 Bellow, *Mr. Sammler's Planet*, 18.

27 Stangneth, *Eichmann before Jerusalem*, 422.

28 Bellow, *Mr. Sammler's Planet*, 10.

29 David Cesarani, *Eichmann: His Life and Crimes* (London: Heinemann, 2004), 327.
30 Yakira, *Post-Zionism, Post Holocaust*, 264–77.
31 Ibid., 274.
32 Ibid., 259.
33 Ibid., 261.
34 Ibid., 284–5.
35 Daniel Jonah Goldhagen, *Hitler's Willing Executioners: Ordinary Germans and the Holocaust* (New York: Alfred A. Knopf, 1996).
36 Judith Butler, *Parting Ways: Jewishness and the Critique of Zionism* (New York: Columbia University Press, 2013), 116.
37 Arendt to Jaspers, 13 April 1961, letter 285, in Hannah Arendt and Karl Jaspers, *Correspondence, 1925–1969*, ed. Lott Kohler and Hans Saner, trans. Robert Kimber and Rita Kimber (New York: Harcourt Brace Jovanovich, 1992), 434–6.
38 Butler, *Parting Ways*, 139. Cf. Elhanan Yakira, *Post-Zionism, Post Holocaust*, 225–6.
39 Arendt, *Eichmann in Jerusalem*, 121.
40 Ibid., 207.
41 Ibid., 223.
42 Yakira, *Post-Zionism, Post Holocaust*, 291.
43 Ibid., 290–1.
44 Arendt, *Eichmann in Jerusalem*, 223–4.
45 Ibid., 226.
46 Ibid., 229–30.
47 Yakira, *Post-Zionism, Post Holocaust*, 234; emphasis in original.
48 Arendt, *Eichmann in Jerusalem*, 231.
49 Yakira, *Post-Zionism, Post Holocaust*, 290.
50 Ibid., 125.
51 Ibid., 127.
52 On the refusal of the German Jewish community to join in the Alliance Israelite Universelle, see Jerrold Siegel, *Modernity and Bourgeois Life: Society, Politics, and Culture in England, France, and Germany since 1750* (Cambridge: Cambridge University Press, 2012), 406.
53 Butler, *Parting Ways*, 139.
54 Ibid., 141.
55 Ibid., 116.
56 *Report of the All-Party Parliamentary Inquiry into Anti-Semitism* (London: 2015), 85–108.
57 Butler, *Parting Ways*, 117–18.

58 Ibid., 122.

59 Cf. Armin Mohler, *Die konservative Revolution in Deutschland 1918–1932: ein Handbuch* (Darmstadt: Wissenschaftliche Buchgesellschaft, 1989), 235–40.

60 Butler, *Parting Ways*, 125; emphasis in original.

61 Ibid., 126.

62 Ibid., 155.

63 Ibid., 154.

64 Ibid., 154.

65 Ibid., 155.

66 Arendt, *Eichmann in Jerusalem*, 277.

67 Butler, *Parting Ways*, 164.

68 Arendt, *Eichmann in Jerusalem*, 279.

69 Ibid., 278.

Chapter Six

Eichmann's Victims, Holocaust Historiography, and Victim Testimony

CAROLYN J. DEAN

Now he had come to tell his story, carefully answering questions put to him by the prosecutor; he spoke clearly and firmly, without embroidery, using a minimum of words.

—Hannah Arendt, 1961[1]

In the past the Jews were envied because of their money, qualifications, positions, and international contacts – today they are envied because of the crematoria in which they were burned.

—Witold Kula, 1996[2]

The desire to be Jewish in place of the Jews becomes acutely competitive as people struggle to attain the prestige of being the elect.

—Pascale Bruckner, 1995[3]

In *Eichmann in Jerusalem* Hannah Arendt asks "what crime is actually involved here?"[4] She argues that the trial failed to grasp the genocide of European Jewry because it could not address how the Nazi regime had transformed the meaning of criminal agency. Eichmann's revelations about Nazi crimes went unacknowledged, and the trial failed to demonstrate how or whether the law could adequately punish a person responsible for unprecedented industrial murder.[5] The trial thus failed to articulate a coherent relationship between law and judgment because it misunderstood the criminal and the nature of his crimes. In Arendt's much-contested view, Eichmann's inability to think foiled prosecutors' desires to portray him as demonic. In the end, she argues, the trial collapsed under the "weight of hair-raising atrocities" because it was no longer a trial of the man who "must suffer for what he has done," but a trial "for what he has caused others to suffer."[6]

A different but related question about how to judge what "the crime actually involved" arises when we consider how the Holocaust also rendered conventional models of victimization – redemption, martyrdom, and resistance – inadequate. This difficulty, rarely articulated for many reasons, may explain as much as does anti-Semitism the postwar suspicion about why Jews did not resist, the deafening silence about the genocide until the Eichmann trial, and why the State of Israel celebrated resistance at the expense of survivors.[7] In the context of Nazi crimes, victims are agents and they are not – they can't be held responsible and yet, in a complex universe of unimaginably reduced agency, the importance of ethical conduct may be heightened rather than reduced even as poor conduct is more easily forgiven. Some victims behaved more admirably than others in a desperate attempt to preserve ideas of honour and dignity. Indeed, survivors who testified at the Eichmann trial make amply clear that they conceived the prosecutor's question about why Jews did not revolt with dismay. In 1990, speaking of his role as a witness in that trial, Moshe Bejsky notes that the prosecutor asked him: "You were 25,000 men, surrounded by only a few hundred SS officers. Why didn't you revolt? But, I think the prosecutor didn't understand the situation; he couldn't imagine it. We were all weak, hungry, hardly human, fearful. Even if we had revolted, we knew what had happened in Krakow. The Germans had machine guns; we would have been destroyed. Even if we had succeeded, how would we leave the camp? The fence was electric. Even if we managed to escape the camp, where would we have gone?"[8] Another witness, Leon Wells, interviewed in 1986, asserted that to ask if one had fought back was "an immoral question."[9]

Arendt exaggerated moral distinctions between innocent victims and Jewish community leaders who could pull strings. She also assumed that Jewish kapos and those in the Sonderkommando were selected because they were criminals, as did Primo Levi immediately after the war. At the same time, the prosecutor's questions about why victims did not rebel, she argues, were needlessly cruel. She does not follow up on this insight because it appears to her so obvious, and because her question concerns how to judge the agents of an unprecedented crime, not its victims. Arendt was accused of "blaming the victim," but we should, for the record, remember that in *Eichmann in Jerusalem* she claims that terrorized and persecuted people do not, as a matter of course, heroically resist their persecutors.

Arendt, however, does prefer victims who speak "purely," "free of sentimentality and self-indulgence," "using a minimum amount of words."[10] Her ironic treatment of K-Zetnik reeks of condescension, not only because she says that he writes about "brothels" and "homosexuals," but also because on the witness stand he is dazed and confused, does not speak to the point, and even faints just when the judge implores him to answer questions.[11] She seems uncomfortable with his lack of control, and his inappropriate behaviour in a court setting merely gives her unsettlement a certain rationale.

Arendt's discomfort, partly implicit in her ironic tone and partly displaced onto her portrait of a kitschy and melodramatic show trial, is hardly unusual in reference to victim testimony. We cannot compare the problem posed by criminal agency with that of victims' decision making, but we can at least enquire into how the Holocaust poses complicated ethical questions about victims and cultural attitudes towards them, some of which Arendt shared. Scholars now interpret the trial's impact by reference to the influence of victim testimony on an international audience.[12]

The 1961 trial marked the beginning of Western perceptions of the Holocaust as a Jewish as well as a human tragedy. Through the 1970s, Auschwitz eventually became the dehistoricized icon of "evil in our time," and the entire concept of "victim" underwent revision. Jewish suffering, once marginalized, became the central reference point for all sorts of rhetorical claims by groups with a history of past persecution, colonization, or discrimination and who felt their pain was long unrecognized.

One of the consequences of this intriguing historical phenomenon has been a sense among public intellectuals and politicians on both the left and the right that Jewish memory, and often all memory of having suffered, has been hyperbolized, or is emphasized at the expense of truly disinterested indignation and rational discussion. This discourse alone suggests that the analysis of victim behaviour in extreme circumstances generates complex responses, as it did in Arendt. In order to assess efforts to evaluate victims' positions historically, I analyse the rhetorical constitution of victims and victimization in two recent and important books on the Holocaust of European Jewry. Both works seek to counter in different ways the presumption that Jewish memory is overwrought. Shortly, I will analyse the work of Saul Friedländer and Jan Gross to assess both the conundrums and potential innovation of their critical interpretations. I do so to argue why the minimalist testimony Arendt preferred has become such a powerful form for recounting atrocities in historiography.

Minimalism is not only a sophisticated style, it is also often conceived as an antidote to the alleged media exploitation of the Holocaust and insurance against the narcissistic representations of the event associated with overwrought memory. Over the past three decades, a cultural consensus has emerged according to which Western European and American culture has entered the "era of the witness": Annette Wieviorka claims that the act of testifying is now a media spectacle, and injury to body and soul a source of recognition and identity in a world with few available forms of self-affirmation.[13] Countless critics argue that rhetorical constraint avoids assigning the Holocaust any meaning other than its own "having happened," and thus somehow guards against false testimony in a media market in which suffering sells and no testimony is authentic or traumatic enough. The privilege accorded to rhetorical constraint seems often to be part of an effort to recount in conceivable terms a place, Auschwitz, which has become "the almost platitudinous reference for the very embodiment of hell on earth."[14]

Such views are also part of a still-powerful view that the grievance structure of rational democratic contestation is being replaced by the unconstrained projection of the victim's wounds, for which minimalism is an antidote. Surely the effectiveness of rhetorical constraint in Holocaust representation as an antidote to sacralization may be fruitfully debated, and an enormous body of criticism now eloquently exposes some of the troubling consequences of confusing the Holocaust and quasi-religious revelations about humankind. But at least one mainstream response by some scholars and public intellectuals to this recent tendency is more than simply a critique of the sort proffered by Wieviorka and is aimed at a clearly defined set of contemporary concerns. In a reductio ad absurdum of the argument against grandiloquence, which prefers some styles to others, some critics believe that all styles that are styles – that are self-reflexive, experimental, ornate, or exuberant – distract from the facticity and authenticity of the Holocaust victim's experience and are particularly egregious when used to represent extreme experiences of suffering and death. This discourse is sufficiently forceful and pervasive to warrant some exploration. I should note here that the point of this exercise is not to advocate for one style or another as the most effective means of representing atrocity, but to ask about the potentially noxious consequences of the cultural privilege accorded to those victims who most effectively mimic the neutral and scientific reportage equated with the objective (rather than implicated) witness's distance from events. This is the style Arendt too prefers, and it is worth asking about its forcefulness beyond its purely evidentiary value. The argument is thus about the ethical implications of a cultural practice in which credible testimony is that in which victims have mastered (or perform mastery of) their own wounds.

The Suspension of Disbelief

The suspension of disbelief best describes accessible, unemotional narration that diminishes defensive and overly emotional responses, especially in history writing. Indeed, the exemplary victim appears to be the survivor who manifests "extraordinary reticence."[15] The editor of a Dutch survivor's memoir writes: "Dr. Micheels is low-key in personality, in writing, and in remembering. Yet his unhistrionic, matter-of-fact style of telling is itself a reassuring demonstration of the patience and indomitability of those who survived and found a way to bring order out of chaos, coherence out of horror, and an affirmation of life out of mass murder."[16]

In writing on memoirs, this tendency is perhaps most powerfully manifest in Tzvetan Todorov's work on Primo Levi. Todorov implies that emotion is inevitable but that only emotional control guarantees the forcefulness and veracity of memory. Assertions that Levi managed to weigh matters judiciously in the aftermath of trauma ignore not only that he is the author of a much darker work on the camps, *The Drowned and the Saved*, in which he departs from his restrained tone, but also that he suffered from prolonged depressions and probably committed suicide, whether or not his depression was related to his experience in Auschwitz, which he denied. Todorov acknowledges that Levi did not have the stamina to meet Albert Speer, but condescends to "understand" this lapse.[17] Indeed, in a 1976 "self-interview" Levi tries to undermine any idea that the lack of rancour in his work indicated forgiveness. He noted that he had not "forgiven any of the culprits," and that he abstained from explicit judgment not because he was without hatred but because he sought to mimic rationality. This was a deliberate and crafted style he used self-consciously to repress hatred and to assume a persona he believed might more effectively "appear" objective. Levi's own words go against the grain of Todorov's presumption that Levi *was* self-controlled rather than that he performed self-mastery. These readings expose the investment in Levi's absence of hatred as a projection that has little to do with Levi and a lot to do with various readers' desire that victims master their experiences.

Although most literary theorists and other scholars know that Holocaust memoirs by definition can provide only mediated perspectives on the experience of their authors, the pressure on such memoirs to appear referential and unmediated is powerful. Indeed, the view that testimony ought to take this form was widespread among survivors who wrote about their experiences, including Levi, who spoke of his fear of "falling into rhetoric."[18] But the idea that works with literary merit may be those which best convey the event is not hotly contested as long as the focus is on the representation of emotions rather than the documentation of evidence, and lots of ink has been spilled about the crucial nature of aesthetic fashioning in the representation of traumatic experience. These discussions, however, neglect the dynamics of the cultural demand for a testimonial style, literary or not, that is unadorned, laconic, and as close to a performance of transparency as possible. The French historian and essayist Georges Bensoussan notes that victims are told not to hate in the name of being reintegrated into the community: "May your suffering be discreet," the victim is counselled, "May your memory be calm and your desire for revenge muted, for it is a matter of assuring the goodwill of humanity."[19]

Victims' Voices

Saul Friedländer seeks to counter the view by which suffering must not disrupt historical synthesis, and yet he cannot really do so. The two volumes of Friedländer's magisterial study of the destruction of European Jewry, *Nazi Germany and the Jews*,[20] offer a deceptively simple narrative that repudiates the suspension of disbelief.[21] He was one of the first historians who sought to speak of Germans and Jews simultaneously, when the history of the Nazi extermination and the history of the Jewish experience had been written about separately, as if the Jewish experience was a peripheral chapter in the history of Hitler's war. And his narrative is masterful, interweaving individual experience, high politics, and the social history of the Jewish genocide in a vast array of nations.

The second volume of Friedländer's study, which concerns all of Europe and the extermination of the Jews, explicitly challenges mainstream historiography by refusing to suspend disbelief and thereby domesticate all the discomfort generated by victims' voices and the suffering they endured. Here Friedländer insists on the historian's loss of mastery at the heart of the most ambitious synthesis of the history of the destruction of modern European Jewry since Raul Hilberg's seemingly exhaustive work, which focused primarily on German perpetrators and the killing apparatus. He says that he will refuse to suspend disbelief and will tell the reader the story as it was, shorn of the redemptive endings that provide comfort.[22] He seeks to accomplish this goal by filling his work with the voices of victims seldom heard and here simply quoted, not interpreted or given meaning, but presented as a form of unfiltered truth capable of disrupting historical narratives by exposing their objectivity as a mode of enforced detachment. As Friedländer puts it: "By its very nature, by dint of its humanness and freedom, an individual voice suddenly arising in the course of an ordinary historical narrative of events such as those presented here can tear through seamless interpretation and pierce the (mostly involuntary) smugness of scholarly detachment and 'objectivity.'"[23]

Throughout his well-ordered, highly readable, and richly documented narrative, Friedländer mimics narrative mastery. But his account is a mimetic adaptation that allegedly disrupts the reader's comfort and expectations by way of a seemingly subversive emphasis on victims' and perpetrators' voices. Both volumes recount hard things straightforwardly in a spare and constrained narrative that emphasizes the "chilling normality"[24] of the words spoken by gentiles about the inferiority or eventual murder of Jews. Thus, for example, a thirteen-year-old Polish boy in the occupied Eastern territories wrote a letter to a district commissar requesting the accordion of a Jewish boy he knew. In so doing, the Polish youth indicated how even the very young understood, in Friedländer's words, that "no law, no rule, no measure protected a Jew."[25] All such voices are interspersed with detailed discussions of debates between high Nazi officials about the progress of the war as well as descriptions of the increasingly bleak situation in which European Jews of various nationalities found themselves. It is thus difficult to distinguish between narrative mastery and the refusal to suspend disbelief: how does the insistence on the reader's discomfort through the introduction of ostensibly dissonant voices both create a masterful narrative that satisfies the reader's demand for clear and objective synthesis and deny readers that very satisfaction?

Narrative description is hardly incompatible with argument and interpretation, and indeed the historian's artistry was (and often still is) judged by his or her ability to make an argument while disguising all the untidy scholarly scaffolding necessary to making it (footnotes, the clear outline of a conceptual design, and so forth). The idea that Friedländer lets the victims' voices speak for themselves is coupled with the ideological claim that they represent "freedom" and "humanness," a claim presented as self-evident. Friedländer's voices are not unfiltered in the narrative: they do not "suddenly arise," as he claims, after all, but are strategically integrated by the historian into the text. They are frail and heroic.

What does his emphasis on voices in this narrative achieve methodologically if their use is a fairly conventional technique hearkening back to the ancient Greeks? What is subversive about voices rendered as righteous exemplars of real humanity in dark times? Why would Friedländer claim that he seeks to undermine mastery by invoking these voices that represent the triumph, in all of their frailty, of good over evil? The voices are meant to exemplify a refusal to domesticate disbelief and undermine the "smug master narrative" by confronting the reader with the strangeness and opacity of horror, but they are also exemplary of humanity that pierces through opacity.

Friedländer rejects the heroism or idealization of victims common to the Israeli school of historiography that mostly told stories of Jewish collective resistance and heroism. But he does not reject heroism altogether: he redefines it as implicit in the powerlessness of voices struggling to understand what is happening to them, sometimes broken, sometimes frail, and mostly uncomprehending even as they grasp the truth that unfolds around them. Friedländer thus embraces victims' frailty. Perhaps it is this embrace that is subversive: at a moment when Jewish victims have been declared the object of too much memory and are still most appreciated when they appear as tragic heroes who fought back, Friedländer ennobles them all, and elevates the most naive and unsuspecting. This gesture is admirable, and it falls well within a discourse of humanity triumphal and an ideology of secular humanism that mobilizes the narrative. It is so familiar and ultimately redemptive that it domesticates the disorientation the voices are meant to introduce.

What do we learn from Friedländer's effort to escape from the documentary impulses of historiography? In spite of itself, Friedländer's minimalism, which, he insists, refuses to domesticate discomfort, replaces traumatic narrative with another narrative that in spite of itself emphasizes the ways the narrator has mastered that discomfort. The voices, which are supposed to represent the "breakthrough" of pain and suffering and undermine detachment, are in the end enfolded into a narrative of frail humanity against whose past and current sufferings we must be vigilant.

In *Fear: Anti-Semitism in Poland after Auschwitz; An Essay in Historical Interpretation,* Jan Gross asks why it would be shameful for Poles to have sheltered Jews, as he discovered from accounts of Poles who begged their Jewish friends not to let other Poles know from whom they received refuge.[26] In *Fear,* he demonstrates how many Poles helped the Nazis find Jews and, during and after the war, also looted or confiscated their property, stole their belongings, and engaged in pogroms against them, most infamously the massacre in Kielce in 1946, instigated perhaps not inconceivably by a claim of blood libel.[27]

Gross insists that he has told, in empirically unassailable fashion, the tale of why Poles murdered Jews. He claims to have done so because he has proven that Poles killed Jews because they felt so guilty about expropriating them that they wanted all reminders of their conduct (that is to say, the few surviving Jews who triggered their memories) expunged. The author insists that his book, *Neighbors,* is nothing but an assemblage of documents that speak for themselves and should force "readers from time to time [to experience] a sense of discomfort."[28] And yet his narrative departs mostly from what it says it is – a chronicle of events, the most minimalist of all styles of history writing. The book is a brutal assault on any attempt to deny what happened rather than a cool-headed, sober, and constrained account of things, a tone that, since *Neighbors,* has evoked a variety of comments. At least two scholars who discuss *Neighbors* argue that Gross's "hyper-empiricist strategy" and "moral outrage" undercut a serious effort to interpret why Poles did what they did.[29]

It is not clear why Gross believes that he has proven that Poles felt guilty about having Jewish quilts on their beds and blood on their hands, and why this guilt might have compelled Poles to kill those Jews who remained in their midst. He documents only that Poles expropriated Jews, benefited from the spoils, and then killed them. Most interestingly, Gross cannot tell this story using the conventions of mainstream historiography, and even his explanation of why Poles killed Jews has no foundation in empirically verifiable experience but can exist only as speculation.

Gross, like Friedländer, chronicles events matter-of-factly, as when he uses the words spoken by Polish officials or ordinary Poles, though he lets voices speak without making any special methodological or ideological claims about them. But his chronicle narrows the events it recounts so hyperbolically that the abundance of detail sheds light on what happened even as it alerts readers to the difficulty of deciphering what they witness and forces them out of the role of distant observers: Gross mimics the very opacity that the murder of neighbours by neighbours continues to generate by those who seek to comprehend it in social scientific terms. His work illuminates the power of the minimalist style his critics term "hyper-empiricism." Perhaps we should not be surprised that Janine Holc, speaking of *Neighbors*, believes that Gross fails to offer causal explanation (she calls his method "undisciplined" and "undisciplinary"). But then she argues that his refusal to connect analytically the decision making of individual Poles who murdered Jews and the collective/ethnic identity that might explain their motives except in fragmentary fashion signals "resistance to, and even prevents, a definitive choice between them."[30]

Unlike Friedländer's narrative, however, Gross's documentation of unpleasant truths has been deemed insufficiently objective, too empathic, and too polemical – that is to say, unconstrained, deeply identified with its subjects, and not wary about taking the victim's side.[31] Because Gross ultimately gets the facts right, most of the debate has been about how his moral outrage may have prevented him from interpreting his sources accurately and thus supplying a persuasive analytical account of why Poles killed Jews after the war. But from Gross's point of view, establishing what happened in and of itself seems to be sufficient not only to hold the perpetrators accountable but to explain why they did what they did. The critics who accuse him of not providing causal explanations are right in many respects. But Gross undermines a conventional construction of causality because his work is not hyper-empiricist but a sophisticated form of minimalism, one which refuses kitsch and voyeurism by presenting horror matter-of-factly, generating empathic unsettlement by refusing to domesticate traumatic violence, and demonstrating that all the interpretation in the world may still take us into a blind alley in explaining extreme events unless we develop new ways of conceptualizing traumatic material. In short, the point is not that Gross ultimately leaves us unsettled but foggy about the meaning of events – this is indeed a problem – but that his work demonstrates the limitations of conventional approaches to disturbingly violent material.

In its most reductive uses, minimalism allegedly resolves the cultural difficulty of how to speak about having been victimized that has confronted Jewish survivors and other victims in different ways since the end of the Second World War. After the war, the cultural stigma attached to Jewish victims rendered them silent in mixed company; now, the pathologies attached to making claims to having been a victim renders victimhood itself a stigma manifest in the very notion that survivors of the Holocaust have to be sacralized if they are not to be relegated to the sphere of the profane. Minimalism meant to counter kitsch often represents victims as already having mastered the symptoms of their suffering, and as already having moved on from their losses. Gross, I would suggest, is controversial because in his work, the victims' suffering is meaningless – in spite of all the entreaties that we cannot understand what happened, we prefer meaning and thus prefer to "witness," even if witnessing in order to prevent future violence can only ever be a metaphorical displacement. I do not wish to make an argument in favour of meaninglessness: rather, I wish to point out simply that minimalism is a style, not a truth, and that our scholarly preferences therefore favour some kinds of victims over others. Primo Levi knew this very well. Arendt, preferring sobriety and equating K-Zetnik's collapse on the stand with kitsch did not conceive her preference as a preference, or the dichotomy between sobriety and kitsch as only one of many ways of conceiving testimony. W.G. Sebald noted rightly that "there is no need to exaggerate that which is already horrible," but found ways of creating solidarity with vulnerability in emotionally laden scenes, especially through the use of animals. But in most discourses and for historians in particular, the opaque and difficult question about how Jews disappeared in the Holocaust is almost always answered by a rendition of how they have returned.

NOTES

1 Hannah Arendt, *Eichmann in Jerusalem: A Report on the Banality of Evil* (New York: Penguin, 2006), 228.

2 Witold Kula, *Rozdzialki* (Warsaw: Wydawn. Tio, 1996), quoted in Antony Polonsky and Joanna B. Michlic, eds., *The Neighbors Respond: The Controversy over the Jedwabne Massacre in Poland* (Princeton, NJ: Princeton University Press, 2004), 9.

3 Pascal Bruckner, *The Temptation of Innocence: Living in the Age of Entitlement* (New York: Algora, 2000), 229. The French original appeared in 1995 as *La tentation de l'innocence* (Paris: Grasset, 1995).

4 Arendt, *Eichmann in Jerusalem*, 288.

5 Ibid., 8.

6 Ibid.

7 Ibid.
8 Testimony of Moshe B., interviewed 1 February 1990 (Fortunoff Archives, Yale University Library, HVT-1832).
9 Testimony of Leon W., interviewed 15 November 1986 (Fortunoff Archives, Yale University Library, HVT- 788).
10 Arendt, *Eichmann in Jerusalem*, 121, 228.
11 Ibid., 223–4.
12 Among countless works, see Lawrence Douglas, *Memory of Judgment: Making Law and History in the Trials of the Holocaust* (New Haven, CT: Yale University Press, 2001).
13 Annette Wieviorka, *The Era of the Witness*, trans. Jared Stark (Ithaca, NY: Cornell University Press, 2006), 135–44.
14 Ruth Franklin, "A Thousand Darknesses: Elie Wiesel's *Night*," in *Re-examining the Holocaust through Literature*, ed. Aukje Kluge and Benn E. Williams (Newcastle upon Tyne: Cambridge Scholars Publishing, 2009), 156.
15 Charles Bigsby, *Remembering and Imagining the Holocaust: The Chain of Memory* (Cambridge: Cambridge University Press, 2006), 374.
16 Louis J. Micheels, M.D., *Doctor #117641: A Holocaust Memoir* (New Haven, CT: Yale University Press, 1980), viii.
17 Tzvetan Todorov, *Facing the Extreme: Moral Life in the Concentration Camps*, trans. Arthur Denner and Abigail Pollak (New York: Henry Holt, 1996), 269–70. "Getting to know a Nazi in a deep and meaningful way would have forced Levi to see him in all of his humanity, and had he done so, he would have had no weapons left to defend himself against the Nazis' intention to destroy him" (269).
18 Primo Levi quoted in Alain Parrau, *Écrire les camps* (Paris: Édition Belin, 1995), 286. For interesting discussions aimed at reducing the sharp delineation between literature and testimony, see Marie Bornand, *Témoinage et fiction: Le récits des rescapés de la literature de langue française (1945–2000)* (Geneva: Droz, 2004); Michael Rinn, *Les récits du genocide: Sémiotique de l'indicible* (Lausanne: Delachaux et niestlé, 1998); and Parrau, *Écrire les camps*. All these texts are valuable French interventions into this question but remain for the most part decontextualized and tend to neglect (while discussing) the real import of the different experiences of Jews and others in the name of comparing their representations.
19 Georges Bensoussan, *L'Auschwitz en héritage: D'un bon usage de la mémoire* (Paris: Mille et une nuits, 2003), 206.
20 Saul Friedländer, *Nazi Germany and the Jews*, vol. 1: *The Years of Persecution, 1933–1939* (New York: Harper Collins, 1997), and vol. 2: *The Years of Extermination:* (New York: Harper Collins, 2007).

21 Historian Richard Evans calls Friedländer a meticulous historian whose work is unusual not because of difficulties of historical method, but because it rises to the level of "literature." By literature Evans means the "skilled interweaving of individual testimony with the broader description of events" (but not the "unreliable testimony of memoirs"), which makes the book read like a novel. Evans, "Whose Orders?" *New York Times*, 24 June 2007. By contrast, in a rather unusual essay, Wulf Kansteiner transforms Friedländer's synthesis into a postmodern work of crafted fragmentation, as if the book subverted narrative totality at every level. Wulf Kansteiner "Success, Truth, and Modernism in Holocaust Historiography," *History and Theory*, 47 (2009): 25–53. Kansteiner claims that Friedländer's success among the very audience who most oppose this sort of experimental work can be attributed to the fact that both "*The Years of Extermination* and contemporary non-fiction TV aesthetics try to engage their audiences emotionally; the readers and viewers are invited to feel their way into the past and get a sense of how the events were experienced by people directly involved in them" (36). It is not clear that inviting viewers to feel their way into the past is particularly disruptive of historiographical convention. I have no desire to deny the interest of some of Kansteiner's often insightful arguments, but the idea that Friedländer's work is the fulfilment of literary criticism historian Hayden White's own is simply not tenable.

22 Friedländer, *Nazi Germany and the Jews*, 2:xxvi.

23 Ibid.

24 The phrase is from Friedländer, *Nazi Germany and the Jews*, 1:5.

25 Ibid. 2:224–5.

26 Jan T. Gross, *Fear: Anti-Semitism in Poland after Auschwitz: An Essay in Historical Interpretation* (New York: Random House, 2006).

27 Ibid., ix–xv.

28 Ibid., xiii.

29 See Janine Holc, "Working Through Jan Gross's *Neighbors*," *Slavic Review* 61 (2002): 453–59; William W. Hagen, "A 'Potent, Devilish Mixture' of Motives: Explanatory Strategy and Assignment of Meaning in Jan Gross's *Neighbors*," *Slavic Review* 61 (2002): 466–75. Gross was asked to respond to these and several other essays, but chose only to respond to one commentary that took issue with his treatment of sources.

30 Holc, "Working Through Jan Gross's *Neighbors*," 458.

31 See in particular the essays by Polish historians and witnesses assembled by Polonsky and Michlic in *The Neighbors Respond*.

Chapter Seven

Truth and Judgment in Arendt's Writing[1]

LEORA BILSKY

Arendt is known for her critique of the use of witnesses in the Eichmann trial. She argued against the decision of the Israeli prosecution to call "witnesses of suffering" whose testimony was not directly related to the determination of the defendant's guilt, undermining in her view the objectives of criminal justice.[2] In other words, Arendt objected to what scholarship later defined as the "didactic purposes" of international criminal law. As a result, she has been portrayed as a legalist, advocating a strict separation between law and history/politics.

With the perspective of time, it seems that Arendt's warnings were not heeded. If we look at international criminal law and truth commissions – the two mechanisms of choice for addressing violence committed by prior regimes – we see that common to both tracks is the recognition of the "clarification of the historical truth" as an objective in international criminal law and transitional justice, and specifically the rise of the individual victim's right to the truth. Thus, while the Eichmann trial has remained associated with Arendt's critique, from a legal perspective, it is precisely the didactic approach inaugurated in the Eichmann trial that is now taken very seriously by international tribunals as well as other transitional justice institutions.[3]

Does this mean that Arendt was wrong, and that there are no legal or jurisprudential insights to be learned from *Eichmann in Jerusalem*?

In this article I would like to offer an alternative reading of *Eichmann in Jerusalem*, one that moves beyond the question of legalism and focuses on the act of judgment. It is in relation to judgment that Arendt's book offers the most promising contribution to the contemporary jurisprudence of international crimes. I will argue that reading Arendt holistically, that is, reading her critique of the Eichmann trial alongside her other works, reveals a very different picture from the one that portrays her as a legalist. I will try to show that Arendt is less concerned with protecting the law from so-called extralegal purposes than with preserving or creating the necessary conditions for politics in general, and for politics in transition to democracy in particular. I will proceed to examine this thesis through Arendt's discussion of three fields: law, moral philosophy, and politics. In all three of them the question of judgment is raised in relation to truth; specifically, judgment entails the rejection of a conception of truth that is dominant in each of the three respective fields. I argue that Arendt's observations about the juridification of politics carry important insights for current developments in international law – among them, the growing recognition of a human right to the truth.[4] I will end by critically examining the emerging right to the truth as experienced in the paradigmatic case of Argentina's transition to democracy. In contrast with the optimistic story international law tells us about the recognition of a human right to truth, I will ask whether the growing legalization of the truth might not actually undermine the democratization in the name of which the right to truth is heralded. Adopting an Arendtian perspective will thus help us distinguish between the new political role of the "truth teller" in the stuggle against organized lies, and the need to preserve a space for political judgment – a judgment of particulars without reference to universal rules – in transitions to democracy.

Truth and Law

Arendt is known as the most famous critic of the Eichmann trial. But there is an ongoing debate as to how to interpret her criticism. Is it a warning against the political uses of law? Is it about the inherent limitations of criminal law to address the nature of "administrative massacres"? Or rather, is it about the failure of the court to understand the novelty in the new category of crimes against humanity, and the new type of criminal ("the banality of evil")? Although Arendt addressed each of these issues, we need to better understand her jurisprudential stance in order to see what brings these issues together as a coherent criticism of the Jerusalem court.

Arendt opens and ends her book *Eichmann in Jerusalem* with a criticism of the direction in which the Israeli prosecution took the trial. She is concerned with what has come to be known as the "didactic purpose of the trial" – the attempt to use the trial to clarify historical truths and construct collective memory. For Arendt, the sole legitimate purpose of the trial was to determine the guilt of the defendant Adolf Eichmann. She was suspicious of the court taking on the role of historian, and in particular criticized Prosecutor Hausner's depiction of the Holocaust as a repetition of the anti-Semitic persecution of the Jews in a long history of their victimization and persecution throughout the ages. She argued that this was "bad history and cheap rhetoric."[5]

However, it is not only to the expanded role of judicial investigation that Arendt objected. She also criticized the Israeli prosecution's decision to put on the stand over one hundred Holocaust survivors to testify about their personal experience under the Third Reich. Such testimonies, she argued, were irrelevant to proving Eichamnn's guilt, and threatened to overwhelm the trial with emotions of suffering, pain and rage, which undermine the ability to judge the defendant fairly and objectively.[6]

The conventional understanding of Arendt's jurisprudential stance is to see her as a "legalist,"[7] following Judith Shklar's definition of legalism as an ethos that holds that law and politics must be separate.[8] However, a closer look at Arendt's arguments reveals difficulties in viewing her as an advocate of legalism.

First, the opposition that Arendt erects between law and history is undermined by her own advocacy of an alternative historical narrative that the trial should promote, one that centres on the rise of the totalitarian state instead of anti-Semitism. Moreover, although she seemingly opposed any "historical excursions" by the court, and objected to the role of victims in the trial, she chose to devote over ten pages[9] of her book to discuss the behaviour of the Jewish councils, Judenrat, a discussion with historical and political importance, but irrelevant to proving the defendant's guilt. Thus, in a previous article I argued that in order to understand the controversy between the Israeli prosecutor, Gideon Hausner, and Arendt, it is better to view it as a "competition of storytellers" – that is, a controversy over historiography, politics, and law.[10] Rather than a battle between justice and politics, or justice and history, Arendt's critique of Hausner should be understood as a controversy about the "right" kind of history needed to make an informed legal judgment about Eichmann's crimes.

But what about Arendt's critique of the reliance on victims' testimonies in the trial? Is this not a clear indication of a legalist stance? Arendt vehemently opposed opening the trial to testimonies the main purpose of which was to allow the survivors to relate their experiences and suffering under the Nazi regime and portrayed the prosecutor Hausner and Judge Landau as two antagonists who asked to pull the trial in two different directions – the political and the legal.[11] Arendt sided with Landau, who for her represented legal limitations. The sharp opposition that Arendt erected between judge and prosecutor, however, is not supported by a closer reading of the Eichmann judgment. In the judgment the court in fact endorses victims' testimonies as relevant to the legal examination, but rejects the expansive didactic role of the trial. In doing so the court articulates a victim-oriented jurisprudence for atrocity trials that responds to the nature of the new crimes without falling into pure didactics.[12] This undermines Arendt's "legalism" from the opposite direction, showing that a legal justification could have been, and indeed was, articulated by the court for the expansive role of victims' testimonies. Thus, again, it is not law versus politics, but rather different conceptions of criminal law that better explain Arendt's critique. Likewise, Arendt's objection to the portrayal of all victims as "pure" as opposed to a frank discussion of the various degrees of collaboration with the Nazis makes less sense as an internal legal critique but points to Arendt's worry – the effect of the trial on the political sphere.

When we adopt a more holistic view of Arendt's critique of the Eichmann trial, it becomes even more problematic to understand her position as "legalist" or "positivist" because her solutions to the legal problems that stood in the way of the court, such as retroactivity, extraterritorial jurisdiction, and the interpretation of crimes against humanity, defy our conventional understanding of legalism. We see that on every issue, Arendt goes beyond a purely legalist position in offering ways for the law to properly respond to the novel crimes of the Nazi regime.[13]

One might think that these examples simply point to contradictions within the book. However, reading *Eichman in Jerusalem* in light of later writings by Arendt, I argue that the attempt to view Arendt's jurisprudence as legalist is insufficient and even misleading. While "legalism" assumes that judging Nazi criminals does not pose a new challenge for the law (as all we need is to apply the correct rules), I would like to suggest the opposite. In my view, the question that concerns Arendt in *Eichman in Jerusalem* is the question of judgment and the possibility of judging the Nazi crimes. Rather than assuming that the law already possesses the tools to judge, Arendt points time and again to the crisis of judgment that the Eichmann trial exposes.

In seeking to come to terms with the problem of judgment, Arendt moves away from both a positivist and natural-law understanding of law. In her view the totalitarian experience in general, and the Third Reich in particular, requires that we rethink basic conception of criminal law, such as the mental state of the accused (mens rea), and the role of conscience. Moreover, her book undermines the basic dichotomy underpinning criminal law between perpetrator and victim as falling under the simple opposition between "satanic evil and complete innocence." She points to the need of the law to deal with the phenomenon of what Primo Levi called the "grey area" – the mass complicity that is indispensable to political violence.[14] Finally, in her discussion about obedience to superior orders, Arendt raises important questions about the relations of criminal law to morality and points to the need to explore the act of judgment as more than just applying pre-given rules to particular situations.

Arendt raises difficult jurisprudential questions: Can we think about the perpetrator of atrocious crimes, such as genocide and crimes against humanity, as a normal person acting from banal motives? And can the law, that is, traditional categories of criminal law that require that actus reus be accompanied by mens rea, convict such a defendant? And what if the most terrible crimes can occur without proper mens rea – does this signal the bankruptcy of our criminal law, or is there a way to revise the fundamental requirement of individual guilt when we deal with collective crimes of that magnitude?[15]

In answering these questions Arendt arrives at the need to develop an alternative theory of judgment that she called, following Kant, reflective judgment.

Reflective Judgment – Truth and Morality

Unlike those who see Arendt as criticizing all the participants in the Eichmann trial, whether prosecutor, witnesses, or judges, from the standpoint of one who knows better, I believe that the Eichmann trial was also a moment of crisis for Arendt, a crisis which helped her identify the questions that need answers. She did not give a satisfactory answer to these questions in her book about Eichmann but returned to them in subsequent articles and in lectures she gave on Kant's *Third Critique*. Reading *Eichmann in Jerusalem* together with her lectures on Kant and judgment[16] allows us to identify this crisis, as well as the way she tried to resolve it.

In the postscript to *Eichmann in Jerusalem*, Arendt reconsiders the defence that was raised repeatedly at the Nuremberg trials, the defence of "obedience to superior orders." The formal legal answer given at Nuremberg was the nullification of the defence for criminals of the Third Reich. The more substantive answer given in Israel in the Kafr Qasim trial in 1958 (regarding the massacre of inhabitants of an Arab village by Israeli soldiers) was the recognition of a duty not to obey an order that is manifestly illegal.[17] However, Arendt believes that this legal doctrine can help judges only in a functioning democracy, when the illegal command sticks out clearly and is "manifest" in its illegality. This response is inadequate in the context of a regime that has turned illegality into state law, that is, a legal system in which the exception has become law.

In contrast to the Jerusalem court, Arendt refuses to ground the obligation to disobey a manifestly illegal order in presupposing the existence of a universal conscience. She writes "the order, to be recognized by the soldier as 'manifestly unlawful,' must violate by its unusualness the canons of the legal system to which he is accustomed."[18] All that can be expected in Arendt's view of the soldier is to know how to distinguish between rule and exception. Accordingly, Arendt reaches the conclusion that the Kafr Qasim precedent cannot help address Eichmann's guilt since the latter dealt with a situation in which the exception became the rule: "We are forced to conclude that Eichmann acted fully within the framework of the kind of judgment required of him: he acted in accordance with the rule, examined the order issued to him for its 'manifest' legality, namely regularity; he did not have to fall back upon his 'conscience,' since he was not one of those who were unfamiliar with the laws of his country. The exact opposite was the case."[19] This goes beyond the problem of legalizing crime and touches the core question about conscience presupposed by criminal law. How does one's conscience change in accordance with legal norms and the norms of civil society? What can we make of the fact that German elites acquiesced with the Nazi regime? Arendt writes: "He did not need to 'close his ears to the voice of conscience,' as the judgment has it, not because he had none, but because his conscience spoke with a 'respectable voice,' with the voice of respectable society around him."[20]

We are therefore faced with a crisis of judgment that goes beyond a positivist understanding of law and challenges the moral foundations of criminal law. A legal system presupposes that ordinary people can distinguish right from wrong. That is, we assume that conscience is different and independent from society's norms. But what if it is not? How do we deal with the process of "coordination" that German society underwent with the crimes of the Nazi regime? This is a question that moves us from law to moral theory.

For Arendt, who came to the trial from the philosophical tradition, it was possible to think differently about the problem of totalitarian law with the help of Kant's moral philosophy, based on each person's ability to judge for himself the law before him according to principles of universal reason. This is the heritage of the Enlightenment expressed in Kant's categorical imperative, which tells us, "Act only in accordance with that maxim through which you can at the same time will that it become a universal law."[21]

Why, in the face of the failure of Nazi law, did Arendt not choose to return to Kant's categorical imperative as a moral guide? Here we approach the depth of the crisis Arendt experienced at the Eichmann trial – the moment at which Eichmann himself cites Kant's categorical imperative in his police interrogation and later in his court's testimony, showing the ease with which Kant's moral philosophy was turned on its head in Nazi Germany.

In the eighth chapter of *Eichmann in Jerusalem,* titled "Duties of a Law-Abiding Citizen," Arendt writes:

> The first indication of Eichmann's vague notion that there was more involved in this whole business than the question of the soldier's carrying out orders that are clearly criminal in nature and intent appeared during the police examination, when he suddenly declared with great emphasis that he had lived his whole life according to Kant's moral precepts, and especially according to a Kantian definition of duty. This was outrageous, on the face of it, and also incomprehensible, since Kant's moral philosophy is so closely bound up with man's faculty of judgment, which rules out blind obedience.[22]

How can Kant's categorical imperative, based on an autonomous independent moral judgment, be reconciled with Eichmann's obedience to superior orders? Can it be that his obedience was not blind, Arendt asked, but was actually guided by his conscience? In court, Eichmann explained that from the moment he was ordered to execute the Final Solution, he ceased living according to Kantian principles. However, Arendt identifies a deeper difficulty, as the categorical imperative received a new and distorted interpretation under Nazi rule, in the new wording provided by Hans Frank: "Act in such a way that the Führer, if he knew your action, would approve it."[23] Arendt writes, "In this household use, all that is left of Kant's spirit is the demand that a man do more than obey the law, that he go beyond the mere call of obedience and identify his own will with the principle behind the law the source from which the law sprang. In Kant's philosophy, that source was practical reason; in Eichmann's household use of him, it was the will of the Führer."[24] In Arendt's view, it is precisely this combination of moral idealism and obedience to orders that accounts for "the horribly painstaking thoroughness in the execution of the Final Solution,"[25] which she traces to "the odd notion, indeed very common in Germany, that to be law-abiding means not merely to obey the laws but to act as though one were the legislator of the laws that one obeys. Hence the conviction that nothing less than going beyond the call of duty will do."[26]

To counter Eichmann's defence of obedience to superior orders, the prosecution brought evidence of Eichmann's refusal to follow Himmler's orders to stop deportations to Auschwitz. This could be an indication that Eichmann was lying, and that it was identification with Nazi ideology that guided his actions, not a sense of obligation to obey superior orders. Yet from Arendt's perspective there is no internal contradiction in this refusal. She writes, "The sad and very uncomfortable truth of the matter probably was that it was not his fanaticism but his very conscience that prompted Eichmann to adopt his uncompromising attitude during the last year of the war ... Eichmann knew that Himmler's orders ran directly counter to the Führer's order."[27]

Here we have a glimpse of the horror: in the interpretation of orders by law-abiding Eichmann, it is Himmler's order to stop deportations that bore a "black flag" of manifest illegality. As a result, for Arendt both law and moral theory fail to respond to the particular challenge posed by the new subject of totalitarianism. She therefore believes that the most urgent challenge for post-Holocaust jurisprudence is to rethink our assumptions about the relations between law and morality. This is the crisis of judgment with which Arendt chooses to end her book.[28]

In my view, even though Arendt clearly identified the crisis of judgment, she was not able to properly address it in her book about Eichmann. The answer she gave at the end of the book as to why, despite all the doubts, it is legitimate to convict Eichmann, is not sufficient.[29] I would like to suggest that we can find the seeds of her more developed answer to the crisis of judgment in her lectures about Kant's political philosophy. Here Arendt tried to sketch the contours of a solution based on Kant's theory of aesthetic judgment, which she interpreted as relevant more broadly to political judgment and to the question of how we (as actors) judge without applying pre-given rules (of law or morality) more generally.

As we can see, the crisis does not derive from Kant's moral philosophy itself, as it is obvious that Eichmann does not take that philosophy seriously and he misinterprets Kant's categorical imperative. The problem Arendt identifies is that Kant's moral philosophy is not sufficient to guide action in the world, and therefore a theory of judgment is required. Kant's moral theory identifies the a priori, necessary, and general moral law, which according to the typography of truths Arendt later suggested, is a rational truth.[30] That Arendt identifies Kant's moral theory with rational truth becomes apparent with another example she gives. Arendt suggests that the Socratic proposition "It is better to suffer wrong than to do wrong" stands at the basis of Kant's categorical imperative, and argues that this proposition is true only for the speaker who is concerned with himself as a thinking being – i.e., the philosopher – and not for the citizen who cares about the world or the community.[31] She concludes this discussion with a general note: "Philosophical truth concerns man in his singularity, [thus] it is unpolitical by nature."[32]

Arendt is concerned with judgment about right and wrong in the absence of either socially accepted or universal legal norms, and in light of the insufficiency of universal moral law to guide such judgment alone. Interestingly it is the first part of Kant's third critique (his theory of aesthetic judgment) that provides her with a solution for the question of judging the particular without pre-given rules.

Turning to Kant's critique of taste as a basis for a theory of political judgment, Arendt exposes the puzzle that lies at the heart of such a move: Why does Kant decide to derive the mental phenomenon of judgment from the most subjective senses of taste and smell, and not from the more objective senses?[33] Arendt's answer to this puzzle points to the discriminatory quality of taste: "because only taste and smell are discriminatory by their very nature, and because they relate to the particular qua particular."[34] But this answer raises another difficulty: how do we overcome the subjectivity of judgment? Here Arendt points to a double movement that is enabled by our faculties of imagination and common sense. While imagination allows a move of internalization of the object of judgment, common sense allows a subsequent move of externalization. Together these faculties allow forming a judgment of the particular that is not dependent on pre-existing rules while escaping the arbitrariness and idiosyncracy of personal preferences. Arendt explains:

> The solution to these riddles can be indicated by the names of two other faculties: *imagination* and *common sense.* Imagination, that is the faculty of having present what is absent, transforms an object into something I do not have to be directly confronted with but that I have in some sense internalized, so that I now can be affected by it as though it were given to me by the nonobjective sense … One then speaks of judgment and no longer of taste because, though it still affects one like a matter of taste, one now has, by means of representation, established proper distance.[35]

In other words, the imagination allows one to both internalize the object of judgment while keeping enough distance to allow reflection on it. However, this is only the first move necessary to arrive at a valid judgment. It has to be accompanied by another movement, one of externalization – that is, of turning to the plurality of viewpoints in the community in light of which to view our judgments. Here one relies on common sense. As Arendt explains,"Judgment, and especially judgments of taste, always reflects upon others and their taste, takes their possible judgments into account. This is necessary because I am human and cannot live outside the company of men."[36] In other words, what enables us to make subjective judgments that are not merely indiosyncratic is our capacity for what Kant called "enlarged thought," that is, the ability to view one's own judgments from the standpoint of others.[37] This act of judgment depends on men in the plural, on the community, which one goes to visit in one's imagination in order to critically examine one's own subjective judgments.

Arendt thinks that judgment can become impartial with the help of the imagination and through a process of representative thinking. She believes that the internal dialogic process of enlarged mentality can help orient the actor's judgments even under conditions brought about by totalitarianism – in which the exception becomes the norm, and society coordinates itself accordingly. Instead of being based on an absolute truth or existing norms, reflective judgment involves forming our judgment in the process of imagining trying to persuade others.

Arendt did not develop her theory of reflective judgment or "enlarged mentality," and she left many puzzles unanswered. Here, however, I would like to return to the dilemma posed by Arendt in *Eichmann in*

Jerusalem with the guidance of this theory of judgment. I briefly return with the help of the theory of reflective judgment to Arendt's analysis of Eichmann's failure of judgment. We saw that the court found that Eichmann had lied about being bound by orders when he organized deportations to Auschwitz, since his acts did not result from literal obedience to orders but from ideological identification with the policy. In other words, the court found that Eichmann had the required mens rea for criminal liability. Arendt, in contrast, explored the possibility that Eichmann had not lied, since he believed Himmler's order to stop deportations was manifestly illegal. That is, Eichmann acted according to his conscience. What, then, would be the basis for morally condemning Eichmann, if he commited his crimes "under circumstances that make it well-nigh impossible for him to know or to feel that he is doing wrong?"[38]

Here we can see how turning to Kant's theory of reflective judgment may help. If we understand judgment as requiring "enlarged thought," we see that even if Eichmann did not lie to the court, his actions involved a failure of judgment to which he has to give account. Eichmann, who was capable of imagining the perspective of his victims for instrumental or manipulative purposes, deliberately failed to do so for the purposes of reflective judgment – to enlarge his judgment so that it could encompass the point of view of his victims. In other words, Eichmann protected his subjective judgments from becoming impartial by refusing to open himself to the point of view of his victims. Arendt provides three examples in her book for this failure, examples that seem trivial at first reading. However, if we read them in light of her lectures on judgment, we can better understand their importance for her condemnation of Eichmann.

First, when Eichmann describes his activities in Vienna to organize the forced immigration of Jews, he uses the term "cooperation" to describe his work with Jewish leaders, as if there had really been a common interest and equality to both sides. Arendt writes:

> A more specific, and also more decisive, flaw in Eichmann's character was his almost total inability ever to look at anything from the other fellow's point of view. Nowhere was this flaw more conspicuous than in his account of the Vienna episode. He and his men and the Jews were all "pulling together," and whenever there were any difficulties the Jewish functionaries would come running to him "to unburden their hearts," to tell him "all their grief and sorrow," and to ask for his help.[39]

Second, his failure to understand the perspective of others stands out even more in his description of his meeting with one of the leaders of the Jewish community in Vienna, Mr. Storfer, with whom he had worked and who was later caught by the Gestapo and sent to Auschwitz when he tried to escape. Eichmann describes their meeting at Auschwitz like this:

> With Storfer afterward, well, it was normal and human, we had a normal, human encounter. He told me all his grief and sorrow: I said: 'Well, my dear old friend … we certainly got it! What rotten luck!' And I also said: 'Look, I really cannot help you … I hear you made a mistake, that you went into hiding or wanted to bolt, which, after all, you did not need to do.' … And then I asked him how he was.[40]

A third example of Eichmann's inability to enlarge his thought and look at things from the perspective of others emerges from a recording of his interrogation at the police, when Eichmann unwraps before Captain Less, a Holocaust survivor from Germany, all the details of his biography, as if trying to obtain sympathy for his story of bad luck, without taking into account the perspective of his audience. Arendt comments: "The presence of Captain Less, a Jew from Germany and unlikely in any case to think that members of the S.S. advanced in their careers through the exercise of high moral qualities, did not for a moment throw this mechanism out of gear."[41]

With the term "banality of evil" Arendt pointed to the way language (with its clichés etc.) loses its communicative function and is used to block the reality of the victim from the perpetrator. Indeed, each of the examples that I referred to above demonstrates this point, as Eichmann uses idioms and clichés to resist the process of enlarged mentality and to block the possibility of visiting through imagination the point of view of his interlocutor. The difficult question Arendt poses to law and moral theory, for which truth plays such an important role, is how to judge such persons who seem to act beyond truth and falsehood, fact and fiction.[42]

It is interesting that to address this problem Arendt reintroduces the notion of "common sense" – but not in its common use, of conventions or common social beliefs. Following Kant, she refers us back to its origins in the Latin term "sensus communis."[43] Accordingly, she argues that the type of reflective judgment explored by Kant requires that the judging subject engage in a process of "enlarged mentality" as a basis for arriving at valid judgments. It is only when one's judgments become "common" that is – inspected from the point of view and opinions of others – that they gain their objectivity. It is in relation to such a notion of common sense that we can best identify Eichmann's flight from judgment. It allows us to notice that even if Eichmann were not lying, he nevertheless should be accountable for his failure of judgment, notwithstanding the changed legal and social norms in Nazi Germany.

Truth and Politics

The phenomena of organized lying in general and social taboo in particular stand at the centre of Arendt's more general reflections on truth and politics. Both, she believed, undermine one's ability to make the distinction between fact and fiction. With a note in the beginning of her essay on the subject, she explains that her thesis grew directly from the controversy brought about by the publication of her book *Eichmann in Jerusalem*.[44] With this essay she purports to return to the question of truth but to locate it in the political sphere. How does she envision the place of truth in politics? At first glance it seems that while her discussion of law and morality is based on a rejection of the coercive power of truth on the act of judgment, in "Truth and Politics" Arendt takes the opposite position and points to the dangers that lies, and in particular organized lies, pose to the integrity of the political sphere.

However, a closer reading of Arendt's argument reveals a more complex relationship between truth and politics. According to Arendt, political debate must be based on truth. For this purpose it is not enough to guarantee freedom of speech, but also to build institutions designed to actively protect the truth: courts (legal truth) and universities (scientific truth).[45] Arendt distinguishes between different kinds of truths: rational or scientific truth, religious truth, and factual truth and draws a genealogy of the relations of politics to each. She claims that whereas antiquity was characterized by a conflict between the philosopher and the citizen concerning rational truth, the modern tension lies between the political ruler and the citizen and concerns factual truth. According to Arendt, of all the types of truth, it is factual truth – a truth entirely dependent on witnesses and testimonies, and the existence of a political space in which views can be exchanged – that is most vulnerable to the onslaught of organized political lies: "[Factual truth] is always related to other people; it concerns events and circumstances in which many are involved; it is established by witnesses and depends upon testimony; it exists only to the extent it is spoken about, even if it occurs in the domain of privacy. It is political by nature."[46] The language Arendt uses draws a close connection between the legal process of "fact finding" and a functioning political sphere. According to Arendt, the modern era of mass communication allows a systematic attempt by rulers to control and shape "factual truths" by reframing the entire context instead of relying on a few discrete lies as was the practice in the past.[47] It is against this background of organized lying that Arendt is able to identify a new political role for the "truth-teller":

> Only where a community has embarked upon organized lying on principle, and not only with respect to particulars, can truthfulness as such, unsupported by the distorting forces of power and interest, become a political factor of the first order. Where everybody lies about everything of importance, the truth teller, whether he knows it or not, has begun to act; he, too, has engaged himself in political business, for, in the unlikely event that he survives, he has made a start toward changing the world.[48]

The importance of the truth teller to politics is connected to the important distinction between past and future. Arendt writes: "Not the past – and all factual truth, of course, concerns the past – or the present, insofar as it is the outcome of the past, but the future is open to action. If the past and present are treated as parts of the future – that is, changed back into their former state of potentiality – the political realm is deprived not only of its main stabilizing force but of the starting point from which to change, to begin something new."[49]

This understanding of the political role of truth telling can explain Arendt's harsh criticism of the treatment of the Judenrat (the Jewish leadership appointed by the Nazis) in the Eichmann trial, as she saw how the issue of their collaboration with the Nazi authorities was transformed before her eyes into a social taboo. In a sense, she sees herself as undertaking the political role of "truth teller" in *Eichmann in Jerusalem*.[50] Maybe in reaction to the Israeli prosecution's attempt to avoid the subject altogether, Arendt went to the other extreme and generally condemned the Jewish leadership, without trying to "enter their shoes" and without making important distinctions between different Judenrate as was made in later historical research.[51]

However, if politics depends on the preservation of factual truth against the onslaught of organized lying, politics should not be reduced to truth finding. Arendt emphasizes that factual truth is only the ground upon which valid political judgment can be made. This becomes clear when we turn our attention to a more recent phenomenon of a struggle against organized lying – the struggle of the Mothers of the Plaza de Mayo.

From the Eichmann Trial Back to Argentina: The Emergence of a Human Right to the Truth

Arendt was concerned with the use of the court in the service of what she regarded as political lies. She saw it as the role of the public intellectual to protest against social taboos and to resist the substitute of truth with myth. But what happens when modern truth tellers rely on courts and the human rights discourse as part of a political struggle against an orchestrated, organized lie by the authorities? How is the truth conceptualized in this context, and how does this conceptualization influence the political debate?

The Israeli authorities had kidnapped Eichmann from Argentina, where he found refuge after the war, in order to bring him to public trial. The struggle of the Mothers of Plaza de Mayo in Argentina dealt with another type of kidnapping – kidnapping on a mass scale. Their struggle provides a paradigmatic case of the modern use of courts by human rights activists against an organized lie, here the lie by the military authorities about the "disappearance" and kidnapping of around thirty thousand suspected leftists by the Argentine military regime in the years 1976–83. The Argentine case can help explain how, on the one hand, the search for the factual truth about the fate of missing persons becomes a political act of the first order. And it will help us understand how, on the other hand, the conceptualization of the truth as a legal, human right threatens the rule of law as well as political debate and judgment in Argentina about the prior regime and the transition to democracy.

My discussion of Argentina is not intended to simply serve as an illustration of Arendt's arguments. The discussion of the rise of a human right to truth in Argentina helps us tie together Arendt's discussion of truth and judgment in the three fields of law, moral philosophy, and politics. It also reveals the relevance of Arendt's discussion of political judgment for pressing contemporary debates in international law and transitional justice. Arendt's essay "Truth and Politics" explores the dangers that a certain understanding of truth poses to the political realm. Thus, contrary to the human rights discourse celebrating the rise of a "right to truth" as part of the end of the era of impunity, Arendt's essay reminds us of the dangers that the legalization of truth poses to politics. In what follows I focus on the case of Argentina, where the right to the truth has been taken to extremes. My argument is not against the struggle to end an organized lie, but rather against the triumphant depiction of the emergence of a right to truth in international law as unambiguous progress for human rights.

It should come as no surprise that the strongest expressions of the right to the truth come from Latin America, which was also the birthplace of truth commissions. Because disappearances were a prevalent mode of repression, the new democracies in Latin America at the end of the 1980s were faced with a colossal lack of information regarding the fate of thousands of victims. To this must be added the practice in a number of countries of kidnapping and changing the identity of children of political dissidents. In order to respond to these types of repression which affect the very fabric of family life, knowledge is key. Hence, it is in connection with disappearances that the most explicit reference to the right to the truth in a human rights treaty has been made. Article 24(2) of the International Convention for the Protection of All Persons from Enforced Disappearances adopted in December 2006 provides that "each victim has the right to know the truth regarding the circumstances of the enforced disappearance, the progress and results of the investigation and the fate of the disappeared person."[52]

The military dictatorship of the juntas in Argentina was known for its repression through torture and forced disapperances. It collapsed in 1983 and the country transitioned to democracy under President Raúl Alfonsín. In 1984 and 1985 Argentina held criminal trials of nine senior junta members and five were convicted. However, when more junior officers began to be targeted for prosecution, the military expressed its discontent with the process and attempted a coup. President Alfonsín responded by granting amnesty to officers through the Full Stop Law of 1986 and the Law of Due Obedience of 1987. In 1990, his successor, President Carlos Menem, pardoned those who had been convicted and were still in prison.

In Arendtian terms, during the years of the "dirty war," Argentina was subjected to an organized lie, which prevented the revelation of information and public discussion of the fate of tens of thousands of disappeared. This organized lying continued in a different way, well after Argentina became a democracy, protected by the general amnesty laws. A number of scholars have described how, in the face of this organized lie, coalitions of local and international NGOs as well as local, foreign, and regional courts and politicians, drove what Naomi Roht-Arriaza has called "wedges" into the Full Stop and Due Obedience laws, exploiting loophooles and exerting pressure on the Argentine government until these laws were set aside and declared unconstitutional by the president and the Supreme Court.[53] What is interesting for our purposes is that in the struggle to defy this organized lie, the coalition of civil society, courts, and politicians has legalized the truth to an unprecedented extent, destroying on its way important individual legal rights as well as endangering political debate.

We can identify three legal campaigns that contributed to the increased legalization of the truth in Argentina.

Habeas Data

As the amnesty laws blocked trials for most human rights violations, the relatives of victims asked the courts to develop legal proceedings aimed at uncovering the truth about the fate and whereabouts of the disappeared. In 1995, in the Lapaco case, family members, supported by local and international human rights groups, presented the first petition arguing that although the amnesty laws had blocked criminal proceedings, they had a right to obtain information from state agencies and to access the remains of their loved ones.[54] Argentine first-instance and appeals courts, relying in part on the Inter-American Court of Human Rights' jurisprudence,[55] agreed, establishing that since the right to mourn the dead is a fundamental need in all human cultures, the state has an obligation to investigate disappearances even if because of the amnesty no one can be prosecuted and punished in a criminal trial on the basis of the information uncovered.[56] However, on appeal the Supreme Court refused to recognize this right, holding that the only point of an investigation is criminal prosecution.[57] In response the families turned to the Inter-America Commission on Human Rights, whose pressure led to a 1999 settlement in which the Argentine government agreed to adopt the necessary laws to grant federal courts jurisdiction "in all cases to determine the truth regarding the fate of persons who disappeared prior to December 10, 1983."[58]

Truth Trials

The Lapaco settlement made it an official obligation on the Argentine state to continue with judicial investigations. This paved the way for what has come to be known as "truth trials" – judicial investigations not involving the establishment of criminal responsibility. These unprecedented court hearings tried to establish what had happened to the disappeared and who was responsible, without there being a defendant.[59] Thousands of such hearings were held, and judges proactively sought out new evidence, visiting torture sites and subpoenaing former and current political and military officers suspected of crimes. And since they could not be formally accused (due to the amnesty laws) they were summoned to testify as ordinary witnesses not enjoying the right against self-incrimination granted to defendants in Argentine criminal law.[60] As witnesses, if they failed to appear they could be arrested and imprisoned for perjury or contempt of court. Later, when the immunity laws were annulled, evidence gathered during truth trials has been used in criminal proceedings, raising questions of due process.[61]

Illegal Adoptions

The lack of criminal trials led to a third innovative legal challenge to the amnesty laws by the organization of the Grandmothers of the Plaza de Mayo to hold military officers responsible for the kidnapping and identity change of the children of the disappeared. According to the organization of Grandmothers, over four hundred children had been kidnapped by the military, either from their homes or after they were born in detention, their identities changed, and handed over to families of sympathizers with the regime. They argued that because the crimes of kidnapping minors and changing their identities had not been covered by the amnesty laws, they were not blocked from pursuing justice for these crimes in a court of law.[62]

The issue of stolen children not only led to new criminal prosecutions. In 2009 legislation was passed to allow the courts to obtain DNA samples from suspected children of the disappeared even against their consent, leading to court injunctions against suspected kidnapped children.[63] Thus, for example, Marcela and Felipe Noble Herrera, heirs to Argentina's largest media empire, who were adopted in 1976, have been subject to a decade of pressure to submit to DNA testing, and have had their home searched by the police to seize personal belongings and conduct a DNA test.[64] Other children who were not interested in knowing their origins have fled the country, to find themselves the subject of extradition proceedings. In the process of trying to establish the "truth" of their identity against their will, their basic rights to privacy and dignity have been infringed, as well as their right not to know their biological origins.

The case of the kidnapped children put the Argentine system in the untenable postion of holding people criminally responsible for kidnapping a child but not for the more serious original crime of murder and disappearance of the parents. As a result, in 2005 the Supreme Court found the amnesty laws unlawful and null.[65]

What began as a search for the "factual truth" about the fate of the disappeared – under the legal theory that in order to determine whether the amnesty laws applied, a court should first determine the truth about the alleged crime – turned into a search for loopholes in the amnesty laws to prosecute illegal adoptions of the children of the disappeared, and ended in nullifying the amnesty laws and opening a new wave of criminal trials twenty years after the events.

The invocation of the "right to truth," its classification as a private right of the families of the victims, and in particular its depoliticization in relation to "innocent victims" such as the children of the disappeared helped mobilize the judicial system, and ultimately the political system as a whole, in resisting an organized lie. However, it did not come without a cost. Ironically, a campaign that was carried out in the name of restoring the rule of law ended up undermining basic guarantees of the rule of law. As a result of the proceedings surrounding stolen children, the criminal justice system became a participant in human rights violations. The search for the truth, conceptualized as an absolute, autonomous human right, gradually released all restrictions intended to ensure basic civil liberties – statutes of limitations, the prohibition of double jeopardy, the non-retroactivity of penal law, and consent requirements to infringing privacy.

This not only affected the legal system in Argentina, but also the possibility of political judgment about Argentina's "dirty war." The unique path that Argentina took has made the mothers and grandmothers the symbol of the struggle, and the search for the identity of the "stolen children" became a metaphor for the search for a new national identity.[66] This debate was cast as a search for factual truth that would obey a high standard of genetic and scientific certainty. It led to discussions of the complex issue of identity in biological and essentialist terms.[67] Likewise, since the search for "truth" was depoliticized, it was used to trump political contestation about the proper path to the future.

How can Arendt's writing help us understand the case of Argentina, and the broader problem it exemplifies? The military regime in

Argentina arose against the background of a conflict among political groups. However, since the repressive regime had constantly accused its leftist political opponents of subversion, civil society organizations saw the need to develop an alternative discourse in their struggle against the regime.[68] Accordingly, the Mothers of Plaza de Mayo developed an apolitical discourse by resorting to human rights and the legal arena. Their legal battle to expose the facts about abductions was to fulfil the important "truth-telling" function identified by Arendt. To do so, they presented the victims of the kidnappings as innocent people and played down the disappeareds' political agency. Later, the Grandmothers focused on the ultimate innocent victim – children – abducted illegally and adopted by families affiliated with the military. The turn to law helped civil society organizations reframe the public debate from one that blamed the victim to one that discussed and exposed the crimes of the previous regime. It thus helped expose the organized lie of the regime.

However, there was a price in terms of political judgment. What we see in the case of Argentina is a pathological situation in which an organized lie turned truth telling, or the search for the truth, into an act of political opposition. Eventually the legal system was enlisted in this struggle. Yet contrary to Arendt's suggestion to use the truth as a sort of boundary or limit on political discourse, in Argentina the truth filled the space of political discourse. Instead of the political community engaging in reflective judgment about its dark past, Argentine political discourse reproduced the binary understanding of society prevalent under the military regime. Already a decade after the junta trials, Jaime Malamud-Goti, presidential adviser to Alfonsín and one of the architects of the trial, came to regret using criminal trials to address Argentina's violent past. In his view, by focusing the blame on the military and obscuring the responsibility of civil society for complicity, criminal trials reproduced the friend/enemy logic of the dirty war and therefore reinforced authoritarianism.[69] The binary structure of criminal law polarized society, with each side striving to occupy the position of perfect victim and demonize the opponent.[70] The legalism of the new politics also created the false impression that law – and in particular criminal law – has clear rules to address situations of political repression, and that all that is needed to address the past is to hold criminal trials. With the emergence of a human right to the truth, the legalization of politics went even further. Politics were reshaped as biopolitics, founded upon the search for genetic and scientific truth, with the expectation that this sort of truth would bring certainty and define political identity. In other words, the legalization of the truth was used to circumvent the difficult task of political judgment of the grey area of complicity with the military regime in which much of Argentine civil society was implicated to different degrees.

Arendt's writing on the Eichmann trial and on reflective judgment helps to point to the difficulty in addressing the grey area, with its banal perpetrators and less than pure victims (requiring reflective judgment), by means of criminal law (a form of determinative judgment). But as I have shown, the overtaking of politics by legalism was unique in Argentina, in that it operated through the formulation of a new human right – the right to the truth. To understand the dangers created by the conceptualization of the truth as a human right, I turned to Arendt's essay, "Truth and Politics," where she assigns factual, scientific truth a legitimate role as basis or boundary on political discourse. Reading that essay alongside her writing on the importance of non-determinative, reflective judgment exposes the danger of the truth taking over political dialogue and judgment, especially in a society facing the difficult transition to democracy.

The debate about abducted children in Argentina clearly demonstrates these dangers. The Grandmothers' campaign offers scientific truth as a simple solution – all that is needed to find the "real" identity of the children is to have a genetic test and return the children to their biological families. However, such an approach ignores the more complex understanding of identity as determined not once and for all at some point in time but as a process built on relationships. Some of the individuals who refused to undergo genetic testing in Argentina introduced such a concept of relational identity.[71] However, the courts found it hard to accept such a position in criminal proceedings against the person charged with complicity in the alleged illegal adoption. The problem became worse when the struggle for the identity of the children came to be understood as a symbol of the broader struggle over the definition of Argentina's identity. The analogy made was that just as a simple genetic test could return abducted children to their families, democracy could be brought back to Argentina simply by ascertaining the factual, genetic truth about the abducted children and prosecuting the abductors. Such an approach not only ignores the important role played by civil society in sustaining the military regime. It also ignores that while facts are important limitations on what can be said in political debate – "the ground on which we stand, and the sky that stretches above us"[72] – they cannot substitute for political judgment. Such judgment, as Arendt explained in her lectures on Kant, requires a process of social dialogue in which individuals seek to understand the different points of view of other members of society. Only by engaging in such a process, can a person or a society judge the very large grey area of cooperation.[73] In this sense, the real threat to democratization is determinative judgment, when it replaces reflective judgment and takes over political discourse.

Conclusion

I suggested at the beginning of this chapter that seeing Arendt's legal theory as legalistic does not do justice to her position in *Eichmann in Jerusalem*. As an alternative, I recommended reading her writings from the perspective of an ongoing conflict between truth and three fields: law, moral philosophy, and politics. This broader perspective allows us to see that the real question at the centre of Arendt's enquiry is not law as such but how to preserve a sphere for political judgment. From this perspective, we can see the relevance of Arendt's writings today when the issue of transitional justice and international criminal law stands at the centre of debate for the international community.

Contrary to Arendt's predictions about the irrelevance of the Eichmann trial as a precedent for international law, it was the Israeli prosecution's view about the expanded role of criminal trials to include didactic goals that shaped international criminal trials since the 1990s. International law in recent decades has gradually released itself from a narrow conception of criminal law, to promote the rights of the victim and adopt the broad didactic goals of clarifying historical truth and shaping collective memory.[74] However, paradoxically, this process has been accompanied by the growth of a new legalism in international law, one that avoids the need to recognize a space of (non-determinative) judgment.[75] This legalism can be seen in the dominance of the human rights discourse over political discourse, the takeover by legal actors of truth commissions and other transitional justice institutions, and the rise of a transnational struggle, led by international and local human rights NGOS, to fight "impunity" through criminal prosecutions, making amnesties and other "softer" ways of reckoning with the past extremely difficult to justify. In the process, the discretion of the local political community to choose how to address and judge its past has been seriously curtailed.

I pointed to the growth of the "human right to the truth" as the latest trend in this process. The danger, as Arendt indicated towards the end of her essay "Truth and Politics," is the collapse of boundaries between legal, political, and scientific discourses, and the takeover of one kind of judgment (legal determinative judgment) over politics as a whole. A universal model of transitional justice imposed by international bodies prevents the creation of spaces in which different communities can engage in reflective judgment – a judgment that recognizes the element of subjective choice, as well as the need to have a discussion that takes into account different viewpoints in the community in the transition to democracy. Here we see the real conflict between truth and politics. As Arendt argued, there need not be a conflict between factual truth and political discourse in principle, as opinions must be based on facts, and facts must be used to limit interpretation.[76] However, according to Arendt there is an inherent conflict in terms of process, between a coercive method based on the truth and a persuasive method that relies on opinions. Here lies the lure of the discourse of truth, as well as the great threat to political debate and judgment.

NOTES

1 תודות. The Israel Science Foundation supported this research under Grant No. 1173/15. I deeply thank my research assistants Natalie Rose Davidson, Rachel Klagsbrun and Miryam Wijler for their help in writing this chapter.
2 Hannah Arendt, *Eichmann in Jerusalem: A Report on the Banality of Evil* (New York: Penguin, 2006), 9, 19, 206–19.
3 Note, however, that Wilson identifies a rise and fall in didactic objectives, and sees the Milošević trial as a turning point. Richard Ashby Wilson, *Writing History in International Criminal Trials* (Cambridge: Cambridge University Press, 2011).
4 According to the Inter-American Commission on Human Rights, "the right to know the truth with respect to the facts that gave rise to the serious human rights violations … constitutes an obligation that the State must satisfy with respect to the victims' relatives and society in general." See *Ignacio Ellacria et al. v. El Salvador*, Inter-American Commission Case 10.488, Report 136/99 (22 December 1999), para. 221; The European Court of Human Rights, the African Commission on Human and Peoples' Rights and the Inter-American Commission on Human Rights have all recognized in one form or another the right to truth of family members of victims disappeared, tortured, or otherwise abused by the government.

For a survey of these bodies' jurisprudence concerning the right to truth, see: Thomas M. Antkowiak, "Truth as Right and Remedy in International Human Rights Experience," *Michigan Journal of International Law* 23 (2002): 977–1014, and Yasmin Naqvi, "The Right to Truth in International Law: Fact or Fiction?" *International Review of the Red Cross* 88, no. 862 (2006): 245–73; The UN has also recognized the human right to truth. For example, the "updated set of principles for the protection and promotion of human rights through action to combat impunity," adopted by the UN in 2005, declares that "irrespective of any legal proceedings, victims and their families have the imprescriptible right to know the truth about the circumstances in which violations took place and, in the event of death or disappearance, the victims' fate." See Commission on Human rights, *Updated Set of Principles for the Protection and Promotion of Human Rights through Action to Combat Impunity*, Report of Diane Orentlicher, UN Doc. E/CN.4/2005/102/Add.1 (2005).

5 Arendt, *Eichmann in Jerusalem*, 19.

6 Arendt writes: "Mr. Hausner had gathered together a 'tragic multitude' of sufferers." *Eichmann in Jerusalem*, 209.

7 See Shoshana Felman, *The Juridical Unconscious: Trials and Traumas in the Twentieth Century* (Cambridge, MA: Harvard University Press, 2002), 120–1; Lawrence Douglas, *The Memory of Judgment* (New Haven and London: Yale University Press, 2005), writes that "Arendt's argument presupposed a strict separation between the legal and the extralegal, between the rule of law and the interests of collective instruction" (2). Both Felman and Douglas are critical of Arendt's legalism.

8 Judith N. Shklar, *Legalism: Law, Morals, and Political Trials* (Cambridge, MA: Harvard University Press, 1964), 1.

9 Arendt, *Eichmann in Jerusalem*, 115–26.

10 Leora Bilsky, "Between Justice and Politics: The Competition of Storytellers in the Eichmann Trial," in *Hannah Arendt in Jerusalem*, ed. Steven E. Aschheim, 232–51 (Berkeley: University of California Press, 2001), 236.

11 Arendt, *Eichmann in Jerusalem*, 4–5.

12 For elaboration see Leora Bilsky, "The Eichmann Trial – Toward a Jurisprudence of Eyewitness Testimonies of Atrocity?" *Journal of International Criminal Justice* 12 (2014): 27–57.

13 Arendt, *Eichmann in Jerusalem*, 253–79. For elaboration, see Leora Bilsky, *Transformative Justice: Israeli Identity on Trial* (Ann Arbor: Michigan University Press, 2004), 117–44. For Arendt's view on universal jurisdiction see Leora Bilsky, "The Eichmann Trial and the Legacy of Jurisdiction," in *Politics in Dark Times: Encounters with Hannah Arendt*, ed. Seyla Benhabib (Cambridge and New York: Cambridge University Press, 2010), 198–218.

14 Arendt refused to see them as "pure victims" who clearly fall on the "white" side of the moral spectrum. Rather, she saw the novelty of the totalitarian system as involving the victims in their own destruction, so that they become morally implicated. Arendt, *Eichmann in Jerusalem*, 125–6. For elaboration see Erica Bouris, *Complex Political Victims* (Bloomfield, CT: Kumarian Press, 2007), 53–73.
15 Arendt, *Eichmann in Jerusalem*, 276–7.
16 Hannah Arendt, *Lectures on Kant's Political Philosophy*, ed. Ronald Beiner (Chicago: University of Chicago Press, 1989)
17 For further discussion of the trial see Bilsky, *Transformative Justice*, 169–97.
18 Arendt, *Eichmann in Jerusalem*, 292–3.
19 Ibid., 293.
20 Ibid., 126.
21 Immanuel Kant, *Groundwork of the Metaphysics of Morals*, trans. Mary Gregor (Cambridge: Cambridge University Press, 1998), 31; Ak. 4:421.
22 Arendt, *Eichmann in Jerusalem*, 135–6.
23 Cited at ibid., 136.
24 Ibid., 136–7.
25 Ibid., 137.
26 Ibid.
27 Ibid., 146–7.
28 "There remains, however, one fundamental problem, which was implicitly present in all these postwar trials and which must be mentioned here because it touches upon one of the central moral questions of all time, namely upon the nature and function of human judgment. *What we have demanded in these trials, where the defendants had committed 'legal' crimes, is that human beings be capable of telling right from wrong even when all they have to guide them is their own judgment, which, moreover, happens to be completely at odds with what they must regard as the unanimous opinion of all those around them.* Those few who were still able to tell right from wrong went really only by their own judgments, and they did so freely; there were no rules to be abided by, under which the particular cases with which they were confronted could be subsumed. They had to decide each instance as it arose, because no rules existed for the unprecedented." Ibid., 294–5 (emphasis added).
29 Arendt suggests that Eichmann's conviction is legitimate on the grounds that he had played a part, and therefore supported a policy of mass murder. The fact that many others would have done the same thing in his position does not lessen his guilt according to Arendt. A crime like the one Eichmann supported wrongs humanity in such a way that it cannot be left unanswered. Under such extreme circumstances, the mere participation of

Eichmann in this new kind of crime is reason enough to convict him even if he did not have the proper mens rea. Ibid., 277–9.

30 Rational truths include mathematical, scientific, and philosophical truths and are differentiated from factual truths. Hannah Arendt, "Truth and Politics," in Hannah Arendt, *The Portable Hannah Arendt*, ed. Peter Baehr (New York: Penguin Books, 2000), 548.

31 Ibid., 558–9. According to Arendt, the philosopher, as a thinking being, is concerned with keeping the conditions for his philosophizing, while the citizen is concerned with the world and public welfare. The Socratic argument says "it is better to be at odds with the whole world than to be at odds with and contradicted by himself." Such contradiction would jeopardize the conditions of philosophizing since this act is understood as dialogue of one with oneself, which requires a basic agreement between the "two sides." But if one cares about the world the argument doesn't work because there's another way out of the contradiction.

32 Ibid., 559.

33 Arendt, *Lectures on Kant's Political Philosophy*, 66.

34 Ibid.

35 Ibid., 66–7; emphasis in original.

36 Ibid., 67.

37 Arendt writes: "You see that *impartiality* is obtained by taking the viewpoints of others into account; impartiality is not the result of some higher standpoint that would then settle the dispute by being altogether above the melée" (ibid., 42; emphasis in original). She continues: "It is accomplished by 'comparing our judgment with the possible rather than the actual judgments of others, and by putting ourselves in the place of any other man.' The faculty that makes this possible is called imagination." Ibid., 43.

38 Arendt, *Eichmann in Jerusalemm*, 276.

39 Ibid., 47–8.

40 Ibid., 51.

41 Ibid., 50. This contrasts with the attitude of officer Avner Less. A new documentary film reveals the process that Captain Less underwent while investigating Eichmann. Through Less's private diary the film shows his struggle in attempting to understand Eichman's point of view, and his engagement with what Arendt called "enlarged mentality." See *Bureau 06*, directed by Yoav Halevy (Israel: Makor Fund for Israeli Films; Open Doors Films, 2013).

42 Arendt wrote earlier that "the ideal subject of totalitarian rule is not the convinced Nazi or the dedicated communist, but the people for whom

the distinction between fact and fiction, true and false, no longer exists." Hannah Arendt, *The Origins of Totalitarianism* (San Diego, New York, and London: Harvest, 1973), 474.

43 "By using the Latin term [*sensus communis*] Kant indicated that here he means something different: an extra sense – like an extra mental capability – that fits us into community. [...] it is the capability by which men are distinguished from animals and from gods. It is the very humanity of man that is manifest in this sense." Arendt, *Lectures on Kant's Political Philosophy*, 70.

It is interesting to note the way in which Arendt contrasts a "common sense" with a "private sense," which marks the state of insanity: "Kant ... remarks in his *Anthropology* that insanity consists in having lost this common sense that enables us to judge as spectators; and the opposite of it is a *sensus privatus*, a private sense, which he also calls 'logical *Eignensinn*,' implying that our logical faculty, the faculty that enables us to draw conclusions from premises, could indeed function without communication – except that then, namely, if insanity has caused the loss of common sense, it would lead to insane results precisely because it has separated itself from the experience that can be valid and validated only in the presense of others" (ibid., 64). This can also explain why Arendt turned away from rational truth as the basis for moral judgment and looked for a conception of judgment based on plurality.

44 Arendt, "Truth and Politics," 545.

45 Ibid., 571–2.

46 Ibid., 553.

47 "We must now turn our attention to the relatively recent phenomenon of mass manipulation of fact and opinion as it has become evident in the rewriting of history, in image-making, and in actual government policy" (ibid., 564). "The traditional lie concerned only particulars and was never meant to deceive literally everybody; it was directed at the enemy and was meant to deceive only him. These two limitations restricted the injury inflicted upon truth ... both these mitigating circumstances of the old art of lying are noticeably absent from the manipulation of facts that confronts us today" (ibid., 565).

48 Ibid., 564.

49 Ibid., 569.

50 Arendt explicitly refers to herself in these terms: "The hostility against me is a hostility against someone who tells the truth on a factual level, and not against someone who has ideas which are in conflict with those commonly held." Carol Brightman, ed., *Between Friends: The Correspondence of Hannah*

Arendt and Mary McCarthy 1949–1975 (New York: Harcourt, Brace, 1995), 148.

51 See, for example, Isaiah Trunk, *Judenrat* (Jerusalem: Yad Vashem Press, 1979) [Hebrew]. Yerushalmi comments that "what is disturbing in Arendt's wholesale condemnation of the Jewish Councils is her uncharacteristic refusal to confront complexity, nuance, context and the historical background which she herself had elucidated in her earlier work." Yosef Hayim Yerushalmi, *Servants of Kings and Not Servants of Servants: Some Aspects of the Political History of the Jews* (Atlanta, GA: Tam Institute for Jewish Studies, Emory University, 2005), 22.

52 G.A. res. 61/177, *International Convention for the Protection of All Persons from Enforced Disappearance*, U.N. Doc. A/RES/61/177 (2006).

53 Naomi Roht-Arriaza, *The Pinochet Effect: Transnational Justice in the Age of Human Rights* (Philadelphia: University of Pennsylvania Press, 2005), 113. See also, Kathryn Sikking and Carrie Booth Walling, "Argentina's Contribution to Global Trends in Transitionl Justice," in *Transitional Justice in the Twenty-First Century: Beyond Truth versus Justice*, ed. Naomi Roht-Arriaza and Javier Mariezcurrena (Cambridge: Cambridge University Press, 2006), 301–24.

54 The petitioners had argued that "the right to the truth in this case means nothing else but the obligation on the part of the State to use all means at its disposal to determine the fate of the disappeared between 1976 and 1983." Cited in Supreme Court Decision in the Lapacó Case. *Suarez Mason, Carlos Guillermo s/ homicidio, privacion ilegal de la libertad, etc.* S. 1085. XXXI, Argentina: Corte Suprema de Justicia (13 August 1998), 3.

55 Notably the Velásquez case: *Velásquez Rodríguez Case*, Inter-Am.Ct.H.R. (Ser. C) No. 4 (1988), Inter-American Court of Human Rights (IACrtHR), (29 July 1988).

56 Roht-Arriaza, *The Pinochet Effect*, 101.

57 "Given that investigation proceedings are intended to determine the existence of a punishable fact and discover its authors … it is not permissible to conduct an investigation in the current state of the present case, as such an investigation would exceed its procedural purpose." Supreme Court Decision in Lapacó Case, *Suarez Mason, Carlos Guillermo s/ homicidio, privacion ilegal de la libertad, etc.* S. 1085. XXXI, Argentina: Corte Suprema de Justicia (13 August 1998), 1.

58 See *Carmen Aguiar De Lapacó – Argentina*. Inter-America Human Rights Commission Case 12.059, Report No. 70/99, (February 29, 2000), para. 17.

59 See Elena Maculan, "Prosecuting International Crimes at the National Level: Lessons from the Argentine 'Truth-Finding Trials,'" *Utrecht Law Review* 8 (2012): 106–21.

60 This constituted a gross violation of due process, since despite the amnesty in Argentina at the time, foreign courts such as those in Spain began prosecuting Argentine officers on the basis of universal jurisdiction. Note however that the practice was not uniform. Some tribunals treated the alleged perpetrators as defendants in criminal trials and accorded them the right against self-incrimination, while others regarded them as witnesses (since formally they were not defendants, and the impunity laws were blocking their indictment). Ibid., 112–13.

61 Ibid., 118.

62 Roht-Arriaza, *The Pinochet Effect*, 108–13.

63 Elizabeth B. King, "A Conflict of Interests: Privacy, Truth, and Compulsory DNA Testing for Argentina's Children of the Disappeared," *Cornell International Law Journal* 44 (2011): 535–68, 540–6.

64 Ibid., 536–7.

65 *Case of Simón, Julio Héctor y otros s/ privación ilegítima de la libertad, etc.*, No 17.768, Argentina: Corte Suprema de Justicia (14 June 2005).

66 According to Gandsman "these campaigns do not simply aim to generate doubt about individual biological identities but intend to raise much larger questions about national belonging." Ari Gandsman, ""Do You Know Who You Are?" Radical Existential Doubt and Scientific Certainty in the Search of the Kidnapped Children of the Disappeared in Argentina," *ETHOS* 37, no. 4 (2009): 441–65, 443.

67 Ari Gandsman, "A Prick of a Needle Can Do No Harm: Compulsory Extraction of Blood in the Search for the Children of Argentina's Disappeared," *Journal of Latin American and Caribbean Anthropology* 14 (2009): 162–84.

68 Patricia Naftali, "The Subtext of New Human Right Claims: A Socio-Legal Journey into the 'Right to Truth,'" in *Diverse Engagement: Drawing in the Margins: Proceedings of the University of Cambridge Interdisciplinary Graduate Conference June 2010*, ed. Matthew Frenchet al. (Cambridge: Cambridge University, 2010), 118.

69 Jaime Malamud Goti and Libbet Crandon Malamud, *Game without End: State Terror and the Politics of Justice* (Norman: University of Oklahoma Press, 1996).

70 See generally Leebaw, who argues that the legalism of international criminal law and the restorative justice paradigm of truth commissions both prevent transitional justice measures from addressing the grey zone between perpetrators and victims. Bronwyn Leebaw, *Judging State-Sponsored Violence, Imagining Political Change* (Cambridge: Cambridge University Press, 2011).

71 Noa Vaisman, "Shedding Our Selves: Perspectivism, the Bounded Subject and the Nature–Culture Divide," in *Biosocial Becomings: Integrating Social and Biological Anthropology*, ed. Tim Ingold and Gisli Palsson (Cambridge: Cambridge University Press, 2013), 106–22.

72 Arendt, "Truth and Politics," 574.

73 In "Truth and Politics" Arendt explains: "Political thought is representative. I form opinion by considering a given issue from different viewpoints, by making present to my mind the standpoints of those who are absent; that is, I represent them … It is this capacity for 'enlarged mentality' that enables men to judge; as such it was discovered by Kant in the first part of his *Critique of Judgment*, though he did not recognize the political and moral implications of his discovery" (ibid., 556).

74 On the recognition of victims' rights alongside defendants' rights in international criminal law see T. Markus Funk, *Victims' Rights and Advocacy at the International Criminal Court* (Oxford and New York: Oxford University Press, 2010).

Central writers in the field today view the didactic purpose of the trial as the main, and sometimes even the ultimate, goal of the legal process. See Lawrence Douglas, "Shattering Nuremberg: Toward a Jurisprudence of Atrocity," *Harvard International Review* (21 November 2007), accessed 12 December 2013, http://hir.harvard.edu/shattering-nuremberg ; Leora Bilsky, *Transformative Justice*; Mark Osiel, *Mass Atrocity, Collective Memory and the Law* (New Brunswick, NJ: Transaction, 1997); Shklar, *Legalism*; and Robert D. Sloane, "The Expressive Capacity of International Punishment: The Limits of the National Law Analogy and the Potential of International Criminal Law," *Stanford Journal of International Law* 43 (2007): 39–94.

75 McEvoy points to this paradox; see Kieran McEvoy, "Letting Go of Legalism: Developing a Thicker Version of Transitional Justice," in *Transitional Justice from Below*, ed. Kieran McEvoy and Lorna McGregor (Oxford and Portland: Hart, 2008), 15–47. Leebaw, *Judging State-Sponsored Violence*, warns about the effects of such legalism on narrowing the space for judgment.

76 Arendt, "Truth and Politics," 555.

Chapter Eight

Arendt, German Law, and the Crime of Atrocity

LAWRENCE DOUGLAS

Arendt and the Crime of Atrocity

Hannah Arendt famously faulted the Eichmann trial as never rising "to the challenge of the unprecedented."[1] At Nuremberg, jurists had forged a new incrimination tasked with naming and condemning the unprecedented nature of Nazi atrocities. While it is true that Nuremberg failed to use the charge of "crimes against humanity" as robustly as some might have hoped, limiting its application to atrocities connected to the Nazis' war of aggression, the international tribunal nonetheless pioneered the notion of crimes that constituted an attack "against the human status" and "upon human diversity as such."[2] Alas, the Jerusalem trial frittered away the opportunity to build on Nuremberg's conceptual breakthrough. In trying Eichmann for, in the first order, "crimes against the Jewish people," the Israelis fundamentally misconstrued the nature of the crimes of the Nazis' "specialist in Jewish affairs."

Whether we agree with Arendt's critique or not, we must ask *why* Arendt believed so strongly in the necessity of framing the proper legal idiom capable of capturing the nature of state-sponsored atrocity. She does not, for example, insist that the correct idiom is essential to rendering legal justice in a conventional sense; she never seriously doubts the justice of Eichmann's conviction, nor does she question the justice of imposing the death penalty. In the case of the Frankfurt-Auschwitz trial (1963–5), in which twenty-two camp functionaries were charged with committing or aiding and abetting murder under conventional German law, Arendt likewise never questions the justice of the convictions; if anything, she laments the handful of acquittals. If judgment framed in wrong or inadequate legal concepts occasions an injustice, it is not an injustice to the accused.

Why, then, the critique of the Eichmann court? Arendt appears to be committed to the position that a court weighing such spectacular crimes must do more than just render justice to the accused. It must also do conceptual justice to the distinctive nature of mass, state-sponsored atrocity. Such trials must frame and deploy the proper legal concepts not in order to adequately judge the accused but to grasp the structure and meaning of an unprecedented phenomenon. At first blush, this concern with using the trial as a tool of conceptual understanding appears to sit uncomfortably with Arendt's louder insistence that the criminal trial must never be used as a history lesson – "the purpose of a trial is to render justice and nothing else; even the noblest of ulterior porose – the 'making of a record of the Hitler regime which would withstand the test of history'… can only detract from the law's main business."[3] Yet it's not clear how seriously we are meant to take this insistence. In her observations towards the end of *Eichmann in Jerusalem* about the vigilante assassins Schalom Schwartzbard and Soghomon Tehlirian, Arendt appears to endorse the idea of deploying history as a defence to criminal charges.[4] Perhaps, then, her concern is meant only to apply to the prosecution's didactic use of history; in any case, the apparent contradiction dissolves when we consider that Arendt's concern is less with the crime of atrocity as an artefact of history, than with a phenomenon that remains present and capable of repetition. This becomes clear toward the end of *Eichmann in Jerusalem* when Arendt writes:

> The unprecedented, once it has appeared, may become a precedent for the future … If genocide is an actual possibility of the future, then no people on earth – least of all, of course, the Jewish people, in Israel or elsewhere – can feel reasonably sure of its continued existence without the help and protection of international law. Success or failure in dealing with the hitherto unprecedented can lie only in the extent to which this dealing may serve as a valid precedent on the road to international penal law.[5]

Only, this statement raises fresh problems. For at the same time that Arendt gives word to the sceptre of genocidal extinction, she also offers a rather conventional if not unconvincing appeal to the legalistic logic of deterrence. What are we to make of this appeal? In "Personal Responsibility under Dictatorship," Arendt notes that legal punishment is typically justified in terms of the "need of society to be protected against the crime, the deterring force of the warning example for the potential criminal, and, finally retributive justice" – only then to observe, "none of these grounds is valid for the punishment of the so-called war criminals."[6] In this essay, written after *Eichmann in Jerusalem* and before her afterword to Bernd Naumann's report on the Frankfurt-Auschwitz trial, Arendt reaches a conclusion that is at once insightful and paradoxical: "Here we are, demanding justice and meting out punishment in accordance with our sense of justice, while, on the other hand, this same sense of justice informs us that all our previous notions about punishment and its justification have failed us."[7]

Arendt's interest in deterrence appears, then, to contradict her position in "Personal Responsibility under Dictatorship' at the same time that it sounds disturbingly naive. Whatever else we might think about Nuremberg, it is quite obvious that it did little to deter Pol Pot, just as the labours of the UN's Yugoslavia and Rwanda tribunals have done little to put a brake on atrocities in Darfur and Syria. As most international prosecutors will readily acknowledge, deterrence remains a rhetorically effective but entirely speculative if not fanciful justification for punishing crimes of atrocity.

I think, then, that we can better understand Arendt's concern with shaping the adequate legal idiom to comprehend crimes of atrocity as born of her belief in the humanizing act of rendering *judgment* – in other words, not as a narrowly instrumental means to some additional goal (deterrence), but as a meaning-sustaining activity in times of crisis. In *Between Past and Future,* Arendt describes the act of judging (*urteilen*) as "one, if not the most important activity in which ... sharing-the-world-with-others comes to pass."[8] It is the task of judgment to grasp and comprehend unprecedented realities without recourse to "reductive commonplaces."[9] Judging makes good on the human project to "begin anew," to fashion fresh standards in the face of "something that has ruined our categories of thought."[10]

This belief in the centrality of judgment to the project of being human is nowhere more remarkably captured than in the last pages of *Eichmann in Jerusalem* in which Arendt assumes the voice of the legal judge, addressing Eichmann in terms that seek to reconcile deliberative judgment (*urteilen*) with the court's verdict (*verurteilen*): "We find that no one, that is, no member of the human race, can be expected to want to share the earth with you."[11] What is remarkable about these words is how they transpose her understanding of judgment as a "sharing-the-world-with-others." As the ultimate refusal to share the world with others, the crime of atrocity demands an act of restorative judgment that both speaks to the perpetrator and ejects him. Such a judgment corrects what Arendt termed the "pernicious … understanding … the common illusion that the crime of murder and the crime of genocide are essentially the same."[12]

The Crime of Atrocity as Ordinary Murder

However critical Arendt was of the Israeli trial, she recognized that German law contributed to this pernicious and common illusion in a far more aggressive manner – at least, when it came to bringing perpetrators of Nazi atrocity to justice. Germany is one of the few countries in the world to have successfully tried and convicted persons for the crime of genocide. These trials, however, are all of recent vintage, involving crimes committed in the Balkans in the 1990s.[13] No perpetrator of Nazi-era atrocities, by contrast, has ever been charged with genocide by a German court, this despite the fact that the incrimination was incorporated into the German legal code in 1954, early in the life of the Federal Republic. German courts are also among the few domestic national courts to have experience with trying persons for crimes against humanity. And yet here we encounter a fresh oddity: these latter trials are all *old* cases, conducted by German courts in occupation zones in the late 1940s. Since the Federal Republic's assumption of sovereignty, no Nazi perpetrator or accomplice has ever stood trial before a domestic court for crimes against humanity or genocide. If Arendt faulted the Israeli court for failing to build on Nuremberg's notion of crimes against humanity, German jurists aggressively repudiated the novel incrimination, insisting that the Nazis' unprecedented acts of state-sponsored atrocity could be adequately addressed through the conventional crime of murder.

This belief was largely born of a misplaced and highly formalistic concern in the early postwar years with the *Rückwirkungsverbot* (the bar against retroactivity).[14] In *Eichmann in Jerusalem*, Arendt rightly argued that *nulla poena sine lege* – no punishment without (pre-existing) law – should be seen as a principle of justice capable of being trumped by superior claims, and not as an absolute limit on sovereign power. Alas, postwar German jurists emphatically rejected this view. Some jurists in the postwar era justifiably associated the complete collapse of liberal legality under Hitler with Nazi jurists' attack on the bar against retroactivity. Carl Schmitt offered the most sweeping and influential attack, arguing in 1935 that *nulla poena* had transformed the German criminal code into a "Magna Carta of criminality," a rigid and ossified thing that could not adapt to changing circumstance and novel challenges.[15] Schmitt's attack resounded in the writings of other Nazi legal theorists, who similarly sought to liberate Nazi jurisprudence from the straitjacket of liberal positivism. In Karl Larenz's influential formulation, the judge was to "recognize the present meaning of the law and thereby assure that no gulf arises between the people and their law."[16] Judges applying the criminal law were encouraged to follow the "sound instincts of the people" (*gesundes Volksempfinden*).[17]

But if German[18] jurists in the postwar period were understandably reluctant to treat the bar against retroactivity with the same cavalier attitude as the Nazis had, their rejection of "crimes against humanity" as an incrimination to be levelled against Nazi perpetrators cannot be explained purely as a jurisprudential matter. Rather, the rejection was of a piece with a larger, in part politically motivated, backlash against Nuremberg and the entire Allies' trial program in Germany. Along with attacking Nuremberg law as retroactive, revanchist German jurists and politicians also consciously instrumentalized the term "war crimes trial," effectively erasing the distinction between acts of extermination and the "excesses" of armed conflict.[19] None of this is all that surprising, inasmuch as the judiciary in the early years of the Federal Republic was stocked with former Nazis.[20] By one estimate, an incredible 80 per cent of the judges in the *Bundesgerichthof*, Germany's highest appellate court, had served in the judiciary or as state officials during the Third Reich.[21] Examples of continuity, or rather, advance, abound. Edmund Mezger, a prominent Nazi jurist who had supported "racial-hygenic measures for the elimination of criminal tribes," retained his prestigious professorship at Munich, and his commentary on the Criminal Code of the Federal Republic became the most popular postwar teaching textbook.[22] Werner Best, the erstwhile in-house counsel to the SS condemned to death in absentia in Denmark, emerged as an influential adviser to the Free Democrats, specializing in questions of Nazi-era crimes (about which he presumably had ample first-hand knowledge).[23] Whether this rapid rehabilitation aided or frustrated the transition to democracy can be debated; as America learned in its disastrous effort to disband Saddam Hussein's army, ambitious campaigns of lustration can create profound power vacuums and resentments in transitional societies. It has become something of shibboleth of the literature of transitional justice that a reckoning with the past is a necessary condition for overcoming the legacy of authoritarianism. And yet avoidance and suppression may perhaps be equally efficacious, at least in the early years of transition. As one prominent German political theorist observed, "The new [German] state had to be constructed against the ideology and politics of National Socialism. It could not be constructed against the majority of the people," who, after all, had been "part of the National Socialist reality."[24]

The legal innovations pioneered at Nuremberg presupposed what Arendt later argued – that ordinary law was incapable of condemning the full range of Nazi atrocity. The German rejection of Nuremberg and the conclusion that prosecutions for crimes against humanity or genocide would violate the bar against retroactivity nonetheless placed the German judiciary in an odd position. (East Germany did not partake in this rejection, though in charging former Nazis with crimes against humanity, the East's trials often amounted to little more than Stalinist shows.)[25] Once German jurists had taken the very incriminations designed to facilitate the prosecution of Nazi exterminators – crimes against humanity and genocide – off the table, the question remained: what charges could be brought? Given the fetishistic attachment of postwar German jurists to the bar against retroactivity, only an incrimination in place during the Third Reich could survive a challenge based on *nulla poena.* In theory, German jurists might have concluded that even the most heinous Nazi atrocities violated *no law* in place at the time; yet such a conclusion, which would have barred *any* prosecution in postwar Germany of even the worst Nazi-era perpetrators, would have made a mockery of the judiciary's effort to rehabilitate itself as an instrument of the rule of law in a fledgling democracy.

And so German jurists relied on the old penal code, and specifically the crime of "murder." On one level, that decision seems straightforward and uncontroversial. After all, "murder" obviously was a crime on the books in the Third Reich, and people had been prosecuted and convicted of murder in the Nazi state under the operative statute. But the conclusion that the statute in place at the time could now be used to prosecute Nazi exterminators was hardly unproblematic. For the argument to work, one had to conclude that those who ordered, organized, and participated in Nazi genocide (and here I'm using genocide as a descriptive, not a legal term) were in violation of German law in place at the time. Whether this was the case has been the source of vehement and continuing debate. Prominent scholars such as Henry Friedländer have insisted, "At no time was it 'legal' to kill Jews or gypsies; no law legalizing such killing was ever promulgated."[26] Others, such as Gerhard Werle, a leading scholar of human rights law, have argued,

"According to the law of the Third Reich, genocide was authorized by law because it was provided legal cover by the will of the political leadership." "In the Third Reich," Werle notes, "the will of the Führer was recognized as a source of law. Regardless of whether it was issued in written or oral form, even a secret order could create and alter law."[27] Werle's argument recalls Schmitt's formulation from 1935, "*Das Gesetz ist Wille und Plan des Führers*" ("Law is the will and plan of the Führer")[28] – but of course towards a very different end, as Werle's point is to show that it is "historically false and juridically a fiction" to believe that the legal standards of "*damals*" (back then) could supply a proper ground for prosecutions in the Federal Republic.[29] By reminding us of the radical jurisprudential challenge posed by what Jaspers called the *Verbrecherstaat* ("criminal state"), Werle insists that only special law, such as that pioneered at Nuremberg, could enable adequate German prosecutions.[30] Werle reminds us of the absurdity of the claim that in ordering or approving acts of extermination, Hitler made himself a criminal under the very law of which he was the ultimate source and mouthpiece. Such an argument conveniently obscures the power of the *Verbrecherstaat* to overwrite and pervert the content of law.

And yet it was precisely this juridical fiction that supplied the foundation for German prosecutions of Nazi criminals. German criminal law, and German law alone, provided the basis for the punishment of Nazi crimes by German courts.[31] The consequences of this approach were far-reaching, both conceptually and practically. As a conceptual matter, this meant that all Nazi crimes, including acts of extermination and genocide, would be treated as "ordinary crimes," no different, except perhaps in scope, from acts of ordinary murder. The fact that such crimes were sponsored by the state would, so the argument went, create no obstacle to prosecution, as the state, it was assumed, was acting in violation of its own valid legal norms when it authorized, organized, and conducted its exterminatory practices. Thus, although the state was found in violation of its own legal norms, the underlying laws of the Reich were "normalized and validated" by this approach.[32]

And so German courts digested acts of state-sponsored genocide through the category of conventional murder. Indeed, after 1960, murder was the *only* charge that could be brought against former Nazis, as the statute of limitations had tolled for all other crimes committed during the Third Reich. Even murder had been controlled by a prescriptive period, which was lifted only thanks to a series of stopgap measures by a German parliament ultimately unwilling to face the international opprobrium and internal rancour that would have resulted from letting the statute of limitations expire on all Nazi-era crimes.[33] Still, the need to treat acts of state-sponsored atrocity as no different from simple murder created immense problems for prosecutors. Investigations were abandoned midstream, charges were brought but later dismissed, trials that did go forward often resulted in bewildering acquittals or frustratingly lenient sentences, and the rare stiff sentence rarely escaped reduction or commutation.

Complicating everything was the extreme and bewildering subjectivity of the doctrine that distinguished between a perpetrator (*Täter*) of murder and a mere accessory (*Gehilfe*). As Werle has put it, the doctrine established a lapidary rule: "He who executed an order is an accessory."[34] Otto Bradfisch was a commander of an extermination unit (*Einsatzgruppe*) responsible for murdering some fifteen thousand Jewish men, women, and children, many of whom he shot personally. Tried by German authorities in Munich, Bradfisch was convicted as an accessory. The result was typical. Of the former members of *Einsatzgruppen* (mobile extermination units) convicted in German courts, 90 per cent were found to have acted as accessories.[35] Equally dreary examples abound in cases involving death camp functionaries. Gustav Münzberger was an SS guard at Treblinka responsible for herding Jews into the gas chamber. In one documented instance, Münzberger shot and killed a mother and her two children who could not fit into the packed chamber. Nonetheless, the court reasoned that although fanatically dedicated to Hitler, Münzberger had not internalized the "will of the perpetrator" and so had acted as an accessory. Alois Häfele was an SS *Untersturmführer* (second lieutenant) at Chelmno, where he helped organize the camp and had personally shoved victims into the gas vans. Because he lacked the "intentions of the perpetrator," he was convicted as an accessory. Robert Mulka was the camp adjutant at Auschwitz, a senior position indeed, who along with twenty-one other camp functionaries was tried at the famous Frankfurt-Auschwitz trial. Supplied with evidence that Mulka had ordered the immediate execution of a prisoner who had conversed with a Jew who had just alighted at the train ramp at Birkenau, the trial court concluded, "By means of the deterring punishment of the prisoner, Mulka wanted to assure the frictionless accomplishment of the ordered extermination action, for which he was responsible."[36] In a different normative universe, this sentence might serve as a prelude to convicting Mulka as a perpetrator of murder. Instead, it parsed his conviction as an accessory. Startling as these results sound, they were made possible if not inevitable by the view that the killer who fires the weapon is not a murderer, unless he acts out of "inner conviction" or some other such subjective agreement with the regime's genocidal politics.

Who, then, was a perpetrator? When it came to the main perpetrators, German law treated the Holocaust as the work of six or seven men: Hitler, Himmler, Heydrich (also at times Kaltenbrunner), Göring, Otto Globocnik, and Christian Wirth. Because German law treated the follower of an order as an accessory, it was well-nigh impossible to convict a "desk killer" as a perpetrator; had, for example, Eichmann been tried in Germany, as numerous commentators hoped and urged, he might well have been convicted as an accessory.[37] Indeed, it was difficult to charge bureaucrats with any crime; they had not killed with their own hand so could not have acted cruelly or treacherously, and had had few opportunities to evince base motives. All this became moot after 1968, as in that year Germany passed a law that *inadvertently* amnestied all so-called desk killers.[38] At the time, German prosecutors were preparing a massive case against former functionaries associated with the *Reichssicherheitshauptamt* (Reich Security Main Office), a gigantic bureaucracy that oversaw the *Einsatzgruppen* and much of the implementation of the Holocaust. What would have been the largest atrocity proceeding in the nation's history, involving potentially three hundred defendants and eighteen separate trials, was brought to a screeching halt by a seemingly innocuous change to the criminal code (Paragraph 50, section 2) that had the effect of treating bureaucratic participation in the killing process as a lesser criminal offence whose statute of limitations had already expired.[39]

To qualify as a perpetrator, then, one typically had to have killed or authorized killing without orders. Only then could a court conclude that one had the "inner conviction" of the perpetrator. Put somewhat differently, to be found guilty of committing murder, one had to act as an *Exzeßtäter*; one had to kill in excess – that is, without orders to do so, or, to put it another way, in violation of SS law.[40] Of course, by the lights of SS justice, the wrong of these "excess acts" was "not the killing of Jewish people, but that of disobedience or more typically lack of discipline."[41] Nonetheless, in judging the actions of those who operated the machinery of death, postwar German courts essentially employed SS standards of legality, limiting the universe of perpetrators to individuals who could have been condemned by the SS's own tribunals.[42] Those who satisfied this standard were a select group of monsters, fanatics, and "bloodthirsty sadists" – sociopaths such as Treblinka's Kurt Franz, the SS officer known as "Lalka" (doll) for his boyish good looks, who would sick his German shepherd on prisoners with the command "Man (i.e., the dog), bite dog (the Jewish inmate)!"[43] In reserving the category of perpetrator to excess killers, German jurisprudence contributed to a distorted image of the SS exterminator as a brutal psychopath, prompted by an unnatural joy in killing – an image that popular culture was more than happy to run with.

As a second matter, this jurisprudence entailed something of a double shift. Because the category of perpetrator came to be reserved for a select group of excess killers, courts treated persons nonetheless deeply implicated in hands-on killing – those who shot Jews in mass graves and pushed them into gas chambers – as mere accessories. The category of accessory was thus filled with persons who had played an active and demonstrable roll in acts of killing – that is, persons who otherwise might have been treated as perpetrators. By contrast, those whom we might have expected to be treated as accessories – "ordinary" members of killing units or guards at death camps – were either acquitted or never tried in the first place. And so while the vast majority of deeply implicated killers could only be convicted as accessories, the larger group that comprised the thousands of lowly foot soldiers of genocide could be convicted of nothing at all.

Arendt was keenly aware of these distortions. "What the old penal code [viz. the statutory definition of murder] failed to take into account," Arendt noted at the time of the Frankfurt-Auschwitz trial, "was nothing less than the everyday reality of Nazi Germany in general and of Auschwitz in particular."[44] As a result of this insufficiency, "a man who had caused the death of thousands because he was one of the few whose job it was to throw the gas pellets into the chambers could be criminally less guilty than another man who had killed 'only' hundreds, but upon his own initiative and according to his perverted fantasies."[45] To correct this mangling of legal categories, Arendt insists, "'mass murder and complicity in mass murder' was a charge that could and should be leveled against every single SS man who had ever done duty in any of the extermination camps."[46] Arendt wrote these words in the mid-1960s, but no German court managed to act on them – that is, until a court in Munich in 2011.

Ivan the Accessory

The legal odyssey of John (Ivan) Demjanjuk had begun back in 1975, when American officials first received sketchy word of the wartime activities of a Ford machinist living in a quiet suburb of Cleveland. Demjanjuk had been born in the Ukraine in 1920 and had entered the United States in 1952, settling in the Cleveland area and becoming a naturalized US citizen in 1958. By the late seventies, American prosecutors had come to identify Demjanjuk as the former Treblinka guard whose cruelty and wanton acts of sadism had earned him the sobriquet, Ivan *Grozny*, "Ivan the Terrible." In the most highly publicized denaturalization proceeding in American history, Demjanjuk was stripped of his citizenship and extradited to Israel, where he was tried as Treblinka's Ivan *Grozny*. In 1988, a special Jerusalem court, using the same statute that had aroused Arendt's ire, convicted Demjanjuk of crimes against the Jewish people and sentenced him to death – making him only the second person in Israeli history to be so sentenced (Eichmann, of course, being the first). For the next five years, Demjanjuk idled in an Israeli prison. In the summer of 1993, the Israeli Supreme Court tossed out his conviction: newly gathered evidence from the former Soviet Union had made clear that the Israelis had the wrong Ivan. A few months later, Demjanjuk returned to the United States, ending Israel's role in one of the most famous cases of mistaken identity in the annals of law.

But the Israeli acquittal hardly spelled the end of Demjanjuk's legal travails. Resettled in suburban Cleveland and his American citizenship restored, Demjanjuk became the subject of a fresh denaturalization proceeding. While Demjanjuk might not have been Treblinka's Ivan the Terrible, evidence conclusively showed he had nonetheless been a "terrible Ivan" who served at Sobibor, a no-less-lethal Nazi death camp. In 2001, Demjanjuk earned the distinction of being the first person in American history to twice lose his citizenship. He remained barricaded in his middle class ranch house in Seven Hills, Ohio, while American officials searched fruitlessly for a country willing to accept him. Poland said *nie*. The Ukraine said *ne*. Finally and rather unexpectedly, Germany, which had long resisted accepting alleged Nazi collaborators from the US, said *ja*. Demjanjuk was flown to Munich, arriving on German soil on 12 May 2009. Two years later to the day, on 12 May 2011, a German court convicted the then ninety-one-year-old defendant of assisting the SS in the murder of 28,060 Jews at Sobibor. Sentenced to five years of prison, Demjanjuk was released pending appeal; ten months later, John Demjanjuk died in a Bavarian nursing home on 17 March 2012 while his appeal was still pending.

John Demjanjuk was hardly an architect of SS policy – indeed, he wasn't even a Nazi. Drafted into the Soviet Red Army after the German invasion in the summer of 1941, Demjanjuk had been taken as a prisoner of war by the Wehrmacht; only after landing in a POW camp was he recruited, along with other Ukrainian and Baltic POWs, to be trained at Trawniki, the SS *Ausbildungslager* (training camp), for service as a death camp guard. As a *Wachmann* (guard) at Sobibor, Demjanjuk operated invisibly on the bottom rung of the hierarchy of extermination. If he behaved cruelly, no evidence has ever been produced to prove this. In fact, Demjanjuk's trial in Munich adduced scant evidence showing exactly what the defendant did at Sobibor, beside the facts that demonstrated, incontestably, that he served as a guard.[47]

What purpose, then, was served by trying Demjanjuk? If Arendt, as we noted at the outset, believed that the classical goals of retribution, correction, and deterrence imperfectly apply to atrocity trials, these reservations would seem to apply with all the greater force in the case of a low-level nonagenarian whose crimes were committed two generations ago. But if Arendt implicitly problematizes the proceeding, she also helps us locate its importance – on the level of legal idiom.

As was the case in all German trials of Nazi-era criminals, Demjanjuk's prosecutors had no choice but to charge the defendant with murder (in this case, as serving as an accessory). Yet while nominally working within the confines of the German statutory construction of murder, the Demjanjuk court in fact achieved something quite radical. In convicting Demjanjuk, the court effectively adopted the jurisprudential theory that Arendt adumbrated nearly fifty years ago. Against the defence's argument that no evidence indicated what precise acts *Wachmann* Demjanjuk committed at Sobibor, the prosecution and court answered in lapidary fashion: *it does not matter.* The mere fact that Demjanjuk served as a guard *necessarily* meant that he was an accessory to murder. The argument was as simple and irresistible as a syllogism: All Sobibor guards participated in the killing process. Demjanjuk was a Sobibor guard. *Therefore* Demjanjuk participated in the killing process.

This theory was specifically tailored to the reality of Sobibor, a pure killing centre, whose small staff of SS men and Trawniki guards oversaw the murder of a quarter-million Jews. It would be difficult to extend the theory even to the case of Auschwitz-Birkenau, which had been a hybrid facility, part death camp, part prison/labour camp. Here the numbers are telling. Of the 1.2 million persons sent to Auschwitz, about 100,000 survived. This is a death rate in excess of 90 per cent; considered as a disease, Auschwitz was astonishingly lethal. But compare this figure to the three pure extermination facilities built as part of Aktion Reinhard. About 1.4–1.7 million Jews were "resettled" to the killing centres of Treblinka, Belzec, and Sobibor. No more than 120 lived, a death rate of 99.99 per cent.[48] That prosecutors lacked evidence about Demjanjuk's specific behaviour at Sobibor was, then, irrelevant as a matter of law. The fact alone that Demjanjuk served as a *Wachmann* at a death camp should suffice to prove guilt. Sobibor guards were accessories to murder because facilitating murder was their *function.*

The theory was simple and its logic irresistible. Still, its embrace by a German court marked a dramatic transformation in the theory of German atrocity prosecutions. Some may find it regrettable that this change was so long in coming; others criticized the fact that the new theory was adopted in the prosecution of an old man who was neither a German nor a Nazi; others still complained of the five-year sentence – for some it was too short, while others saw no need to inflict punishment in addition to the conviction itself. Yet however we might think about these matters, there is no denying that the Demjanjuk trial marked a fundamental conceptual reorientation. For sixty years, German jurists tortured history by pigeonholing Nazi atrocities into the conventional murder statute; now, while still working with the strictures of murder, prosecutors found a way to accommodate the logic of genocide. The Demjanjuk trial rectified, in Arendt's terms, the "pernicious ... understanding" and the "common illusion" that the "crime of murder and the crime of genocide are essentially the same."[49]

Now armed with the Demjanjuk precedent, German investigators have begun investigating dozens of guards and low-level killers whom the old model had essentially shielded from legal scrutiny. German prosecutors have announced the possibility of filing charges against as many as thirty former guards.[50] Recent newspaper accounts have described the use of state-of-the-art computer imaging technology to establish sight lines of former Auschwitz guards who continue to dispute having known of the workings of the gas chambers and crematoria.[51] Whether any of these cases will actually go to trial remains far from clear.[52] All the cases obviously involve old men; the youngest would be nudging ninety by the time the case went to trial. In December 2013, German prosecutors suddenly dropped charges against Samuel Lipshis after the former SS guard at Auschwitz-Birkenau was diagnosed with incipient dementia. More recently, Germany sought the extradition of Johan Breyer, an American by birth who was raised in Europe and later served in the SS, allegedly participating in a massacre of Jews. On the very day that a federal judge in Philadelphia upheld Germany's extradition request came word that Breyer had died.[53]

Even assuming a healthy defendant, it is not clear how well the Demjanjuk precedent will travel. To use the Demjanjuk precedent against an Auschwitz guard, it would be necessary to show that he had performed *Rampendienst* – that is, worked the train platforms – during, say, the summer of 1944, when trainloads of Jews from Hungary were hurried straight to the gas chambers. Only in such cases did Auschwitz become a pure killing centre in which all participants by necessity must have served the exterminatory process. Whether any of the present cases satisfies this condition remains unclear.

But even if none do, the importance of the Demjanjuk decision remains undiminished. For the significance of this jurisprudential correction should not, I believe, be measured simply in terms of the prosecutions it sponsors or the convictions it secures; its importance, pace Arendt, lies in the renewal of judgment as a meaning-positing act. While still nominally working within the troubled German framework that treated the Holocaust as an "ordinary" crime, the Munich court managed to shatter the old paradigm and comprehend the Holocaust as a crime of atrocity. Demjanjuk was rightly convicted not because he committed wanton murders but because he worked in a factory of death. To convict only in the presence of proof of evil or viciousness is to treat the Holocaust trial as a garden-variety crime. Demjanjuk's Munich trial, by contrast, understood that mass killing is not a personal act of evil but an exterminatory process. When it comes to state-sponsored atrocities, guilt is not to be measured by acts of cruelty or nastiness; guilt follows *function*. Indeed, Demjanjuk was what Eichmann never was – a replaceable cog in an exterminatory apparatus. And for this he was rightly convicted.

NOTES

1 Hannah Arendt, *Eichmann in Jerusalem: A Report on the Banality of Evil* (New York: Penguin, 1992), 263.

2 Ibid., 268–9. It should be noted that Arendt understood crimes against humanity in a manner different from at least some of the jurists at Nuremberg who pioneered the concept. Indeed, Nuremberg jurists themselves disagreed about the very understanding of "humanity," some believing the term referred to a core notion of humaneness, while others thought, like Arendt, it referred to a capacious notion of humanity, writ large. This debate was reflected in the struggles to translate the term into German, with some translations using "Verbrechen gegen die Menschheit"

(humanity) and others "Verbrechen gegen die Menschlichkeit" (humaneness). See http://www.stiftung-evz.de/fileadmin/user_upload/EVZ_Uploads/Handlungsfelder/Handeln_fuer_Menschenrechte/Menschen_Rechte_Bilden/huhle-verbrechen_gegen_die_menschheit.pdf.

3 Arendt, *Eichmann in Jerusalem*, 233, http://www.worldcat.org/title/eichmann-in-jerusalem-a-report-on-the-banality-of-evil/oclc/405280&referer=brief_results.

4 Ibid., 253.

5 Ibid., 273.

6 Hannah Arendt, "Personal Responsibility under Dictatorship," in *Responsibility and Judgment*, ed. Jerome Kohn (New York: Schocken, 2003), 25.

7 Ibid., 26.

8 Hannah Arendt, *Between Past and Future: Six Exercises in Political Thought* (New York: Viking Press, 1968), 221.

9 Mary G. Dietz, "Arendt and the Holocaust," in *The Cambridge Companion to Hannah Arendt*, ed. D. Villa (Cambridge: Cambridge University Press, 2000), 87.

10 Hannah Arendt, "Understanding and Politics," *Partisan Review* 20 (1953): 379. See also M.P. d'Entrèves, "Arendt's Theory of Judgment" in Villa, *Cambridge Companion to Hannah Arendt*, 245.

11 Arendt, *Eichmann in Jerusalem*,279.

12 Ibid., 272.

13 See, for example, the case of *Public Prosecutor v. Djajic*, Bayerisches Oberstes Landesgericht, 23 May 1997, and the discussion in L. Reydams, *Universal Jurisdiction: International and Municipal Legal Perspectives* (Oxford: Oxford University Press, 2003), 150–7.

14 *Grundgesetz für die Bundesrepublik Deutschland, vom 23.5.1949, veröffentlichte und bereinigte Fassung. Zuletzt geändert durch Gesetz vom 21.7.2010*, BGBl I, 944.

15 Carl Schmitt, "Der Führer schütz das Recht. Zur Reichstagsrede Adolf Hitlers vom 13. Juli 1934," *Deutsche Juristen-Zeitung* 39 (1934): 1947. See also Bernd Rüthers, *Entartetes Recht: Rechtslehren und Kronjuristen im Dritten Reich* (Munich: C.H. Beck, 1994).

16 Quoted in Rüthers, *Entartetes Recht*, 36.

17 Hall YLJ 187.

18 By "German" and "Germany" I am referring to the Federal Republic; East Germany will be designated as such.

19 See N. Frei, *Vergangenheitspolitik: Die Anfänge der Bundesrepublik und die NS-Vergangenheit* (Munich: DTV, 1999).

20 J. Reinhold, *Der Wiederaufbau der Justiz in Nordwestdeutschland 1945 bis 1949* (Königstein: Athenaum, 1979), 103ff, 130ff.

21 Joachim Perels, *Das Juristische Erbe des "Dritten Reiches": Beschädigungen der demokratischen Rechtsordnung*, Wissenschaftliche Reihe Des Fritz Bauer Instituts, Bd. 7 (Frankfurt and New York: Campus Verlag, 1999), 215.

22 Gerhard Wolf, *Befreiung des Strafrechts vom nationalsozialistischen Denken?* (Humboldt Forum Recht, 1996), 2.

23 Perels, *Das juristische Erbe des "Dritten Reiches,"* 20.

24 Hermann Lübbe, "Der Nationalsozialismus im deutschen Nachkriegsbewußtsein," in *Historische Zeitschrift* 236 (1983): 586.

25 Hermann Wentker, "Die jurisitsche Ahndung von NS-Verbrechen in der sowjetischen Besatzungszone und in der DDR," *Vierteljahrshefte Für Zeitgeschichte* Jahrgang 35, no. 1 (2002): 60–78.

26 Henry Friedländer, *Nazi Crimes and the Law* (Cambridge: Cambridge University Press, 2008), 22.

27 Gerhard Werle and Thomas Wandres, *Auschwitz vor Gericht: Völkermord und bundesdeutsche Strafjustiz* (Munich: Verlag C.H. Beck, 1995).

28 Wolf, "Befreiung des Strafrechts vom nationalsozialistischen Denken?" 11. Also Schmitt, "Der Führer schütz das Recht," 924.

29 Werle, *Auschwitz vor Gericht*, 37.

30 Friedländer's claims can in part be reconciled with Werle's more radical critique of Nazi law. For while Friedländer insists that "killing Jews and gypsies" was never "legal," he never says it constituted a punishable crime under then-operative law; and while Werle argues that genocide was authorized by the will of the Führer, he never says it was fully "legal."

31 Werle, *Auschwitz vor Gericht*, 31.

32 Peter Reichel, *Vergangenheitsbewältigung in Deutschland: Die Auseinandersetzung mit der NS-Diktatur von 1945 bis heute* (Munich: C.H. Beck, 2001), 25.

33 Ralph Vogel, ed., *Ein Weg aus der Vergangenheit: Eine Dokumentation zur Verjährungsfrage und zu den NS-Prozessen* (Frankfurt am Main: Ullstein, 1969), http://www.worldcat.org/title/weg-aus-der-vergangenheit-eine-dokumentation-zur-verjahrungsfrage-zu-den-ns-prozessen/oclc/1005919&referer=brief_results.

34 Werle, *Auschwitz vor Gericht*, 32.

35 Joachim Perels, "Perceptions and Suppression of Nazi Crimes by the Postwar German Judiciary" *Nazi Crimes and the Law* (New York: Cambridge University Press, 2008), 95.

36 Kerstin Freudiger, *Die juristische Aufarbeitung von NS-Verbrechen* (Tübingen Mohr Siebeck, 2002), 169.

37 For a discussion of the anamolous murder conviction of Hermann Krumey, who worked as Eichmann's assistant in the deportation of the Hungarian Jews, see ibid.

38 See generally Jorg Friedrich, *Die kalte Amnestie: NS-Täter in der Bundesrepublik* (Berlin: List, 2007).

39 On the question of the inadvertent affects of the change, see also Hubert Rottleuthner, "Hat Dreher gedreht?" https://edoc.bbaw.de/volltexte/2011/1875/pdf/307_Rottleuthner_Hat_Dreher_gedreht.pdf.

40 See Rebecca Wittmann, *Beyond Justice: The Auschwitz Trial* (Cambridge, MA, and London: Harvard University Press, 2012).

41 Werle, *Auschwitz vor Gericht*, 38; see also Angelika Benz, *Der Henkersknecht der Prozess gegen John (Iwan) Demjanuk in München* (Berlin: Metropol-Verlag, 2011), 165.

42 See G. Werle and T. Wandres, *Auschwitz vor Gericht*, 31–3.

43 Gitta Sereny, *Into That Darkness: From Mercy Killing to Mass Murder* (New York: McGraw-Hill, 1974), 202.

44 Hannah Arendt, "Auschwitz on Trial," in *Responsibility and Judgment*, ed. J. Kohn (New York: Schocken, 2003), 243.

45 Ibid.

46 Ibid., 243–4.

47 This evidence includes Demjanjujk's Trawniki ID that indicates his assignment to Sobibor; a Sobibor Transfer roster, indicating Demjanjuk's transfer from Sobibor back to Trawniki; and the record of interrogations that the Soviets did with another guard, Ignat Danilchenko, who has since died. After being trained at Trawniki and before being assigned to Sobibor, Demjanjuk first served at Majdanek, where there is a record of his being disciplined. After Sobibor, Demjanjuk was assigned as a guard at Flossenbürg; German prosecutors presented the testimony of a fellow Ukrainian guard, Alex Nagorny, who testified in Munich and also presented several documents, including the Flossenbürg transfer roster, the assignment of weapons to the guards, and a list of guard duties, all of which name Demjanjuk. This latter evidence does not prove Demjanjuk's assignment to Sobibor, but it does challenge his insistence that he never served as a guard anywhere at any time.

48 Timothy Snyder, *Bloodlands* (New York: Basic Books, 2010).

49 Arendt, *Eichmann in Jerusalem*, 272.

50 "Last Justice: Germany to Prosecute 30 Auschwitz Guards," *Der Spiegel*, 3 September 2013, http://www.spiegel.de/international/germany/nazi-murder-germany-may-prosecute-30-former-auschwitz-guards-a-920200.html.

51 Melissa Eddy, "Chasing Death Camp Guards with New Tools," *New York Times*, 5 May 2014, http://www.nytimes.com/2014/05/06/world/europe/chasing-death-camp-guards-with-virtual-tools.html?_r=0.

52 Klaus Wiegrefe, "The Auschwitz Files: Why the Last SS Guards Will Go Unpunished," *Der Spiegel*, http://www.spiegel.de/international/germany/the-german-judiciary-failed-approach-to-auschwitz-and-holocaust-a-988082.html.

53 Eric Lichtblau, "Philadephia Man Accused in Nazi Case Dies," *New York Times*, 23 July 2014, http://www.nytimes.com/2014/07/24/us/philadelphia-man-accused-in-nazi-case-dies.html?module=Search&mabReward=relbias%3As%2C%7B%221%22%3A%22RI%3A5%22%7D.

Chapter Nine

Whose Trial? Adolf Eichmann's or Hannah Arendt's? The Eichmann Controversy Revisited

SEYLA BENHABIB

The Never-Ending Controversy

It is rare to encounter a work of twentieth-century philosophy which has reached as wide an audience and caused as much furor as Hannah Arendt's 1963 volume on *Eichmann in Jerusalem: A Report on the Banality of Evil*.[1] Based on her coverage of the trial of Adolf Eichmann in Jerusalem from 11 April to 15 December 1961, this acrimonious and tangled controversy cast a long shadow on her otherwise illustrious career as a public intellectual and academic.

Although she was and continues to be severely attacked by the Jewish community,[2] this book is Arendt's most intensely Jewish work, in which some of the deepest paradoxes of retaining a Jewish identity under conditions of modernity came to the fore in her search for the moral, political, and jurisprudential bases on which the trial and sentencing of Adolf Eichmann could take place.[3] Gershom Scholem's phrase that Hannah Arendt "lacked Ahabath Israel,"[4] "loving belonging to the Jewish people," is indeed cruel. Arendt never denied her Jewishness; if anything, for her it was so much a part of the order of the given that she was puzzled by Scholem's claim that "I regard you wholly as a daughter of our people."[5] To which Arendt replied: "The truth is that I have never pretended to be anything else or to be in any way other than I am, and I have never even felt tempted in that direction … To be a Jew belongs for me to the indisputable facts of my life … There is such a thing as a basic gratitude for everything that is as it is; for what has been *given* and not *made*; for what is *phsei* and not *nomō*. To be sure such an attitude is prepolitical, but in exceptional circumstances – such as the circumstances of Jewish politics - it is bound to have also political consequence, though, as it were, in a negative way."[6] But Arendt did not "merely belong to them," as Judith Butler named her review of *The Jewish Writings*:[7] in the interwar years, she was a political activist, a left Zionist who pleaded for a bi-national state in Palestine; after migrating to the United States in 1941, she advocated for a Jewish army to fight against the Nazis in the name of the Jewish people; and subsequent to Judah Magnes's death and the extinction of the dreams of a "bi-national state that would be a part of the Mediterranean comity of peoples,"[8] Arendt lost the platform from which she could speak. The State of Israel was busy building and consolidating a new nation and was beleaguered by constant threats of war. World Jewry, aghast at the horrors of the Holocaust, was in no position to criticize Israel but exercised almost unconditional solidarity with it. The generation of German-Jewish intellectuals such as Judah Magnes, Martin Buber, and even at times Scholem himself, who had envisaged some kind of bi-national polity in Israel-Palestine, was disappearing as were many Holocaust survivors. In Israel, the trial was indeed used by the Ben-Gurion government as a form of political education, mobilizing sentiment for the project of nation building and the triumph of the Zionist ideal.[9]

Equally important, the Eichmann trial was the first time since the Holocaust that the pretence of normality that had begun to reign in Israel, Germany, and the world about these events was shattered and the painful task of recollection and rearticulation begun. As many historians of the Holocaust have noted about this period, after more than half a century of discussion, research, and publicity, it is hard for us to even imagine how scanty such public knowledge and scholarship were in the early 1960s.[10]

Psychoanalysis teaches us that recollection and the narration of trauma have their own temporality: uncovering why trauma is recalled at specific moments and not in others is part of the therapeutic process. Human memory is activated by certain triggers, which can lead to unblocking the repressed memories of the past. It is odd that despite all the ink that has been spilled by Jewish and Israeli historians over Arendt's *Eichmann in Jerusalem* (and in the continuing attempts to refute Arendt in recent works by David Caesarani and Deborah Lipstadt),[11] it is hardly taken into account that Arendt herself was a survivor, and her "Olympian distance" – as Ralph Ellison once named it[12] – may also have been a defence mechanism against the traumatic possibility of falling into the hands of the Gestapo. After she fled from the women's camp in Gurs in the south of France, had she been caught, Arendt faced sure death by deportation to Auschwitz. She was fortunate enough that, unlike her close and unlucky friend, Walter Benjamin, who committed suicide in the French-Spanish border, she and her husband, Heinrich Blücher, were able to reach the United States in 1941.[13] Arendt, who rejected psychoanalysis,[14] would most likely be offended by this interpretation, yet there is so much evidence in her language, in the construction of narrative voice in *Eichmann in Jerusalem*, that reveals a storm raging within her, that this reading is hard to resist. Arendt's much-misunderstood sarcasm as well as her thinly veiled contempt for Eichmann himself were like layers of additional skin that she had to clothe herself in so that she could provide one of the first and most dramatic accounts of the destruction of European Jewry.[15]

Just as memory and the process of recollection (*Erinnerung*) have their own temporality, so do the reading and reception of texts. It is by now possible to construct the historiography of successive readings of *Eichmann in Jerusalem*. In the mid- to late 1960s, Arendt's book was interpreted in the light of Stanley Milgram's famous experiments about the facility with which cruelty and torture could be exercised by seemingly ordinary individuals who obeyed authority and silenced their own conscience. Milgram, in fact, began carrying out these experiments in 1961 at the same time as the Eichmann trial was proceeding in Jerusalem and published his own results in 1963, thinking that references to Arendt's study would increase his credibility.[16] Three decades later, Christopher Browning's famous analysis of the Reserve Police Batallion 101 in his book *Ordinary Men: Reserve Police Batallion 101 and the Final Solution in Poland* (1992), on the one hand, and Daniel Goldhagen's *Hitler's Willing Executioners* (1996), on the other, largely written as a refutation of Browning's claims, would define the hermeneutic horizon against the background of which Arendt's thesis about "the banality of evil" would be reread.[17]

Browning and Goldhagen are identified with different schools in their interpretations of the centrality of anti-Semitism and the Holocaust to the Third Reich. The "functionalist" historical school started by Hans Mommsen emphasizes that the Final Solution and the extermination of European Jewry were not the driving forces behind many developments in the Third Reich.[18] Goldhagen and, more recently, Saul Friedländer[19] claim, by contrast, that "apocalyptic anti-Semitism" was indeed the central impetus for the National Socialist ideology of the

Reich. Richard Wolin as well has characterized Arendt's position as belonging with the "functionalist historians." Yet a cursory examination shows that Arendt's own writings contain elements of both kinds of analysis, with the emphasis on ideology predominating in her early work and the latter work focusing more on institutional and systemic factors in the functioning of national socialism. It is simplistic therefore to reduce it to one or the other school of interpretation.[20]

The latest instalment in this controversy, which once more refocuses the debate on the matter of Eichmann's personality and anti-Semitism, is the impressive scholarly work by Bettina Stangneth, *Eichmann vor Jerusalem*.[21] A closer analysis of Stangneth's findings will also help shed further light on the thesis of "the banality of evil."

Eichmann *before* Jerusalem

Discussions of the German edition of Stangneth's book (2011) have centred around the neo-Nazi circle of sympathizers who gathered in Argentina, their connections to postwar Germany, their hopes to influence political events there, and the claim that successive German governments resisted bringing Adolf Eichmann to trial. "Many who were caught in the network of the criminal state from which so many had profited, felt themselves as accomplices," Stangneth writes, "even if the time after 1945 had not been a period of painful questions for them personally. In this atmosphere of collective silence even the resurgence of a name which had become a symbol disturbed one."[22]

Eichmann himself wanted to be tried in Germany, knowing that he would not be condemned to death because statutes considering Nazi crimes to be "crimes of state" forbade imposition of capital punishment upon individuals simply obeying laws that were legal at the time of the Third Reich.[23] Attempts by Fritz Bauer, the Attorney State General of Hessen, who was on Eichmann's trail and who may have been the first to tip Israelis to Eichmann's whereabouts, were thwarted by the Adenauer government.[24] Stangneth notes that more than 2,425 pages of documentation are still held in a dossier by the German Central Intelligence Service, which refuses to make them public.[25] As late as 10 September 2009, a decision was made by the office of the German chancellor not to release this material on the grounds that "the abstract … interest in the discovery of truth," had to be balanced against "the good of the State; the protection of informants and the personal (privacy) rights of concerned third parties." These aspects of Stangneth's book, which directly address the culture of silence, repression, and postwar Germany's failure "to work through the past," have all been neglected by American commentators. Instead the trial of Adolf Eichmann has turned once more into the trial of Hannah Arendt – as if Hannah Arendt, not Adolf Eichmann, needed to stand trial before the judges of Jerusalem!

For example, the historian Deborah Lipstadt avers that "if previous researchers have seriously dented Arendt's case, Ms. Stangneth 'shatters it.'"[26] The intellectual historian Richard Wolin, heralding "the demise of a legend," announces that Arendt, "perhaps out of her misplaced loyalty to her former mentor and lover Martin Heidegger ... insisted on applying the Freiburg philosopher's concept of 'thoughtlessness' (*Gedankenlosigkeit*) to Eichmann. In doing so, she drastically underestimated the fanatical conviction that infused his actions."[27]

But can Eichmann not be a convinced Nazi anti-Semite and also banal? In what sense did Arendt mean that Eichmann "was not stupid. It was sheer thoughtlessness – something by no means identical with stupidity – that predisposed him to become one of the greatest criminals of that period"?[28] Stangneth does not address such questions, nor does her book throw much light on the larger philosophical issues underlying Arendt's analysis, but she is respectful of Arendt's work: "Arendt read the protocols of the interrogation and the trial unlike anyone else. And with this she fell into a trap, because Eichmann in Jerusalem was no more than a mask. She did not recognize this, but impressively it was clear to her that she had not understood the phenomenon as well as she wanted to."[29] What, then, was this phenomenon?

Stangneth brings to light new evidence about Eichmann's persona and thinking based mainly on the so-called Argentina papers. After 1979 large chunks of interviews conducted with Eichmann in 1957 by Willem S. Sassen, a Dutch Nazi journalist who had become a German citizen, became available. It took nearly twenty years for this material to emerge more or less complete because, with the death of Eichmann's lawyer Servatius, his posthumous papers were deposited in the national German archives in Koblenz. Sassen himself had also given everything in his possession back to the Eichmann family by then.[30] These included over one thousand pages of typed conversation with handwritten comments, as well as tape recordings (the originals of which would emerge only in 1998), and an additional five hundred pages of handwritten material and commentary, some by Eichmann and some by Sassen.[31] The interviews and Eichmann's own notes were in preparation for a book to be published by the Argentine-based neo-Nazi press Dürer Verlag, run by Eberhard Ludwig Ceasar Fritsch.[32] Since the late 1950s the goal of this publishing house and of the circle of old Nazis and Nazi sympathizers assembled around it, was to influence events in Germany, and especially to counter the charges of the mass murder of the European Jews. Eichmann was composing a book with the title "Others Have Spoken, Now I will" (*Die anderen sprachen, jetzt will ich sprechen*). He had asked Sassen to publish these documents if he were to die or fall into the hand of the Israelis.[33] After Eichmann's arrest, Sassen prepared a photographic film of the convolute of a thousand pages but decided to sell only about one hundred pages. Eichmann's wife, Vera, who was now destitute financially and alone with her four sons in Argentina, approved of the sale. Eventually only 150 pages of handwritten material and 600 pages of typescript, which amounted to no more than 60 per cent of the interviews and 40 per cent of the handwritten documents, were sold to *Life* magazine. This did not include additional papers and archives, which had been buried rapidly by Eichmann's son in the family's garden upon his arrest. Only after thirty years would they be made available to the British historian and Holocaust denier, David Irving, in October 1991.[34]

Sassen, who quickly came under suspicion of having betrayed Eichmann, proceeded to sell some additional material to the German magazine *Der Stern* and two other Dutch publications. With the publication of the *Life* magazine series, Eichmann, who was by then in an Israeli jail, suffered a nervous breakdown, but he and his lawyer, Servatius, managed to come up with a defence to cast doubt on the veracity of the Sassen interviews.

Arendt was unable to read either the entirety or even a significant portion of this material but was quite familiar with the interview in *Life*. She knew that "Eichmann had made copious notes for the interview, which was tape recorded and then rewritten by Sassen with considerable embellishments," and she also knew that although the notes were admitted to the trial as evidence, "the statement as a whole was not."[35] Israel's state prosecutor, Gideon Hausner, had a bad copy of the more complete material, yet he and the court continued to assume that the *Life* magazine materials and the transcripts were the same. They were not.[36] Stangneth further explains that of the 713 typed and 83 handwritten pages in Israel's possession, Hausner could use only 83 pages. Eichmann and Servatius had managed to convince the court that this was inadmissible evidence, supposedly because the recorded statements were uttered under the influence of alcohol and with Sassen's encouragement to Eichmann to make sensationalist pronouncements for publicity purposes. Stangneth concludes that both had lied successfully: Eichmann by pretending to be a down-and-out exile, given to drunken exaggerations of his role in the murder of European Jews, and Sassen, an ambitious journalist out to make money and fond of journalistic fabulations.

The Argentine Papers give us new insights into the intensity of Eichmann's anti-Semitic world view, insights that Arendt missed. Stangneth cites a statement by Eichmann's former friend and colleague, Dieter Wisliceny, during the Nuremberg trials: "[Eichmann] said: He would jump laughing into the grave because the feeling that he had five million people on his conscience would please him extra-ordinarily."[37] This then led Göring to comment: "This Wisliceny is a small pig, who only appears big, because Eichmann is not here."[38]

Would full access to this material have led Arendt to change her assessment that Eichmann was banal and "thoughtless"? Not if one understands and uses German as she did, and not if one understands the philosophical contexts within which she meant precisely what she said.

Consider the following: Commenting on Eichmann's claim that he was not a "mass murderer," Stangneth writes that his "inner morality is not [based on] an idea of what is right or a universal moral category, not even a form of self-examination, [but on] the recognition of a dogma which is uncontested by National Socialists, namely that each *Volk* has the right to defend itself with all possible means and one's own people has the most right to do so." Conscience is nothing other than this "morality of the Fatherland that lives in every human being," which Eichmann also calls "the voice of the blood."[39]

In a farewell message to sympathizers in Argentina, Eichmann also "threw caution to the winds" and declaimed: "I say to you honestly… I was the 'conscientious bureaucrat.' I was that indeed … [but] within the soul of this conscientious bureaucrat lay a fanatical warrior for the freedom of the race from which I stem … what my Volk requires … is for me a holy commandment and a holy law."

It is this strange mixture of bravado and cruelty, of patriotic idealism and the shallowness of racialist thinking that Arendt sensed because she was so well attuned to Eichmann's use of language. As Stangneth puts it, "With her sense of language and concepts educated through classical German literature, Hannah Arendt describes how Eichmann's language is like a changing torrent of thoughtless greyness, cynically violent thoughts, internalized self-pity, unintended comedy and in part incomprehensible human pitifulness."[40]

Precisely because Eichmann's world view was a self-immunizing mixture of anti-Semitic clichés circulating since *The Protocols of the Wise Men of the Elders of Zion* (and which Eichmann knew to be a forgery), an antiquated idiom of German patriotism, and even a craving for the warrior's honour and dignity, Arendt concluded that Eichmann could not "think," not because he was incapable of rational, calculating intelligence but because he could not think for himself beyond clichés. He was banal precisely because he was a fanatical anti-Semite, not despite it.

Although Arendt was wrong about the depth of Eichmann's anti-Semitism, she was not wrong about these crucial features of his persona and mentality. She saw in him an all-too-familiar syndrome of rigid self-righteousness; extreme defensiveness fuelled by exaggerated metaphysical and world-historical theories; fervent patriotism based in the belief in the "purity" of one's *Volk*; paranoid projections about the power of Jews and envy of them for their achievements in science, literature, and philosophy; and contempt for Jews' supposed deviousness, cowardice, and pretensions to be the "chosen people."[41]

This syndrome was banal in that it was widespread among National Socialists. Nevertheless, by coining the phrase "the banality of evil" and by declining to ascribe Eichmann's deeds to the demonic or monstrous nature of the doer, Arendt knew that she was going against a tradition of Western thought that saw evil in terms of ultimate sinfulness, depravity, and corruption. Emphasizing the fanaticism of Eichmann's anti-Semitism cannot discredit her challenge to a tradition of philosophical thinking; it only avoids coming honestly to terms with it.

Thoughtlessness – Kant or Heidegger?

There is a famous exchange between Judge Raveh and Eichmann about Kant's moral philosophy that Arendt cites in *Eichmann in Jerusalem*. She quotes Eichmann as saying, "I meant by my remark about Kant that the principle of my will must always be such that it can become the principle of general laws."[42] Arendt notes that Eichmann's meaning perverts Kant's categorical imperative: Whereas in Kant's philosophy the source of the Categorical Imperative is practical reason, "in Eichmann's household use of [Kant], it was the will of the Führer."[43]

When Arendt uses the phrase "the inability to think" to characterize Eichmann's reduction of conscience to the "voice of blood," and of the categorical imperative to the command of the führer, she is taking as given the Kantian terminology, in which to think means to think for oneself, to think consistently, but also from the standpoint of everyone else.[44] These preoccupations antedate the Eichmann trial. In 1960 Arendt had published an essay called "The Crisis in Culture: Its Social and Political Significance" in her collection *Between Past and Future*.[45] Portions of this essay had appeared earlier as "Society and Culture" in *Daedalus*, and there are significant passages in her posthumous *Denktagebuch* from the late 1950s on the relationships between thinking, judging, and thinking from the standpoint of others.[46]

These reflections on Kant's moral philosophy, as remote as they might at first seem to the case of Eichmann, are especially relevant to understanding Arendt's use of "thoughtlessness." After writing that Kant's *Critique of Judgment* contains "perhaps the greatest and most original aspect of Kant's political philosophy," Arendt continues: "In the *Critique of Judgment*, however, Kant insisted upon a different way of thinking, for which it would not be enough to be in agreement with one's own self, but which consisted of being able to 'think in the place of everybody else' and which he therefore called an 'enlarged mentality'" (*eine erweiterte Denkungsart*).[47] Furthermore she added: "That the capacity to judge is a specifically political ability in exactly the sense denoted by Kant, namely, the ability to see things not only from one's own point of view but in the perspective of all those who happen to be present ... these are insights that are virtually as old as articulated political experience."[48]

Not only Eichmann but all those who wore the ideological blinkers of totalitarianism were incapable of thinking in this Kantian and Arendtian sense. Ideological thinking immunizes itself against the world by fitting all evidence into a coherent scheme that cannot be falsified, and renders one blind to differences and perspectives that do not fit into one's *Weltanschauung*. It was this ideologically conditioned thoughtlessness that permitted Eichmann to sit for days on end with an Israeli officer, Captain Less, and tell him the sad story of his own life and the wrongs he believed had been done to him. Arendt comments: "The longer one listened to him, the more obvious it became that his inability to speak was closely connected with his inability to *think*, namely, to think from the standpoint of someone else."[49]

Commentators, such as Richard Wolin, stress not the Kantian but the Heideggerian sources of Arendt's use of "thoughtlessness." "It is on the basis of Heidegger's fatalistic critique of modern technology as an unalterable condition of modern life that Arendt derives her view of Eichmann as a human automaton, or, following Eichmann's own self-description during the trial, as a mere 'cog' in the Nazi machinery of extermination," Wolin writes.[50] Arendt actually believed none of the "cog in the machine" theory and considered Eichmann quite responsible for his actions.[51] Wolin's eagerness to prove that Arendt's views of Eichmann's "thoughtlessness" and that her theory of Nazi totalitarianism were largely indebted to Heidegger drive him to a factual blunder, namely, his claim that it was only after 1970, almost a decade after the trial, that Arendt turned to the Kantian categories of thinking, judging, and in particular "thinking from the standpoint of others." As we have seen, however, Arendt was preoccupied with these themes before, during, and after the trial.

In 1954 Heidegger published the essay "What Is Thinking?" in which he indeed writes that "most thought-provoking in our thought-provoking time is that we are still not thinking."[52] The German text explicitly says: "überall herrsche nur die *Gedankenlosigkeit*," using the same term as Arendt did in the Eichmann case.[53] Yet for Heidegger that we are still not thinking stems from the fact that "the thing itself that must be thought about turns away from man, has turned away long ago,"[54] meaning that the inability to think is a form of "the forgetting of Being." For Heidegger, the thoughtlessness of modern man is not the inability to think from the standpoint of others; quite to the contrary, such thoughtlessness stems from being all too beholden to what others may think and turning away from Being itself.

Undoubtedly, Arendt knew this text but, far from following Heidegger, she gave the category of thinking quite a different meaning than he did.[55] This is because she never changed her mind about the fact that with the concentration camps and the Holocaust something had emerged in human history which had altered the essence of politics and perhaps even human nature itself. It was not this evil which was banal, but the quality of mind and character of the perpetrators. Even though the full depth of Eichmann's Nazi fanaticism were not publicly known when she wrote, Arendt never thought of him as a mere "cog in the machine" (which as Bettina Stangneth shows Eichmann invented as a way of defending himself);[56] nor, however, did she honour him by ascribing to him diabolical dimensions.

Her preoccupation with the Kantian as opposed to the Heideggerian meanings of thinking stems from her attempt to understand the connections between thinking, judging, and acting morally. Writing in the Postscript to *Eichmann in Jerusalem* that she would have welcomed a discussion of the concept of the "banality of evil," she continues: "Eichmann was not Iago and not Macbeth, and nothing would have been farther from his mind than to determine with Richard II 'to prove a villain' … That such remoteness from reality and such thoughtlessness can wreak more havoc than all the evil instincts taken together, which, perhaps are inherent in man – that was, in fact, the lesson one could learn in Jerusalem."[57] In using the phrase "the banality of evil" and in explaining the moral quality of Eichmann's deeds not in terms of the monstrous or demonic nature of the doer, Arendt became aware of going counter to the tradition of Western thought, which saw evil in metaphysical terms as ultimate depravity, corruption, or sinfulness. She asked again: "Might the problem of good and evil, our faculty of telling right from wrong, be connected with the faculty of thought? … Could the activity of thinking as such, the habit of examining whatever comes to pass or attract attention, regardless of results and specific contents, could this activity be among the conditions that make men abstain from evil-doing or even actually 'condition' them against it?"[58] She asked again: "Do the inability to think and a disastrous failure of what we commonly call conscience coincide?"[59] Arendt's reflections on these issues are anything but conclusive.

It is one of the perplexities of these "exercises in political thought" that although Arendt emphasized the relevance of *enlarged thought* and *taking the standpoint of others* as being crucial for political and public judgments, in her 1971 essay on "Thinking and Moral Considerations," written a decade after the Eichmann trial, she reverted to a Platonic model of the unity of the soul with itself. In this essay, following Socrates in the *Gorgias*, she described conscience as the harmony or oneness of the soul with itself.[60] But as Mary McCarthy observed, Arendt was too quick in assuming that out of the self's desire for unity and consistency alone a principle moral stance would emerge.

More than a decade earlier, McCarthy had asked Hannah Arendt about Raskolnikov's old problem in Dostoevsky's *Crime and Punishment*:[61] "Why shouldn't I murder my grandmother if I wanted to? Give me one good reason." Arendt responded with a professorial gesture that acknowledged the depth as well as difficulty of McCarthy's question: "The philosophic answer would be the answer of Socrates: Since

I have got to live with myself, am in fact the only person from whom I shall never be able to part, whose company I shall have to bear forever, I don't want to be a murderer; I don't want to spend the rest of my life in the company of a murderer."[62] McCarthy is not convinced: "The modern person I posit would say to Socrates, with a shrug, 'Why not? What's wrong with a murderer?' And Socrates would be back where he started."[63]

Adolf Eichmann admitted during the trial that he would have killed his own father if he were ordered to do so – but only if his father had actually been a traitor to the cause. In Eichmann's case, unlike Socrates, there was a voice that supervened over his conscience, in fact a voice that altogether replaced individual conscience: this was the voice of the party and the movement. Eichmann never considered himself a mere murderer of innocent Jewish women and children; he called himself an idealist and was at pains to emphasize that he fought a war against the enemies of the Reich – no matter how far from reality it seemed to describe helpless, vulnerable, and destitute Jewish masses, now huddled in ghettos and camps throughout East-Central Europe, as the "enemies" of the Reich. Eichmann was shrewd and he certainly "thought" for himself when it came to his own benefit and advantage; but he did not think for himself in that he did not have a moral compass that was independent of the party and the movement.

Nor could Eichmann think from the standpoint of others, since they were already defined and categorized for him in certain ways. They had ceased to be moral beings worthy of equal respect and consideration. They had become dehumanized. Yet the trial transcripts also reveal how difficult and surreal this process of dehumanization was. Repeatedly, Eichmann is at pains to emphasize his proper and dignified conduct, and even friendly dealings with officials of the Jewish community in Vienna and Budapest.[64]

It would seem then that the capacity to take the standpoint of the other is not just a cognitive ability at which some are better than others. It is true that some people project so much of themselves onto others that they cannot distinguish between "me" and "you"; whereas others are so empathetic and have such weak ego boundaries that they cannot tell where the "I" ends and the "you" begins. Eichmann's dehumanization of the Jews and his inability to take the standpoint of others was a case of extreme paranoid projection through which the other became merely a blank screen for the fears and delusions of the self. "Taking the standpoint of the other" then is not simply a cognitive capacity but one that involves complex psychological and motivational dimensions as well.

Under what conditions do individuals lose such capacities? Under what circumstances does "thoughtlessness" of such magnitude emerge that individuals wash away the boundaries between self and other, demonize the other, become immune to reality, seek for a kind of coherence that the facts do not permit, and get lost in self-justifications that cannot be falsified?

Certainly these psychological syndromes are more common than we would like to think, but it is also clear that they alone, without the massive sociocultural upheavals and economic dislocations in social and political life, do not lead to mass murder and genocide. Arendt, therefore, did not believe that modernity or modern technology alone had given rise to totalitarianism. This is why *The Origins of Totalitarianism*,[65] in which she deals with the rise of Nazism and Soviet totalitarianism historically, is an unwieldy work. It is not a mono-causal account but a rich exploration of many elements and configurations in modern societies – such as the collapse of the rule of law in the nation-state, the rise of anti-Semitism, race thinking in the encounter with Africa, and the practice of administrative massacres in Western colonies, and so forth – all of which come together in some fashion to enable totalitarian politics. There is no teleology to Arendt's account just as there are no easy answers to her characterization of Eichmann's "banality."

The trauma of the Holocaust of European Jewry is so deep in us that like a wound that one scratches before it has healed, it will keep bleeding. Hannah Arendt's *Eichmann in Jerusalem* scratches where it has not healed and probably never will. This is why the controversy will "die down, simmer," but "erupt" again and again, in Irving Howe's wise words.[66]

NOTES

Thanks to my student Clara Picker for excellent bibliographic help, and to Roger Berkowitz, Corey Robin, and Jim Sleeper for further conversations on the Eichmann controversy.

1 Hannah Arendt, *Eichmann in Jerusalem: A Report on the Banality of Evil* (New York: Penguin, 1994 [1963]), revised and enlarged edition.

2 "Nearly every major literary and philosophical figure in New York chose sides in what the writer Irving Howe called a 'civil war' among New York

intellectuals – a war, he later predicted, that might 'die down, simmer' but will perennially 'erupt again.' So it has." Roger Berkowitz, "Misreading 'Eichmann in Jerusalem,'" *New York Times Opinionator*, 7 July 2013. See Irving Howe, "The New Yorker and Hannah Arendt," *Commentary*, October 1963, 318–19, 22. See also Anson Rabinbach, "Eichmann in New York: The New York Intellectuals and the Hannah Arendt Controversy," *October* 108 (Spring 2004): 97–111.

3 Some formulations and discussions in this essay have previously appeared in: Seyla Benhabib, "Arendt's *Eichmann in Jerusalem*," in *The Cambridge Companion to Hannah Arendt*, ed. Dana Villa (Cambridge: Cambridge University Press, 2000), 65–86.

4 Gershom Scholem, "'Eichmann in Jerusalem': An Exchange of Letters between Gershom Scholem and Hannah Arendt," *Encounter* 22 (January 1964): 51–6, reprinted in Hannah Arendt, *The Jew as Pariah: Jewish Identity and Politics in the Modern Age*, ed. Ron H. Feldman (New York: Grove Press, 1978), 241. The new and expanded edition of this volume, Hannah Arendt, *The Jewish Writings*, ed. Jerome Kohn and Ron H. Feldman (New York: Schocken Books, 2007), contains Arendt's reply to Scholem and other documents in the controversy but not Scholem's letter (see 465ff).

5 Ibid., 52.

6 Arendt, "A Letter to Gershom Scholem," in Kohn and Feldman, *The Jewish Writings*, 466.

7 Judith Butler, "I Merely Belong to Them," *London Review of Books*, 10 May 2007, 26–8.

8 Cf. Hannah Arendt, "Zionism Reconsidered" (1941) in Kohn and Feldman, *The Jewish Writings*, 372. See also my discussion of Arendt's politics in this period in S. Benhabib, *The Reluctant Modernism of Hannah Arendt* (Thousand Oaks, CA, London, and New Delhi: Sage 1996 [2002]), 35–47.

9 Tom Segev, *The Seventh Million: The Israelis and the Holocaust*, trans. Haim Watzman (New York: Henry Holt and Company, 1991). Leora Bilsky gives an excellent analysis of the broader political as well as jurisprudential issues involved in the Eichmann trial in: *Transformative Justice: Israeli Identity on Trial* (Ann Arbor: University of Michigan Press, 2004). See also Idith Zertal, *Israel's Holocaust and the Politics of Nationhood* (New York and Cambridge: Cambridge University Press, 2005).

10 See Michael R. Marrus, *The Holocaust in History* (Toronto: Lester and Orpen Dennys, 1987), 4–5: "Up to the time of the Eichmann trial in Jerusalem, in 1961, there was relatively little discussion of the massacre of European Jewry … Since then scholarship has proceeded apace … Hannah Arendt's *Eichmann in Jerusalem*, originally an assessment of the trial for the *New*

Yorker, prompted a debate in the historical literature that echoes to our own times."

11 David Cesarani, *Becoming Eichmann: Rethinking the Life, Crimes and Trial of a "Desk Murderer,"* (Raleigh, Essex: Da Capo Press: 2007 [2006]); Deborah Lipstadt, *The Eichmann Trial, Jewish Encounters* (New York: Schocken, 2011).

12 Ralph Ellison, "The World and the Jug," in *Shadow and Act* (New York: Random House, 1964), 108.

13 See Seyla Benhabib, "Arendt and Adorno: The Elusiveness of the Particular and the Benjaminian Moment," in *Understanding Political Modernity: Comparative Perspectives on Arendt and Adorno*, ed. Samir Gandesha and Lars Rensmann (Stanford, CA: Stanford University Press, 2011).

14 Cf. Arendt: "Psychology, depth psychology or psychoanalysis, discovers no more than the ever-changing moods, the ups and downs of our psychic life, and its results and discoveries are neither particularly appealing nor very meaningful in themselves." Hannah Arendt, *The Life of the Mind, Thinking* (New York: Harcourt, Brace and Jovanovich, 1977 [1971]), 1:35. I thank Clara Picker's research paper, "Arendt, Eichmann and the Problem of Thinking Under Modern Conditions," for calling my attention to this quote.

15 See Léon Poliakov, *Harvest of Hate: The Nazi Program for the Destruction of the Jews of Europe*, Foreword by Reinhold Niebuhr (New York: Syracuse University Press, 1954).

16 David Cesarani's discussion of Stanley Milgram's experiments on "obedience" and his attempt to present them as consonant with Arendt's analysis are helpful. Cesarani, *Becoming Eichmann*, 352–4.

17 Christopher Browning, *Ordinary Men: Reserve Police Batallion 101 and the Final Solution in Poland* (New York: HarperCollins, 1993); Daniel Jonah Goldhagen, *Hitler's Willing Executioners: Ordinary Germans and the Holocaust* (New York: Alfred Knopf, 1996).

18 See Mommsen's introduction to the 1986 German revised edition of *Eichmann in Jerusalem*, reprinted as "Hannah Arendt and the Eichmann Trial," in Hans Mommsen, *From Weimar to Auschwitz: Essays in German Historiography* (Princeton, NJ: Princeton University Press, 1991), 254–78.

19 Saul Friedländer, *Nazi Germany and the Jews: 1933–1945*, abridged edition by Orna Kennan (New York: HarperCollins, 2009).

20 Cf. Richard Wolin, "The Banality of Evil: The Demise of a Legend," *Jewish Review of Books*, 4 September 2014, http://jewishreviewofbooks.com/articles/1106/the-banality-of-evil-the-demise-of-a-legend/ (accessed on September 14, 2014). While *The Origins of Totalitarianism* is more intentionalist, *Eichmann in Jerusalem* contains "functionalist" elements

that stress the bureaucracy and impersonal machinery of death that made the Holocaust possible, but Arendt never disputes the centrality of anti-Semitism for understanding the Third Reich as a whole. See the important chapter in *The Origins of Totalitarianism* , with an introduction by Samantha Power (New York: Schocken Books, 2004 [1951]) called "Ideology and Terror," 593–617.

21 Bettina Stangneth, *Eichmann vor Jerusalem: Das unbehelligte Leben eines Massenmörders* (Zurich-Hamburg: Rowohlt Taschenbuch, 2014 [2011]), trans. as *Eichmann before Jerusalem: The Unexamined Life of a Mass Murderer* (New York: Alfred Knopf, 2014). I have used the German edition; all translations are mine. There is a double meaning in Stangneth's title: on the one hand the title can be read to mean that Eichmann stands before [the judges of] Jerusalem and on the other, it can also be read to mean Eichmann before (in the sense of anterior) to Jerusalem. See also my intervention in this debate, criticizing Richard Wolin and Deborah Lipstadt, "Who's on Trial? Eichmann or Arendt?" http://opinionator.blogs.nytimes.com/2014/09/21/whos-on-trial-eichmann-or-anrendt/?_php=true&_type=blogs&_r=0.

22 Ibid., 530–1.

23 Ibid., 263.

24 Ibid., 163. Note that Arendt herself thought that "according to well-informed circles" in Europe … "it was the Russian Intelligence service that spilled the news" (*Eichmann in Jerusalem*, 238). Stangneth's research shows that in addition to Fritz Bauer, Simon Wiesenthal and his colleagues were on Eichmann's trail as well.

25 Ibid., 533.

26 Quoted in Jennifer Schuessler, "Book Portrays Genocidal Nazi as Evil, but Not Banal," *New York Times*, 3 September 2014, C5.

27 Richard Wolin, "The Banality of Evil: The Demise of a Legend," *Jewish Review of Books*, 4 September 2014, http://jewishreviewofbooks.com/articles/1106/the-banality-of-evil-the-demise-of-a-legend/ (accessed 14 September 2014).

28 Arendt, *Eichmann in Jerusalem*, 287–8.

29 Stangneth, *Eichmann vor Jerusalem*, 21.

30 Ibid., 514–15.

31 Ibid., 471.

32 Ibid., 151.

33 Ibid., 473.

34 Ibid., 517.

35 Arendt, *Eichmann in Jerusalem*, 238.

36 Stangneth, *Eichmann vor Jerusalem*, 496–7.

37 Ibid., 93. As evidence mounted that Eichmann, "the specialist for Jewish affairs," had provided the first hypothetical numbers of the Jews murdered, and after Robert Jackson, the American chief prosecutor in the Nuremberg trials, named Eichmann "this dark figure, who was in charge of the extermination program," Eichmann and his cohort were alarmed and dismayed. According to Bettina Stangneth, in 1949 Léon Poliakov also published the first more or less accurate estimate of the Holocaust's figures under the title "A. Eichmann ou le rêve de Caligulas" (*Adolf Eichmann or Caligula's Dream*) (ibid., 97). These mounting assertions around his name as well as the undeniable facts of the Holocaust that began to appear all over the world press convinced Eichmann and his circle of neo-Nazis to try to counter this Jewish "propaganda" by telling their story. Arendt believed that Eichmann himself "had made many efforts to break out of his anonymity" (*Eichmann in Jerusalem*, 238).

38 Stangneth, *Eichmann vor Jerusalem*, 93.

39 Ibid., 264.

40 Ibid., 259.

41 Many attempts to understand this syndrome were made by famous psychologists such as Bruno Bettelheim and members of the Frankfurt School, who worked on the "authoritarian personality." Cf. Bruno Bettelheim, "Individual and Mass Behavior in Extreme Situations," *Journal of Abnormal and Social Psychology* (1943): 38, 417–52; T.W. Adorno, Else Frenkel Brunswik, Daniel Levinson, and R. Nevitt Sanford, *The Authoritarian Personality*, abridged edition, in *Studies in Prejudice*, ed. by Max Horkheimer and Samuel Flowerman (New York and London: W.W. Norton, 1950), reissued as a Norton paperback in 1969 and 1982. I discuss the parallelisms as well as differences between Arendt's and Horkheimer and Adorno's analyses of anti-Semitism in Seyla Benhabib, "From *The Dialectic of Enlightenment* to *The Origins of Totalitarianism*: Theodor Adorno and Max Horkheimer in the Company of Hannah Arendt," in S. Benhabib, *Dignity in Adversity: Human Rights in Troubled Times* (Cambridge, UK, and Malden, MA: Polity Press, 2011).

42 Arendt, *Eichmann in Jerusalem*, 136.

43 Ibid., 137.

44 Immanuel Kant, *Kritik der Urteilskraft* (1790), trans. and with an Introduction by Werner S. Pluhar (Indianapolis/Cambridge: Hackett, 1987), par. 40, "On Taste as a Kind of Sensus Communis," 160.

45 H. Arendt, "The Crisis in Culture: Its Social and Political Significance," in *Between Past and Future: Eight Exercises in Political Thought*, introduction by Jerome Kohn (New York: Penguin, 2006 [1961]).

46 Hannah Arendt, *Denktagebuch 1950–1973: Erster Band*, ed. Ursula Ludz and Ingeborg Nordmann (Munich and Zurich: Piper Verlag, 2002), Notebook 22, 571–84.

47 Arendt, "The Crisis in Culture," 217.

48 Ibid., 218.

49 Arendt, *Eichmann in Jerusalem*, 49; emphasis in original.

50 Richard Wolin, "Thoughtlessness Revisited: A Response to Seyla Benhabib," *Jewish Review of Books*, 30 September 2014, http://jewishreviewofbooks.com/articles/1287/in-still-not-banal-a-response-to-seyla-benhabib/?utm_source=Jewish+Review+of+Books&utm_campaign=4142abc423-Fall_2014-Wolin&utm_medium=email&utm_term=0_538f7810ff-4142abc423-.

51 Arendt, *Eichmann in Jerusalem*, 91–3, 114, 140, 145.

52 Martin Heidegger, "Was heisst Denken?" in *Vorträge und Aufsätze* (Pfullingen: Verlag Gunther Neske, 1954 [1978]), 125. This text is based on a brief radio lecture which Heidegger gave in May 1952 in the Bayrischer Rundfunk and which was published in the journal *Merkur* in 1952. The English translation is based on the lectures Heidegger gave in the winter semester of 1951 at the University of Freiburg and which were published as Martin Heidegger, "Was Heisst Denken," in *Gesamtausgabe. I. Abteilung. Veröffentlichte Schriften 1910–1976*, 8 (Frankfurt am Main: Vittorio Klostermann, [1954] 2002), 8:1–266. Cf. Martin Heidegger, "What Is Called Thinking?" trans. J. Glenn Gray (New York: Harper Perennial, 1968 [1976]), 5–6. I have compared the two editions of "Was heisst Denken?"and noted discrepancies.

53 Heidegger, "Was heisst Denken?" 126. There are some sentences included in this essay which are neither in the lecture version of the German nor in the English translation. Heidegger writes that "in our thought-provoking time we are still not thinking," means that "what is worth thinking about (das Bedenkliche) shows itself in this assertion. The assertion should by no means be interpreted to mean, therefore, in the prejorative sense that everywhere only thoughtlessness (Gedankenlosigkeit) prevails" (125–6). These sentences are not contained in the corresponding German lectures on p. 7 nor in the Grey translation on pp. 5–6.

54 Heidegger, "Was heist Denken?" 127; English translation of the lectures, 7.

55 In the Introduction to *The Life of the Mind*, the first volume on *Thinking*, Arendt explains again how the puzzles of the Eichmann trial led her to focus on thinking and moral concerns. In this work, however, as opposed

to *The Human Condition* in which she was concerned with the *vita active* (the life of activity), she turns to the *vita contemplative* (the life of the mind). Yet rather than just following Heidegger, she situates herself between Kant and Heidegger. She interprets Kant's distinction between "reason" (*Vernunft*) and "intellect" (*Verstand*) to correspond to the distinction between thinking and knowing. Whereas thinking aims at generating meaning, intellect is concerned with truth. "The need of reason is not inspired by the quest for truth but by the quest for meaning. And truth and meaning are not the same," she writes (15). The basic metaphysical fallacy is to interpret "meaning on the model of truth." This then leads her to the remarkable claim that "the latest and in some respects most striking instance of this occurs in Heidegger's *Being and Time,* which starts out by raising 'anew the question of the meaning of Being.' Heidegger himself, in a later interpretation of his own initial question, says explicitly: "'Meaning of Being' and 'Truth of Being' say the same" (15). It would be beyond the scope of this essay to follow all the epistemological questions that Arendt's claims raise but we see one more time that thinking for Arendt is not the same as thinking for Heidegger.

56 Stangneth, *Eichmann vor Jerusalem*, discusses Eichmann's reference to himself as "eine kleine Zahnrädchen im Getriebe," that is, a "small cog in the machinery" of the Nazi high command (282). Neither Arendt nor Stangneth accepted this account of Eichmann's actions, and in fact, Stangneth shows that it was Willem Sassen who first came up with this phraseology (487).

57 Arendt, *Eichmann in Jerusalem*, 287–8.

58 Hannah Arendt, *The Life of the Mind: Thinking* (New York and London: Harcourt, Brace Jovanovich [1971] 1978), 1:5.

59 Hannah Arendt, "Thinking and Moral Considerations: A Lecture," *Social Research* 38/3 (Autumn 1971), reprinted in *Social Research, 50th Anniversary Issue* (Spring/Summer, 1984): 8.

60 Arendt, "Thinking and Moral Considerations," 180–9.

61 Mary McCarthy wrote to Arendt on 10 August 1945 and Arendt responded in *Between Friends: The Correspondence of Hannah Arendt and Mary McCarthy, 1949–1975*, ed. Carol Brightman (New York: Harcourt, Brace Jovanovich), 19.

62 Arendt to McCarthy, ibid., 22.

63 McCarthy to Arendt, ibid., 27.

64 Cf. the story of Mr. Storfer, a member of the Jewish community of Vienna, who wrote to Eichmann upon being deported to Auschwitz. When Eichmann informs him that he cannot be released, Storfer requests that he

be given less heavy work to do. His assignment would now be to keep the gravel paths clean, but he would also have the right to sit down on one of the benches to rest. Arendt quotes Eichmann: "Whereupon he was very pleased, and we shook hands, and then he was given the broom and sat down on his bench. It was a great inner joy to me that I could at least see the man with whom I had worked for so many long years, and that we could speak to each other." Six weeks after this normal human encounter, Storfer was dead – not gassed, apparently, but shot. Arendt asks: "[Is] this a textbook case of bad faith, of lying self-deception combined with outrageous stupidity? Or is it simply the case of the eternally unrepentant criminal … who cannot afford to face reality because his crime has become part and parcel of it?" (*Eichmann in Jerusalem*, 51–2).

65 Hannah Arendt, *The Origins of Totalitarianism*, with an introduction by Samantha Power (New York: Schocken, 2004 [1951]).

66 Howe, "The New Yorker and Hannah Arendt."

Contributors

Seyla Benhabib born in Istanbul, Turkey, is the Eugene Meyer Professor of political science and philosophy at Yale University since 2001, and was director of its program in ethics, politics, and economics from 2002 to 2008. Professor Benhabib is the recipient of the Ernst Bloch Prize for 2009 and of the Meister Eckhart Prize for 2014 (two of Germany's most prestigious philosophical prizes) as well as the Leopold Lucas Prize in 2011. She was a Guggenheim fellow in 2013 and senior research fellow at NYU's Straus Center for Justice and Legal Studies. Professor Benhabib is the author of numerous award-winning books, many of which have been translated into German, Spanish, French, Italian, Swedish, Russian, Serbo-Croation, Hebrew, Japanese, and Chinese. Her most recent publications are: *Dignity in Adversity: Human Rights in Troubled Times* (Polity, 2011) and, together with David Cameron et al., *The Democratic Disconnect: A Plea to Revive Citizenship and Accountability in the Transatlantic World* (Transatlantic Academy: Washington, DC, 2013).

Russell A. Berman is a Walter A. Haas Professor in the humanities at Stanford, appointed in the Departments of Comparative Literature and German Studies. He is also senior fellow at the Hoover Institution. He has written widely on German literature and culture of the nineteenth and twentieth centuries, on critical theory, and on contemporary politics. He is the editor of *Telos*.

Leora Bilsky is a full professor at the Tel Aviv University Faculty of Law, where she serves as director of the Minerva Center for Human Rights at Tel Aviv University. Her main areas of research and teaching are international criminal law, political trials, transitional justice, feminist legal theory, and the relationship between law, history, and memory. She is the author of *Transformative Justice: Israeli Identity on Trial* (Michigan University Press, 2003), and is currently working on a book-length project on the Holocaust restitution litigation of the 1990s as well as on the right to truth in international law.

Daniel Conway is a native of Terre Haute, Indiana, and received his BA in philosophy and economics from Tulane University, and his PhD in philosophy from the University of California, San Diego. He has held faculty appointments at Stanford University, Harvard University, Pennsylvania State University, and Texas A&M University, where he is professor of philosophy and humanities with affiliate appointments in the religious studies program and the interdisciplinary graduate program in social, cultural, and political theory. He has lectured and published widely on topics pertaining to nineteenth-century philosophy, social and political philosophy, philosophy and literature, and philosophy of religion. He is the author of three books, the editor (or co-editor) of thirteen volumes, and the author of over one hundred articles, essays, and entries to scholarly journals, edited volumes, dictionaries, and encyclopedias. His research has been supported by grants from the National Endowment for the Humanities, the Oregon Humanities Center, the Deutscher Akademischer Austausch Dienst (DAAD), the National Humanities Center, the Andrew W. Mellon Foundation, the Institute for the Arts and Humanities at Penn State University, and the Melbern G. Glasscock Center for Humanities Research at Texas A&M University. He has held visiting appointments at Harvard University, University of Oregon, University of Warwick, the National Humanities Center, UMass Amherst, and Amherst College.

Carolyn J. Dean is a Charles J. Stille Professor of history and French at Yale University. She is the author of several books, most recently *Aversion and Erasure: The Fate of the Victim after the Holocaust* (Cornell, 2010). Her research interests range from the history of gender and sexuality to genocide studies and the Holocaust of European Jewry. She is also the author of many articles concerning the relationship between history and theory, where most of her work is situated. She is currently working on a series of essays on recent narratives about human dignity and atrocity photography, and a larger book-scale project on the history of homophobia since the nineteenth century in Europe and the United States.

Lawrence Douglas is a James J. Grosfeld Professor of law, jurisprudence and social thought at Amherst College. A graduate of Brown University and the Yale Law School, Douglas is the prize-winning author of several books, including *The Memory of Judgment: Making Law and History in the Trials of the Holocaust*, a widely acclaimed study of war crimes trials, and two novels, *The Catastrophist* (2007) and *The Vices* (2011). His most recent book, *The Right Wrong Man*, was published in January 2016. He has also co-edited twelve books on contemporary legal issues, and has lectured in many countries, including addresses to the International Criminal Tribunal for the Former Yugoslavia and the International Criminal Court. The recipient of major fellowships from the National Endowment for the Humanities, the American Council of Learned Societies, the United States Holocaust Memorial Museum, and the Institute for International Education, Douglas has served as a visiting professor of law at the University of London and at Humboldt Universität, Berlin. His work has appeared in numerous publications, including *Yale Law Journal*, *Washington Post*, *Los Angeles Times*, *Frankfurter Allgemeine Zeitung*, *New Yorker*, *Times Literary Supplement*, and *Harper's*.

Richard J. Golsan is a university distinguished professor and distinguished professor of French at Texas A&M University. His research interests include the history and memory of the Second World War in France and Europe and the political involvements of French and European writers and intellectuals with anti-democratic and extremist politics in the twentieth and twenty-first centuries. His most recent book is *French Writers and the Politics of Complicity* (Johns Hopkins, 2006). Golsan served as a Visiting Professor at the University of Paris III-Sorbonne Nouvelle in 2001. He has served as editor of the *South Central Review* (SCMLA) since 1994, and is also director of the Melbern G. Glasscock Center for Humanities Research at Texas A&M and the Centre Pluridisciplinaire, funded by the French government.

Valerie Hartoun is a professor of communication at the University of California San Diego and author of *Visualizing Atrocity: Arendt, Evil, and the Optics of Thoughtlessness* (New York University Press, 2012). Hartouni's research interests include the fields of political theory, legal theory, and history. Her early research was situated at the intersection of feminist, cultural, and science studies, focusing specifically on the disruptive cultural impact of "new" reproductive and genetic technologies. She has also been pursuing a more literary project on practices of dying, specifically, "some of the ways in which modern death is both staged and enacted as a particular kind of performance, structured according to certain plot devices that render it most one's own and most not."

Sarah M. Misemer is an associate professor in the Department of Hispanic Studies at Texas A&M University. She is the author of *Secular Saints: Performing Frida Kahlo, Carlos Gardel, Eva Perón, and Selena* (Tamesis, 2008) and *Moving Forward, Looking Back: Trains, Literature, and the Arts in the River Plate* (Bucknell University Press, 2010). Professor Misemer has published numerous articles on contemporary River Plate, Mexican, Spanish, and Latino theatre in journals such as *Latin American Theatre Review, Gestos, Revista Canadiense de Estudios Hispánicos, Symposium: A Quarterly Journal in Modern Languages, Letras Peninsulares, Revista Hispánica Moderna,* and *Hispanic Poetry Review*. Misemer is also the editor for the Latin American Theatre Review Book series and serves on the editorial board for the *Latin American Theatre Review* journal. Her main areas of research include contemporary Argentine and Uruguayan theatre, performance, and literature.

Henry Rousso is a senior research fellow at the Centre National de la Recherche Scientifique, and member of the Institut d'Histoire du Temps Présent (IHTP, Paris), which he directed from 1994 to 2005. He coordinates the European Network on Contemporary History (EURHISTXX), sponsored by the CNRS and a dozen European institutions and universities. Rousso's works focus on the history and memory of traumatic pasts, especially the Second World War. His main books include: *The Vichy Syndrome: History and Memory in France since 1944* (Paris, 1987; Cambridge: 1991); *Vichy: An Ever-Present Past,* with E. Conan (Paris, 1994; Hanover, 1998); *The Haunting Past: History, Memory, and Justice in France* (Paris, 1998; Philadelphia, 2002); *Stalinism and Nazism* (ed.) (Brussels, 1999; Lincoln, 2004); *Vichy: L'événement, la mémoire, l'histoire* (Paris, 2001); *Le dossier Lyon III: Le racisme et le négationnisme à l'université Jean-Moulin* (Paris, 2004); *Le régime de Vichy* (Paris, 2007; Munich, 2009); *Juger Eichmann: Jérusalem, 1961* (Paris, 2011); and *La dernière catastrophe: L'histoire, le présent, le contemporain* (Paris, 2012).

Dana Villa is a Packey Dee Professor of political theory at the University of Notre Dame. He is the author of *Arendt and Heidegger: The Fate of the Political* (1995), *Politics, Philosophy, Terror* (1999), *Socratic Citizenship* (2001), and *Public Freedom* (2008), all from Princeton University Press.

He is also the editor of *The Cambridge Companion to Hannah Arendt* (Cambridge University Press, 2001) and the co-editor of *Liberal Modernism and Democratic Individuality* (Princeton, 1996). His articles and essays have appeared in such journals at *American Political Science Review, Political Theory, New German Critique, Review of Politics,* and *Revue Internationale de Philosophie.*

Index

Note: HA refers to Hannah Arendt; AE refers to Adolph Eichmann; and *EiJ* refers to *Eichmann in Jerusalem.*

German and European Studies

General Editor: Jennifer J. Jenkins

1 Emanuel Adler, Beverly Crawford, Federica Bicchi, and Rafaella Del Sarto, *The Convergence of Civilizations: Constructing a Mediterranean Region*
2 James Retallack, *The German Right, 1860–1920: Political Limits of the Authoritarian Imagination*
3 Silvija Jestrovic, *Theatre of Estrangement: Theory, Practice, Ideology*
4 Susan Gross Solomon, ed., *Doing Medicine Together: Germany and Russia between the Wars*
5 Laurence McFalls, ed., *Max Weber's 'Objectivity' Revisited*
6 Robin Ostow, ed., *(Re)Visualizing National History: Museums and National Identities in Europe in the New Millennium*
7 David Blackbourn and James Retallack, eds., *Localism, Landscape, and the Ambiguities of Place: German-Speaking Central Europe, 1860–1930*
8 John Zilcosky, ed., *Writing Travel: The Poetics and Politics of the Modern Journey*
9 Angelica Fenner, *Race under Reconstruction in German Cinema: Robert Stemmle's* Toxi
10 Martina Kessel and Patrick Merziger, eds., *The Politics of Humour in the Twentieth Century: Inclusion, Exclusion, and Communities of Laughter*
11 Jeffrey K. Wilson, *The German Forest: Nature, Identity, and the Contestation of a National Symbol, 1871–1914*
12 David G. John, *Bennewitz, Goethe, Faust: German and Intercultural Stagings*
13 Jennifer Ruth Hosek, *Sun, Sex, and Socialism: Cuba in the German Imaginary*
14 Steven M. Schroeder, *To Forget It All and Begin Again: Reconciliation in Occupied Germany, 1944–1954*
15 Kenneth S. Calhoon, *Affecting Grace: Theatre, Subject, and the Shakespearean Paradox in German Literature from Lessing to Kleist*

16 Martina Kolb, *Nietzsche, Freud, Benn, and the Azure Spell of Liguria*
17 Hoi-eun Kim, *Doctors of Empire: Medical and Cultural Encounters between Imperial Germany and Meiji Japan*
18 J. Laurence Hare, *Excavating Nations: Archeology, Museums, and the German-Danish Borderlands*
19 Jacques Kornberg, *The Pope's Dilemma: Pius XII Faces Atrocities and Genocide in the Second World War*
20 Patrick O'Neill, *Transforming Kafka: Translation Effects*
21 John K. Noyes, *Herder: Aesthetics against Imperialism*
22 James Retallack, *Germany's Second Reich: Portraits and Pathways*
23 Laurie Marhoefer, *Sex and the Weimar Republic: German Homosexual Emancipation and the Rise of the Nazis*
24 Bettina Brandt and Daniel Purdy, eds., *China and the German Enlightenment*
25 Michael Hau, *Performance Anxiety: Sport and Work in Germany from the Empire to Nazism*
26 Celia Applegate, *The Necessity of Music: Variations on a German Theme*
27 Richard J. Golsan and Sarah M. Misemer, eds., *The Trial Never Ends: Hannah Arendt's* Eichmann in Jerusalem *in Retrospect*